LADY'S CHOICE

Ethel Waxham's Journals
and Letters,
1905–1910

LADY'S

Ethel Phoebe Waxham, Wellesley, 1905.

COMPILED & EDITED BY BARBARA LOVE &

FRANCES LOVE FROIDEVAUX

CHOICE

ETHEL WAXHAM'S JOURNALS & LETTERS,

1905–1910

FOREWORD BY JOHN McPHEE

INTRODUCTION BY CHARLES E. RANKIN

UNIVERSITY OF NEW MEXICO PRESS

ALBUQUERQUE

Printed and bound in the United States of America

11 10 09 08 07 06 05   5 6 7 8 9 10 11

ISBN-13: 978-0-8263-1786-5

Library of Congress Cataloging-in-Publication Data

Waxham, Ethel, 1882–1959.
Lady's choice : Ethel Waxham's journals & letters,
1905–1910 / compiled and edited by Barbara Love &
Frances Love Froidevaux ; foreword by
John McPhee ; introduction by Charles E. Rankin.—1st ed.
p. cm.
Correspondence includes letters between Ethel Waxham and John Love.
Includes bibliographical references and index.
ISBN 0-8263-1393-0
ISBN 0-8263-1786-3 (pbk.)
1. Waxham, Ethel, b. 1882—Correspondence.
2. Teachers—Wyoming—Correspondence.
3. Teachers—Colorado—Correspondence.
4. Teachers—Wisconsin—Correspondence.
I. Love, John, 1870–1950.
II. Love, Barbara, 1949–   .
III. Froidevaux, Frances Love, 1942–   .
IV. Title.
LA2317.W35A3   1992
371.1'0092—dc20
[B]
92-36499
CIP

Design: Linda Mae Tratechaud

CONTENTS

ACKNOWLEDGMENTS

The compilation of this manuscript has included people from several generations and has involved both public institutions and private memories. We would like to thank the many people who helped us assemble this historical and personal record. The Wyoming Council for the Humanities Centennial Project granted us research funds and the Writing Center, Department of English, University of Wyoming, Laramie, Wyoming gave us access to their computer facilities.

John McPhee brought selections from the original journals to an audience beyond the immediate family. Several people helped in our research efforts: Tom Bell, Director of the Fremont County Museum, Lander, Wyoming; Archivists Wilma Slaight and Jean Berry at the Margaret Clapp Library, Wellesley College, Wellesley, Massachusetts; Marguerite Mitchel, Director Hugh Stephens Library, Stephens College, Columbia, Missouri; Ken Marble, Margie, Whitney and Wayne Rowell, current residents at the Red Bluff Ranch; Dr. and Mrs. R. L. Hillier, research advisers; Emmett Chisum, Research Historian, American Heritage Center, Laramie, Wyoming; Mr. and Mrs. Jack Corbett, Mills family descendants, Jeffrey City, Wyoming; Zach and Roberta Tobias, Love family descendants, Sargent, Nebraska; and Helen Sanderson Butler (daughter of Arthur H. Sanderson) Tulsa, Oklahoma. Charles Rankin's insightful Introduction helps situate the text within contemporary trends in western literature.

We are grateful to Barbara Guth and her staff at the University of New Mexico Press for their guidance, enthusiasm, and encouragement.

Family members also collaborated on this project, and we appreciate their patience and understanding. Claude M. Froidevaux contributed the cartography. We are especially indebted to our parents, J. David and Jane M. Love, and to our aunt, Phoebe Love Holzinger, for their willingness to share their memories and insight toward people and events before our time. Their respect for history has preserved a legacy fascinating and valuable to present and future generations.

FOREWORD

In the late nineteen-seventies and early nineteen-eighties, I collected material in Wyoming for a book about the geology there. Almost without exception, those journeys were made in the company of John David Love, of the United States Geological Survey, who had started life in 1913 on a solitary ranch in the center of the state and had long since achieved a reputation of preeminence among Rocky Mountain geologists. My intention was to try to present the natural history of his region through his eyes and his experience. It is not uncommon for a geologist to reflect in the style of his science the structure of his home terrain.

We had been making field trips together for a couple of years when he reached into a drawer in his office in Laramie and handed me a journal that had been started by his mother long before she was married—when she had first come to Wyoming. She had been born more than a hundred years before I saw her manuscript, and needless to say I never met her, but the admiration and affection I came to feel toward her is probably matched by no one I've encountered in my professional life. This was not merely because she had the courage to venture as a young teacher into very distant country, or because she later educated her own bright children, or because she was more than equal to the considerable difficulties of ranch subsistence, but also because she recorded these things—in her journals and later writings—with such wit, insight, grace, irony, compassion, sarcasm, stylistic elegance, and embracing humor that I could not resist her.

She arrived in Wyoming in the autumn of 1905, when she was twenty-three—a slim young woman stepping down from a train in Rawlins, in order to go north by stagecoach into country that was still very much the Old West. In Massachusetts, a few months before, she had been graduated from Wellesley College and had been awarded a Phi

Beta Kappa key, which now hung from a chain around her neck. Her field was classical studies. In addition to her skills in Latin and Greek, she could handle a horse expertly, but never had she made a journey into a region so remote as the one that lay before her. Immediately, she began to interpret her impressions of the journey, of the people of the country, of the landscape through which she moved:

> Mountains were far away ahead of us, a range rising
> from the plains and sinking down again into them.
> Almost all the first day they were in sight.

> In the door was Mrs. Frink, about eighteen, with
> Frink junior, a large husky baby. Ida Franklin, Mrs.
> Frink's sister and almost her double, was beside her,
> frivolous even in her silence.

Insight was her long suit, and in no time she understood Wyoming. For example, another entry says:

> He came to the country with one mare. The first
> summer, she had six colts! She must have had calves,
> too, by the way the Ehlers' cattle increased.

These remarks were dated October 22, 1905—the day after her stagecoach arrived.

Three quarters of a century later, this unpublished journal was a large gift to me, and with the permission of her son and daughter I used fragments from it to help recreate her family's world. My work, though, did not include a hundredth part of what was there. My presentation could only suggest her. In years that have followed, two of her granddaughters have sifted through attics and other archives to discover packets of letters to and from her, various forms of writing by and about her, and another journal. Their work in arranging, annotating, and editing what they found has not only been loving in nature but restrainedly skillful in accomplishment. They have elected to present her here between 1905, when she began her first journal, and 1910, when she decided to marry John Galloway Love, a cowboy from Scotland who, in the Wind River Basin of Wyoming, had presented his credentials to her seemingly within moments of her arrival. The boundaries of this volume (another will follow) are deliberate and significant, for they enclose a young American woman of nearly a century ago in something like a complex of competing magnets. Self-possessed, cool, detached, she clearly knows that this is her time, and she takes it. As this chronological flow of journal entries, letters, and poems progresses, she is not only wooed by the cowboy but also importuned by a Wyoming mother who sees the young schoolteacher as a match for her own son, and who attempts to assassinate the character of John Love by referring to him as a gossip. Possibly she helps to effectuate a marriage she hopes to prevent. Letters are arriving all the while from Wellesley friends who are now in places like medical school and Paris. She experiments with teaching jobs in other states, in one instance at a sort of nunnery in Wisconsin, with macabre, humorous results. Always, she is writing— an incidental skill that would later become an ambition. Always, as well, John Love is writing to her. Indirectly, she is being asked to choose between a very isolated family life and the realm of other possibilities easily within reach of (as someone puts it in a letter to John Love) "her combination of strength and the gentlest charm—welded by that flashing mind."

Recently, when her granddaughters sent to me the annotated manuscript of this volume, I raced through the innumerable letters and the later journal that I had never seen, looking for that flashing mind and the person I felt I knew. When she described one of the faculty members at the school in Wisconsin as "a square prunes-and-prisms lady with a mouth like a buttonhole," I was reassured that I had found her.

Elsewhere, when a difficult woodstove at last began to function properly, she wrote:

The stove has developed a conscience.

When she taught Latin and Greek for a time at Central High School in Pueblo, Colorado, and lived in the home of one Mrs. Butler, she wrote to John Love:

Mrs. Butler . . . is a little war-horse of a woman with
a long, thin husband. I'm telling you about her, because she has been improving him for about twenty
years, and it is beginning to tell on him.

Reading again the journal that she kept when she was twenty-three, I found everywhere the sense of landscape that resembled her touch with people:

The dampness had brought out the darkness of the red soil, and the blackness of the green cedars. The sagebrush, too, along the way, was as black about the branches as if a fire had passed over the hills. The bluffs loomed dark and moody against the gray sky, but far away at the Big Bend the hills were the color of pale straw. The mountain looked yellowish green, softened by a sifting of snow. It is strange how the whole face of the country will be changed by a little dampness, like the face of a person intensified but softened by tears.

It should be said that while this lady's choice was a classic universal dilemma, John Love's side of it was something close to an all-or-nothing gamble. He was thirty-five years old when he fell in love with her. He lived in a place so far from community that he did not glimpse a woman for months at a time. He presented himself to her without guile, and she dealt in kind with him. For five years, he took no for an answer but never changed his question. When his letters developed closing salutations that were unacceptably intimate—for example, "Ever Yours"—and she verbally rapped his knuckles for it, thereafter he said, "Sincerely." Abidingly, he carried within him the heart and the humor, not to mention the brain, of the Scots. He was a match for her. Evidently, she knew it.

As this volume ends, she accepts him, his ranch, and a fulfillable vision of their life together. Her granddaughters quote from something she wrote years later, describing an embroidered sampler that existed only in her imagination and depicted the ranch and its hands and her family and certain symbols of a time in the Wind River Basin.

I will wait impatiently for the sampler. Meanwhile, these distinct themes from her single life will more than do.

JOHN MCPHEE

INTRODUCTION
CHARLES E. RANKIN

Ethel Waxham's story is decidedly out of step with current historical studies. It deals with an urbane, upper middle-class, well-educated white woman whose brief experience teaching in a Wyoming country school parallels in reality the fictive experience of Molly Wood in Owen Wister's *The Virginian*. Absent is the focus on ethnicity and the underclass of many historical studies of western women today. Absent also is the sense of pessimism that sometimes characterizes the new western history—the belief that somehow the pioneer generation did it all wrong. At first, one cannot help but think this manuscript should have found publication in the 1940s or earlier, as did a handful of other firsthand accounts of the early West by women, rather than in our own time when such works seemingly have nothing new to tell us. What can be learned, one might ask, from a story that corresponds to *The Virginian,* the novel that set the pattern for formulaic westerns?

Contemporary trends be what they may, the reader of this book is about to encounter a meaningful narrative, and one constructed quite unconventionally, for assembled here are a number of sources not usually available in sufficient quantity and quality to carry a story by themselves without substantial editorial intervention. Between her graduation from one of the East's most prestigious women's colleges in 1905 and her marriage to Wyoming sheep rancher John Love in 1910, Ethel Waxham pursued her education, taught school in several diverse settings, and held off the attentions of her determined Wyoming suitor. While doing so, she created an extensive written record of letters, journals, and poetry. The editors, two of Waxham's granddaughters, have elected not to convert this material into historical fiction or family history. Instead, they have presented it largely as they found it. They have arranged everything in chronological order and supplemented it with photographs, family reminiscences, discrete annotation, and a minimum of unobtrusive bridges to assist the reader in following the story from one set of circumstances to the next. The result is a fascinating narrative presented through actual sources that brings to life, vividly, the experiences of a young, sensitive, career-oriented woman in the early twentieth century.

Lady's Choice is much like a number of other autobiographical accounts of western women in that it offers a relatively positive portrayal of the pioneer West. Unlike previous autobiographical accounts of western women, however, this one is not written through the veil of years as a latter-day reminiscence of by-gone days, as with Agnes Morely Cleaveland's *No Life for a Lady* (1941). Nor has it been written, like Nannie T. Alderson's *A Bride Goes West* (1942), in collaboration with a skilled interviewer and writer like Helena Huntington Smith. Like Elinore Pruitt Stewart's *Letters of a Woman Homesteader* (1914), this book is compiled from first-person sources written at the time of the events they record. But unlike even Stewart's book, which is a compilation of letters to a single friend, Ethel Waxham's story is told through a host of different sources. In addition to Ethel's own letters are letters to her from an unusual cross-section of people—contemporary friends like Mary Alice Davis and Louise Dudley, suitors like Sanford Mills and John G. Love, and would-be mentors like Mary B. Mills. Supplementing this correspondence are Waxham's two journals, one kept while she was teaching school at Red Bluff Ranch, Wyoming, in 1905–1906, and another maintained while she taught Latin and Greek at Kemper Hall in Kenosha, Wisconsin, in 1907–1908. In addition, there is Ethel's poetry. "I Know a Land," for example, captures in a clean, simple form an intuitive appreciation for the land and the lay of the seasons upon it that many others undoubtedly have felt but have been unable to capture so well in words.

The whole contributes to what we know generally about employment opportunities for women in education in the early twentieth century and the limitations imposed on those opportunities by social expectations related to a woman's proper place. Women could enter the teaching profession fairly easily, but a number of factors undermined their chance to rise above an entry-level position. Women were seen as the proper moral, ethical, and patriotic instructors of youth, and where else could they better fulfill that role, conventional wisdom asked, than teaching young children? Like Ethel, most women who entered teaching at the turn of the century were young, seeking either to fill the time between the conclusion of their own education and their marriage, or, whether intending to marry or not, effectively filling that time anyway. Married women, meanwhile, were not encouraged to stay in teaching. Salaries were low, employment conditions difficult and spare, and the rewards generally not great enough to entice a woman to abandon the thought of marriage in favor of pursuing a long-term career in education.

Lady's Choice thus offers a sense of how the social conventions of the day could limit career opportunities for upper middle-class white women and channel their aspirations toward certain choices. Indeed, one cannot help but wonder whether Ethel Waxham would have chosen marriage and life on a remote Wyoming ranch had she found her career options more numerous and fulfilling. Ethel acknowledged such limitations, much as she commented on most things, with knowing irony. In defense of taking her last teaching position as a single woman in 1909 before finally agreeing to marry John Love, Ethel inquired, "You do not think that the only reason for teaching is the salary?" then added, "One does it for one's precious self-respect, and the exercise of one's faculties, and for half a hundred reasons not included in the salary—which nevertheless one accepts and spends very quickly."

Ethel's story also adds to what we know about Victorian courtship, its special proprieties, decorums, and intrigues, and about the dynamics of keeping journals and maintaining a diverse correspondence, much of it intimate yet remarkably formal. Like the overland emigrants of a few decades earlier, Ethel began a journal when her life seemed to hold the greatest potential for change. It helped her record that change and provided a means of maintaining self-control in new and untested situations. In addition, her journal was the most intimate of companions. It furnished the assurance of a familiar yet private reference point—an unviolated place where her innermost thoughts and critical judgments could be communicated without fear of betrayal. Ethel twice kept a journal for both these reasons—in the limited sphere of the Mills ranch and in the repressive atmosphere of Kemper Hall.

Ethel's writing is also valuable for its sheer quality. Unlike the writings of the rural working-class women Elizabeth Hampsten and others have studied, who wrote of the near-at-hand and lacked authorial distancing, Ethel wrote descriptively and used such literary devices as metaphor, generalization, irony, anthropomorphism, and local color. Her literary style is not self-conscious, however, and does not admit to the saccharine sentimentalism so prevalant in the Victorian era. She wrote as an insightful, detached observer, and consciously for the entertainment of the reader. As she admitted to John Love in one such letter, "When I came home I found two piles of letters that needed immediate attention—not answers like, 'yours of the 1st inst. received—Forward goods at once—yours truly etc.,' but answers to make other people as glad as I am to get their letters." Ethel's scene setting and character portrayal let the reader participate in the events she describes, much as a reader of fiction interacts with the lives of literary characters. With Ethel's writing, the reader is provided a full view of the events taking place, rather than being forced to peer through a keyhole of fleeting reference so characteristic of the writings of working-class rural women. Deepening our comprehension further are the letters of people writing to Ethel, which provide insights into such matters as popular perceptions of the West, youthful aspirations, the not-so-routine concerns of a bachelor sheep rancher, and the cultural and social insecurities of westerners themselves.

In as much as Ethel's story is concerned most with life's choices, it seems fitting that her pursuit of career introduces her to Wyoming and to what would become her most attractive options. In autumn 1905, Ethel took a rather typical position to teach in a country school at Gardiner S. Mills's Red Bluff Ranch in Fremont County, Wyoming. "You understand all the conditions," Mr. Mills wrote to her, "a six (or may be a seven) month school at $50 a month, board $20—quite an isolated life." Obviously, the promised rewards were not overwhelming. Ranch hands earning a dollar a day plus board received as much, and Mr. Mills's emphasis on isolation was no exaggeration. His Red Bluff Ranch was more than a hundred miles from the railroad, its Twin Creek School was hardly a first-class facility, and its students, while a colorful assortment of varied ages and personalities, were not stellar. The challenge in teaching lay in overcoming desultory mediocrity while instilling an elementary education, not in preparing Rhodes scholars for intellectual excellence. But then, that was not why Ethel took the job. Rather, she was in search of experience, not for the sake of career so much as in hopes of expanding her horizons. She had spent the previous summer working at a settlement house in the slums of New York City and now she would risk the wilds of the remote West teaching in a one-room school. Well-educated and raised in a family setting that encouraged an awareness of the larger world, Ethel wanted to experience more of that world firsthand.

Departing from her family home in Denver in October 1905, Ethel began her first journal anticipating a singular experience. As she admitted later, "my friends were scandalized at my going to the 'unknown wilderness' of Wyoming to teach in a district school and live among strange and therefore unpleasant people!" Indeed, as a family friend noted admonishingly, "Ethel dear, You are too delicately absurd, 120 miles from the RR—Shades of the Virginian!" But even before she plunged into that "unknown wilderness," Ethel discovered the West to be more familiar than strange. When the train deposited her in Rawlins, Wyoming, where she would begin the rest of her journey to Red Bluff Ranch by stage, she discovered acceptable local color, not uncouth absurdity deserving only of contempt. "Backwoods? Frontier? Never!" she confided in her first journal entry. "The hotel had steam heat and electric lights, lace curtains and a bell boy in buttons. Three stories high it is. What matter if the pitchers lack noses?" Two months later, during an annual teachers' institute in Lander she was forced to admit that the contrast between eastern conventions and western wilds was not so extreme after all. "It truly surprised me to find here a moral code as rigorous as that in the New Star theatre in New York."

Her seven months as a country schoolteacher was a grand success, but it is difficult to imagine Ethel staying on beyond her single term to do it over again. Her journal entries, poetry, and letters are full of the exotic sense of remoteness, the power of the weather, which could be so cruel yet so beautiful, the striking qualities of the landscape, and the characterizations and portraits of the colorful people she encountered and the stories they told. But they also reveal her loneliness and isolation. After six months at Red Bluff Ranch, she was reaching her limit. "News, such news!" she wrote on March 18. "Two men appeared yesterday, one, a Mr. Harsh, from Derby after oats. To be sure we were at school and did not see him, but it was some connection with the rest of the universe." Then, two days later, "Even Dante will pall! I've been going through 'Hell' lately for diversion." She left Wyoming and the Twin Creek school in May in search of more rewarding encounters.

Unfortunately, Ethel's commitment to improving society as an educator and her idealistic view of gaining self-knowledge through experience foundered amidst daunting discouragement at her next teaching assignment the following year. A private school run by nuns, Kemper Hall offered regimentation, parsimony, suffocating stuffiness, rigid discipline, and arbitrary rules, and it taught her that teachers are not respected even by the institutions that hire them. On the wall of the Kemper supervisor's office hung a sign warning: "The sins of the teachers are the teachers of sins." Some months later, well through the academic year, Ethel conceded to John Love, "I am quite out of love with the [teaching] profession at present, and make faces at Kemper Hall behind its back." By contrast, Wyoming beckoned. Kemper Hall, Ethel wrote, "is about as nearly opposite to the Twin Creek School on the ranch as can be imagined."

Ethel survived Kemper only to grow weary from the dull routine of supervising her father's home in Denver a year later. She confessed to her Wyoming suitor, "Life isn't worth living unless things are neat and sweet and clean round about, but somehow it takes most of the living time to keep them so." Another year found her still in Denver, lamenting her lack of options. "I wish I were in Venice at twilight, in a gondola," she wrote to John Love,

> or watching northern lights in the land of midnight suns—or seeing moonrise from a Swiss chalet among the Alps—or enjoying the early morning bustle of a harbor in Algiers—can't you see the sails?—or wish I were a lizard lying on the hot rocks in New Mexico, a gold fish swimming around the South Seas—or anything in the world but this.

The four years since leaving Red Bluff Ranch had been full enough for Ethel. She had held other teaching positions, obtained her master's degree in literature from the University of Colorado at Boulder, and served dutifully in between times as domestic supervisor of her father's household. Yet it was what she had not done with that time that haunted her. Meanwhile, John Love's letters, often written by the light of midnight oil in a sheep wagon, arrived regularly from Wyoming. Through her suitor's correspondence, the remote West increasingly came to represent freedom, viability, and a challenging future not only because pleasant memories resided there but also because her options for other new experiences were narrowing. After one last semester as a high school teacher in Pueblo, Colorado, Ethel agreed to marry John Love and live thereafter on a remote western ranch.

Parallels to *The Virginian* are striking; it is as if life were imitating art in as much as Ethel's story takes place between 1905 and 1910, and *The*

Virginian was published in 1902. A well-bred, educated woman, seeking fulfillment through a career in education, goes west to teach in a one-room school and becomes romantically involved with the consumate western man. The reality was not a perfect mirror to the fantasy, of course. Born in Illinois, Ethel had lived in Denver and Albuquerque. Although she had attended a refined eastern college, she was not, like Molly Wood of Vermont, an easterner. Similarly, unlike the Virginian, John Love was from the North (Portage, Wisconsin), not the South, and he drew his livelihood primarily from sheep, not cattle. Unlike Owen Wister's hero, Love was a self-made man with no apparent mentor, and his courtship of Ethel Waxham took five years, not one, as the Virginian's did of Molly Wood. Moreover, John Love never had to kill anyone, and Ethel did not fall in love with him right away. Indeed, she may not have been as thoroughly enraptured as he when they finally did marry in 1910, and certainly, when she left Red Bluff Ranch in the spring of 1906, John Love was but one of many pleasant people she had encountered and could expect, perhaps, never to meet again. Beyond Wyoming, she had hoped, lay a still unfolding career and ever greater prospects. Little did she realize that nowhere else would her horizons be so broad.

The writers of contemporary western literature believe that we, as westerners, need a new story, but they caution that the story cannot divorce itself entirely from the old. In its never having been published before, of course, this story is new. But it is new in more ways than that. Unlike the formulaic tale of *The Virginian,* Ethel Waxham's narrative shows the complexities of women's experiences at the turn of the century, the play of opportunity and constraint, and the timeless struggle of an individual's willingness to gamble the known, familiar, and comfortable for a chance at greater fulfillment. History as narrative is history as story, and Ethel's story invites us to compare our own lives with those of the people we encounter from the past. She reminds us that dreams, aspirations, gentleness, and self-possession are not the property of fiction alone. They can be found in the lived experience of the past and speak to us just as forcefully as they ever did. So personal a portrait emerges here that we are encouraged to consider how Ethel Waxham was typical and how she was unique. The answer is that Ethel's experiences were generally representative, at least for women of her economic class and social status, but that her descriptions of them were truly exceptional in their color, depth, insight, and honesty.

PROLOGUE

Ethel Waxham was born August 11, 1882 in Rockford, Illinois. She was the second of three daughters of Frank and Lizzie Leach Waxham, who moved from Rockford to Denver, Colorado, in the late 1880's because of Lizzie's ill health, and was educated in the public schools in Chicago (Hyde Park High School), Albuquerque, and Denver. The death of her mother in 1898 echoes later in poetry and accounts of dreams. Her father, a prominent physician associated with St. Joseph's Hospital and the University of Colorado Medical School in Denver, became known for his work in developing effective tracheotomies and treating birthmarks with dry ice. After Ethel's graduation (1901) from East Denver High School, she attended Wellesley College in Massachusetts, graduating in 1905 with a degree in Classical Literature and a Phi Beta Kappa key. She was proficient in Latin, Greek, French, and German.

A woman of diverse interests and talents, ecclectic friendships and perceptive vision, Ethel wrote, "I do not want to see one side of life only, but many. A person cannot expect to run the whole gamut of human experience; what you cannot have or do not wish for, may be had from sharing the lives of other people" (in a letter to John G. Love February 15, 1907).

This desire to see more than one side of life prompted her to leave the comfortable surroundings of a Denver doctor's household, complete with electricity and telephone. Through a Wellesley program, she spent the summer of 1904 working in a settlement house in the slums of New York. Then, following her graduation from Wellesley in 1905, she accepted a teaching position at the Twin Creek School, near Hailey, Wyoming.

After teaching in Wyoming from October 1905 to April 1906, Ethel returned to Colorado where she earned a master's degree in literature from the University of Colorado in Boulder (May 1907). Her thesis,

1

written in French and English, discussed "The Dramatic Theory and Practice of Maurice Mæterlinck." She then took a job teaching Latin at Kemper Hall, a strictly regimented Anglican girls' school, in Kenosha, Wisconsin (September 1907–June 1908). From June 1908 to November 1909 she studied housekeeping from an academic's viewpoint as she cared for her father and small half-sister in Denver. She next accepted a job teaching Latin at Central High School in Pueblo, Colorado.

During these years, she continued her correspondence with John Love, the sheep baron she had met in Wyoming. "Mr. Love," as she called him throughout the nearly five years of their courtship, was born in Portage, Wisconsin, October 2, 1870. He was the youngest, and only boy, in the family of four children of Barbara Galloway Love and John Watson Love. His mother, a sister-in-law of John Muir, the naturalist, died shortly after her son's birth. His father, who had studied medicine at Edinburgh University in Scotland, led his life as a professional photographer, lecturer, orator and world traveler. After Barbara's death, father and young son returned to Edinburgh; the daughters remained in America and eventually became homesteaders and school teachers near Broken Bow, Nebraska. When John Watson Love died suddenly in 1880, young John was only ten. He was placed in the John Watson School for Orphans of Indigent Professional People in Edinburgh, where memorization was a key element in his instruction. Sixty years later, he could recite "The Lady of the Lake" in its entirety, along with many other Scottish and English ballads. Returning to America in his teens, he worked on his sisters' farms until 1890. He enrolled in the University of Nebraska in Lincoln, where Willa Cather was one of his classmates. He was expelled in 1891 for planting a sign in the Dean's flower garden and refusing to name his accomplices.

In the spring of 1891, using all his savings, he bought two beautiful black matched carriage horses and a buggy, packed his worldly possessions in a small trunk, and drove to Wyoming. The first night, near the present town of Douglas, he camped beside an alkali spring. Before morning both horses were dead, presumably from either the water, or from seleniferous vegetation, or death camas, which are present in that area.

On foot and broke, he left his carriage, new harnesses, and trunk beside the bodies of his beloved horses and walked westward for one hundred miles to the Sweetwater country in central Wyoming. He was not yet twenty-one years old. For a while he herded sheep in the Ferris mountains for a Scotsman named Jack McTurk. Then he worked as a

"Persephone" presented at Wellesley College during Ethel Waxham's senior year (1904–05). Ethel Waxham is in right foreground. Florence Risley, also known as Big Bear, the author of the play, is at left.

cowboy for the 71 Cattle Company on the Sweetwater River for several years.

In 1897 he filed on a ranch homestead on Muskrat Creek. When his friends asked him why he had chosen "that God-forsaken lonesome place," he replied with calm assurance, "Because it has lots of room and that is what I want." He was thirty-five years old when he met Ethel Waxham, a meeting foreshadowed by the address given months earlier at Ethel's Wellesley graduation.

On June 27, 1905, William DeWitt Hyde, President of Bowdoin College, was the speaker at Wellesley College's Twenty-seventh Commencement. He chose as his theme "Apollo or Idas: The Choice of the College Woman": Should she find happiness by following Apollo, a symbol of aristocratic education which shines down on the world from above, or by joining Idas, a shepherd representing the toil, sorrow and wealth of humanity?

Hyde told the graduates,

Your choice today is between aristocracy and democracy,—between the sense of superiority and the feeling of community, between the effort to shine and the willingness to share. In the home, in the market, in society, even in charity work and in the social settlement, this deep distinction runs through all you do. . . . In the last analysis it is nothing less than whether in the most comprehensive relation to your environment you stand off and say, "you and I" with the accent of implied superiority on the "I," or clasp hands with your environment in a genuine acceptance of the pronoun "we."

He explained, basing his theme on Stephen Phillips' poem "Marpessa," that in turn Apollo and Idas, the god and the shepherd, present their suits.

Precisely so these two radically different attitudes toward life confront the college woman at the noon hour of the day she graduates. Many, perhaps most of you stand ready to place the keeping of your lives in the hands of the divine Apollo. To shine down on the world with the light of literature, or music, or art, or failing that, in the gentle ministry of the social settlement, the charity organization, is the ideal to which you have devoted your future lives.

To feel that we belong above and apart; . . . yet that we send down an illuminating radiance, a healing effluence,—that appeals to us as something diviner than just being one of the toiling suffering masses on whom the light is shed. To travel, and get impressions of art and music; to read, and get stories of literature and science; to give lectures, or write articles, or work out some social reform—be honest now, is not something of this sort the ideal of life that is hovering over you as the best use to which a college woman can put her college education?

All I ask is that, before you accept it as the highest

4

[ideal], you hear what can be said for the humble, homely human sharing of the world's experience from within, as one of the rank and file. Then comes the great statement of woman's mission in the world, not as one of remote and isolated illumination, as of a sun in the heavens, but of sympathy, enlargement, and inspiration, as of a modest common candle lighting its little sphere in the surrounding dark.

College life is abnormal. . . . All your days "like perfect lilies under water stir." You have been these four years sheltered from God's wind, the darlings of his breezes. What have you known of the dreary drudgery that underlies the happy life of a growing family of children? . . . What do you know, you who have been the special objects of hundreds of thousands of dollars of invested capital and scores of expert instructors, and sympathetic advisers,—of the coldness and hardness and indifference of a world where each is supremely intent on his own selfish ends, and treats you merely as an obstruction, a rival, or at best as a tool? You must bear on your own back your share of the world-burden, and feel in your own heart your part in the world-sorrow, in normal experience within the home, the shop, the market, before you have the slightest possibility of being able profitably to shine down upon it from above with artistic radiance or social reformation.

Whether for man or for woman, but far more for woman than for man, true and lasting happiness is to be found not in the brilliant intellectual or social performance, but in the plain hand in hand walking with a comrade along the dusty streets of daily duty, and in the peaceful glades of private life.[1]

The Marpessa of the poem rejects Apollo's transitory glitter—"It is not in the power of the human mind to be perpetually brilliant"—and concludes

> *But if I live with Idas, then we two*
> *On the low earth shall prosper hand in hand*
> *In odours of the open field, and live*
> *In peaceful noises of the farm, and watch*
> *The pastoral fields burned by the setting sun* . . . [2]

Ethel Waxham's thoughts on the speech are not known, but she kept the transcript of it, bringing it back with her to Denver. Also among her books was a small, green, leather-bound volume of the poem "Marpessa." In hindsight, between 1905 and 1910, she seems to have been wrestling with the choice the speaker presented of either following Apollo, who had already recognized her intellectual gifts with one of the first Phi Beta Kappa keys granted at Wellesley, or of joining Idas the shepherd, reaping the rewards of working with people.

The summer following her graduation from Wellesley she spent at her comfortable family home in Denver, working as her father's medical assistant. Her older sister Vera had recently married, and the household consisted of Ethel, her younger sister Faith, their father Dr. Frank Waxham and his second wife Alice, who was so disliked by the Waxham girls that she is never mentioned in Ethel's journal. Two weeks before Ethel departed for Wyoming, her baby stepsister Ruth Eudora Waxham was born.

In her unpublished story "Rome Was Not Built in a Day," written much later, Ethel gave her own account of what happened next:

In September of 1905, a voice asked over the telephone.

"Is this Miss Waxham?"

"Yes," I answered. I had succeeded to the title after my older sister Vera left to be married.

"We have a school for you, in Wyoming. Please come to our office for particulars."

I was astonished. I had never heard of the teachers' agency, nor applied for a position. Later I learned that my sister had done so.

No wonder the agent told nothing over the telephone! Few persons might have been interested in a one-room, log cabin school, more than a mile from the nearest house; a term of six months from October

6

to April, a salary of fifty dollars a month, nearly half to be paid for board; seven pupils, all in different grades, two of them in high school; a day and night stage ride of approximately one hundred and twenty-five miles from Rawlins.

It was intriguingly different from anything I knew. After college, my first September in sixteen years dragged by, unscheduled. Anyone with a B.A. was supposed to be able to teach school. Why not? I went.

1

En Route: 1905

GARDINER S. MILLS
Hailey, Fremont Co., Wyoming
October 9, 1905

Miss Ethel Waxham
1901 Colfax Ave.
Denver, Colo.

My Dear Miss Waxham,

Your letter of October 2nd together with one from Mr. Coy of the Fisk Agency reached me last night, and I reply by the first mail hoping we are not too late to secure your services.

I have written Miss Allie Davis [County Superintendent of Schools]—Lander, Wyo.—and think there will be no difficulty in having your Wellesley diploma endorsed. There should be none. It will be necessary for you to attend the Teachers' Institute at Lander during Christmas week, but the school board pays your salary during the week, so that will be no extra expense to you.

You understand all the conditions—a six (or it may be a seven) month school at $50 a month, board $20—quite an isolated life.

We would like to begin school on the 23rd if you can get here by that time.

Yours very truly
Gardiner S. Mills
Clk. Dist. No. 11.

In the same envelope:

MARY B. MILLS
Red Bluff Ranch

My dear Miss Waxham—

I have written you officially, for Mr. Mills, as he is very busy. Now I will put in a little friendly word.

Mr. Mills desires me to say that on reaching Rawlins, go to the Ferris Hotel and tell them you wish to leave for Hailey and they will have the coach come for you at the hotel. Bring with you on the coach only what you will need for a little while and have your trunk come by freight. Go to Hugus & Co. with your trunk check and have them send it (the trunk) to Gardiner S. Mills, Hailey.

Dear Miss Waxham, no matter what clothes you wear to Rawlins, put on your heavy flannels for the stage ride. You leave Rawlins one morning and get to Hailey about seven the next morning.

Let Mr. Mills know and he will meet you there the day you arrive—if you should have to stay over you will be in very good hands with Mrs. Signor and her daughter Miss Edith.

Bring warm clothes and heavy shoes, your riding skirts— if you have not one, you can make here. The girls find denim a good material for them—if you get the material in Denver eight yards of denim is sufficient.

Sincerely hoping we are not too late with the letters I remain

Very Sincerely Yours
Mary B. Mills

Ethel Waxham's journal begins:

October 19, 1905. The train ride from Denver was marked only by the slow change of scenery. Long's Peak was always on the left, but seemed to move little by little from the peak beside it. The plains were always the same. At last the mountains disappeared behind the train; patches of snow a

THE COLORADO SCHOOL JOURNAL   1

1905   Twenty-fourth Year

The Fisk Teachers' Agencies

Denver Office, NATHAN B. COY, Manager, 405 Cooper Building

Leading Teachers' Agency of the Rocky Mountain region.   Qualified teachers always in demand.
Register now.   Manual and full information on application.

The stagecoach Ethel Waxham took from Rawlins to the stage station and post office at Hailey, Wyoming. In the background is the Hailey Hotel and Roadhouse, social center for the area.

Ethel Waxham on horseback in Denver. Perhaps as a diversion after her mother died, Ethel's father bought her a thoroughbred horse, which she spent many happy hours riding, grooming, and training. She rode astride, wearing a split brown leather skirt, considered most daring in those days, and a broad-brimmed hat cocked at a rakish angle. A broken nose acquired in a fall was one of her lifelong mementoes of this horse.

long way ahead on the plains, and when we reached them, other patches and larger took their places on the horizon. The plains grew more rolling and finally were irregular and tumbled. Then we drew into Cheyenne. Four hours we waited. The Germans with their baskets—market baskets of sandwiches and meat and hunks of pie and coffee in a newspaper-wrapped coffee pot—disappeared. The Salvation

Army lady left, and the Japanese boy. At last we started, and climbed through the ever increasing hills to Laramie. There it was almost dark; too dark to see the Medicine Bow Range beyond when we passed there. The train reached Rawlins about ten. There a Negro met the train with a handcar to take suitcases to the Ferris Hotel. Backwoods? Frontier? Never! The hotel had steam heat and electric lights, lace curtains and a bell boy in buttons. Three stories high it is. What matter if the pitchers lack noses?

October 20. At twenty minutes after seven a two-horse stage bundled up to the door and we proceeded to be packed in with the other merchandise. Passengers are entered on the waybill—billed, like the express. The stage had a seat for the driver, more than half filled with boxes and mail bags, a seat behind for passengers, and much room behind for suitcases and baggage of all sorts. Oysters and eggs and grapes were stored away in boxes under the seats. The whole was enclosed in canvas top and canvas curtains that flapped away at the sides, between driver and passengers and in front of this, the driver himself. Only four years ago they used the old thoroughbrace coach which was hung on leather straps and held the passengers shut up inside. The driver, Bill Collins, a young fellow with a four days beard, untied the bowknot of the reins around the wheel, and swung up on the seat, where he ensconced himself with one leg over the mail bags as high as his head, and one arm over the back of his seat, putting up the curtain between. "Kind a' lonesome out here," he gave as his excuse.

The other passenger beside myself was a woman of fifty or sixty, white-haired, face weather worn, bright brown eyes, Mrs. Welty.[1] She was post mistress at Dubois, the post office farthest from the railroad of any in the U.S. The town of Dubois consists of a saloon, blacksmith shop, store and a post office. Mrs. W.'s husband used to be physician to the Indians, the Shoshonis. Her son, Frank, keeps the store. The ranch she took up herself and improved upon. It did not take

13

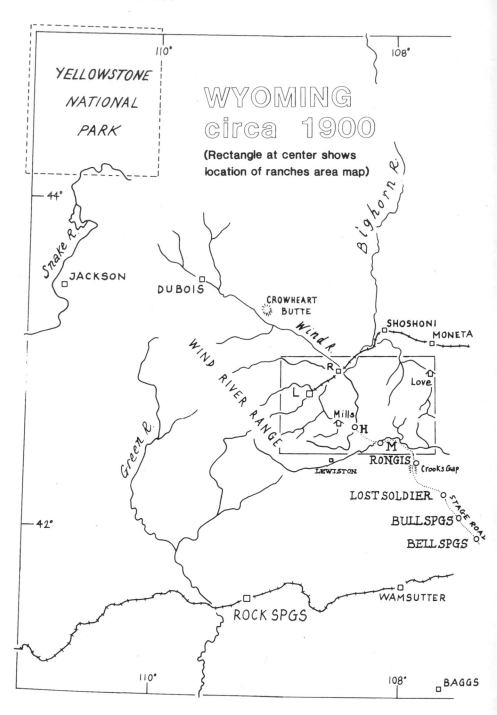

YELLOWSTONE
NATIONAL
PARK

WYOMING
circa 1900

(Rectangle at center shows
location of ranches area map)

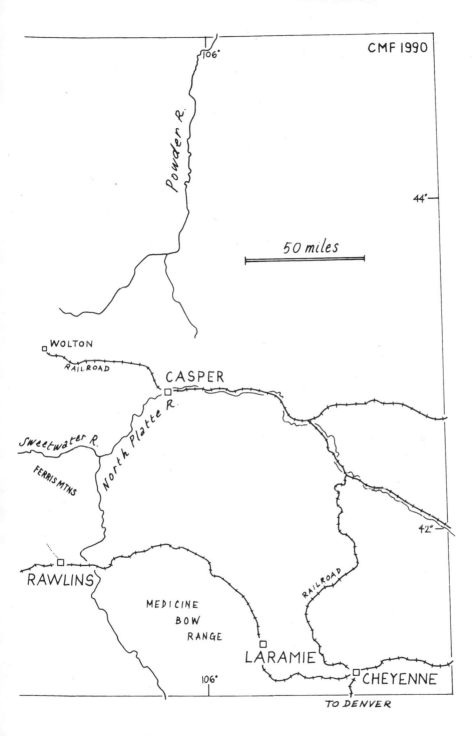

CMF 1990

106°

Powder R.

44°

50 miles

WOLTON
RAILROAD

CASPER

North Platte R.

Sweetwater R.

FERRIS MTNS

42°

RAWLINS

MEDICINE
BOW
RANGE

RAILROAD

LARAMIE

CHEYENNE

106°

TO DENVER

long for her to strike up a conversation with both the driver and myself. She came down often she said—every two years. Her interests were wide; she selected her denim and cloth riding skirts generally from catalogues of goods from Altmans and Sterns in New York. Her younger daughter, Alice, is champion woman rider in Wyoming now married to one Bill Hawley.

Such gossip about people within a range of more than two hundred miles. Where was Brockey Jones, and did the Loverings go home? They had just had trouble with the Loverings, etc.

Mrs. Welty has a little blue horse of her own now—only one. Last summer she was thrown three times by bucking broncos—bless her white hairs—so now she has one somewhat reliable horse. Her eyes are the brightest—"There's a man on foot! What is he doing around here? It's a long way to Rawlins," she said, where my own eyes saw only sage brush.

The first part of our ride was among rolling sweeps of prairie growing ever higher. Besides the man, we met two sheep herders with thousands of sheep each. "See them talking to their dogs," said the driver. They raised their arms and made strange gestures while the dogs, at the opposite sides of the flock, stood on their hind legs to watch for orders. The Seminoe[2] mountains were far away ahead of us, a range rising from the plains and sinking down again into them. Almost all the first day they were in sight, first in front of us, then at the right, until we had passed the end of the range. They looked then within walking distance, but were really twenty-five miles away. We passed several freight teams with from six to eight horses, though sometimes they have as many as twenty-two. A string of horses or a string team, is a long line of horses carrying freight; they have only one long rope to guide them, called a "string." The drivers call out "Gee" and "Haw" to make them turn.

We passed a fire of sagebrush where someone had cooked a rabbit for dinner. The smell is unlike any other, the unpleasant odor of burning sage. The dry curling roots are what they use. The other weed on the plains is greasewood, a little larger than the sage. There is a woman freighting along the road. Her husband deserted her, leaving her nothing but the freighting outfit, so she travels the road all year like the men. She usually goes near another outfit, to get help in case of breakdown. The freighters' horses are sad looking specimens, thin, hardworked, cast off from anything else, often blind.

The first house along the road from Rawlins is Bell Springs where we changed horses. The buildings are low and picturesque, built out from the bluff, mud-roofed. After leaving Bell Springs, we drove until noon without seeing anyone except a couple of freighters and a man riding on the hills far away. For several hours before we came to the road house we could see it in the distance, a white speck among the hills. It did not look larger when we reached it. The only incident along the way was the discovery of a rope wound around a sagebrush. Whiskey Mountain rose ahead of us. "One of the passengers asked me the name of that mountain," remarked the driver, "and I told him that it was in this coach where I could put my hand on it, but he could not guess."

Turn after turn of the road brought Bull Springs nearer. At last we drove up, and the men changed horses while Mrs. Welty and I hurried in to get warm, for we were chilled through. Outside, hung from the roof, was half a carcass of a steer, high enough so that it was out of reach of the dogs. The house was less preposessing than the first. In a cluttered kitchen, a fat, forlorn silent woman served us wearily with a plentiful but plain meal, and sat with her arms folded watching us eat. The driver tried to cheer her up by such remarks as, "There's too much fat on this piece of meat. Give it to the dogs," or "These onions is too small," or "What you so mad over?" She said she was sick, and had fed twenty-seven people the day before. No wonder. "Makes you tired even to look at so many people," consoled Mrs. Welty. We ate our baked potatoes and giant biscuits, onions and carrots and canned apple pie in half silence, glad to be through.

The stage horses were changed and we started on toward Lost Soldier. Bill Collins told us then that our next driver was to be Al Dowerty [Dougherty] or Peggy. In the winter of '86 when Dowerty had been driving the stage with mail, he had lost the way in a blizzard and wandered far from the road. His fingers became frozen and his toes. Finally the horses could not pull the stage any farther. Dowerty cut them loose, left all the wraps with the lady passenger and started off with one of the horses. He hung on to the harness and made the horse pull him through the snow. When he was too much exhausted to hold on any longer, he would stop the horse and rest. At last his fingers were useless and he was pulled along by an arm hooked through the harness. The horse dragged him near the town, where, within a hundred feet of the station, it would not stop when he tried to make it. He fell exhausted in the snow, called out for help and was rescued. Lost the fingers of both hands, except for thumbs and little fingers, lost one foot and half of another, but is still driving the stage. A party went out to find the stage and its passenger, but the woman had frozen to death.

Sometimes it is said that there were two other passengers—men.

Early along the way, the talk turned to the Hog Back. No coaches had blown over for some time. One of the drivers, though, had recently to chain his coach to a tree to prevent its going over. Another just in time transferred his passengers to a sleigh when the coach blew over. Only a few years ago there was every trip a dead horse or broken coach at the bottom of the Hog Back. A freight team went over the side a little while ago about Thanksgiving time. The load was partly supplies for Thanksgiving dinner, turkeys, oysters, fruit, etc. The driver called to the team behind for help. When it came he was calmly seated on a stump peeling an orange while the wagon and debris were scattered below. Often the sides—canvas—of the coach have to be unfastened there to allow the wind to sweep through. At the very top, going up, Mrs. Welty was once in a carriage with a balky

Alice Jane Amoss Welty.

horse. The horse refused to move. Only the brake kept the passengers from being hurled down backwards to certain death. The driver tried to get a man to hold the brake and reins while he chained the horses together. The man refused to take the responsibility. He said he would do what he could with the chain, however. So he put a chain around the neck of the balky horse and attached it to the other, following the directions of the driver. Then they whipped up and the willing horse dragged both the carriage and the balky horse to safety. Always going down the wheels are rough-locked by a chain so that they slip along without turning. A brake is not always sufficiently reliable.

In such talk the hours passed. We had forty-five miles with three relays of horses and the same driver. That part of the trip took about eight hours. As we drew near Lost Soldier, the driver told us one of the three stories which account for the name. The soldiers[3] were camped on the creek there once in winter when their supplies ran low and they needed meat. They sent a man out on a horse to hunt for game. They

19

waited but he did not return. They went out in search of him at last. But not yet has any trace ever been found of either horse or rider. So the creek was called "Lost Soldier Creek," and the ranch—when the roadhouse came to be there,—and the post office, are now called "Lost Soldier."

We rattled into the place at last, and were glad to get in to the fire to warm ourselves while the driver changed the load from one coach to another. With every change of drivers the coach is changed, making each man responsible for repairs on his own coach. The Kirks keep Lost Soldier. Mrs. Kirk is a short stocky figureless woman with untidy hair. She furnished me with an old soldier's overcoat to wear during the night to come. She and Mrs. Welty gossiped about the people they knew at the fort. I looked about the house. The walls were covered with whitewashed material of some sort, and an old red tablecloth served as a portière in front of what must have been bunks in the living room.

Before long we were started again with Peggy Dowerty for driver. He is tall and grizzled. They say that when he goes to dances they make him take the spike out of the bottom of his wooden leg. Our way lay up to Crook's Gap, the coldest part of the road where the night before, the thermometer had registered zero. The road was sandy, so from this place on, we had four horses to the coach. This was a team of broncos, and a wicked little team. Almost at first they kicked over the traces and tried to run away, and it was an exciting moment when we held on to the reins from the back seat while Dowerty climbed down over the wheel with his wooden leg to see what he could do. This started his swearing, and ye gods, how he could swear. We switched him off to telling stories of the cold winter of '86 and the old times. The freighters suffered then as never before. One of them lost thirty head of mules, sixteen in one evening. They were only a little way from camp, but the snow was so deep that they could not reach it. Some were found on the prairie so covered with ice that it was impossible to tell whether they were horses or mules. The men took them to a corral at Lost

Soldier, I believe, where they thawed them out. The freighters ran out of firewood, and to prevent their freezing to death, cut down the telegraph poles along the way and burned them. Dowerty himself used to haul poles to them. He was driving along one night in the snow when he saw by tracks in the snow that some carriage had left the road and gone off to the desert. He followed, and about three miles away discovered a party of officers and women stuck in a snow drift. The mules had their backs turned to the storm and refused to go. The women were huddled in the bottom of the carriage, crying. Dowerty hitched on in front and helped pull them out and start them right. "The winters have not been so severe lately," he said. "No," said Mrs. Welty, "and we haven't had a blizzard this summer."

Supper we were to have at Burnt Ranch, where Mrs. O'Neil had been burnt out once. Supper seemed to grow farther and farther away as we travelled on. The sun set and the stars rose, and the cold grew more intense. The driver stopped his reminiscences and swore again at the horses. We passed a house where a phonograph was going inside, the home of the mother of our first driver. We heard afterwards that they were probably having a dance there. About half past nine, stiff with cold, we reached the supper station. Inside we thawed out, while the man was sorting the Burnt Ranch mail. The name of the post office is Rongis.* "Here's a letter for Jones," he said. "He's in the pen."†

"Got out," said Dowerty. "He's in again, will be glad to get this most likely." Supper was soon ready, a canned supper, with the usual dried apple pie and monstrous biscuits and black coffee.

About ten we started out again, more wrapped up than ever, with a new relay of horses. We sat close to each other to keep warm, and leaned against the sacks of mail behind us. Now and then we would get a doze of a minute until our

*Signor spelled backwards.
†Probably the Wyoming State Penitentiary in Rawlins.

driver would swear at the horses, or the coach would bounce over some unevenness of the road, or get into some rut. The driver had had only two hours sleep and talked little. Once we met a stage going in the other direction. "What's your load?" asked the other driver. "Livestock," answered Dowerty. After a moment's talk we passed on. "The moon is skedooled for eleven," said our driver. "Guess we won't get none." But about twelve the moon did rise, and I watched for hours the shadow of the suitcase handle against the canvas to see the moon's change of position. The hours dragged by, and the cold grew worse. Any movement of the feet was a rest. Between three and four we reached Myersville. There were no lights. We held the horses while Dowerty went over to the bunk house to wake the other driver and change loads. His wooden leg sounded sharply on the frozen ground.

October 21. When we roused the man in the house, he came out at last half-dressed and frowsy to sort the mail and build a fire for us. It seemed as if we would never get warm again. When we were called out to get in the stage, the new driver stood by the horses. By the lantern he looked a most unprepossessing specimen. "Lost whip," he grumbled and went off to the stable to look for it. "Here," yelled Dowerty, "don't leave your horses, dumbhead!" The three men joined in the search while we sat slumbering in the coach. No whip appeared. Finally we started without one. The driver had been on the road only once, did not know his horses, and had no whip. The Hog Back was ahead. The driver started out the wrong way. Then he forgot the name of the place where he was going and tried to reassure us by saying that if he did miss the way he thought he could find Atlantic City, which is some twenty-eight miles from Hailey. There was no more sleep for us then, not an eye wink. This new driver never put on the brake. "Have to make time going down the hills anyhow," he said. The team crept along. He would stand up and try to lash them with the loose ends of the reins. "Oh good gracious," he would cry. It seemed as if the night would never brighten into day.

"Peggy" Dowerty and the stagecoach Ethel Waxham took from Rawlins to the stage station and post office at Hailey, Wyoming.

We crossed the Sweetwater. Never a house did we come to all the way. The road was only eighteen miles, but it lengthened out interminably. When morning came, there was no sun, only dark clouds. We neared the Hog Back, passing a freighter's camp, where the men were getting ready to hitch up. The harnesses for the horses lay along the ground where the horses belonged. Covered with frost were the harnesses. "Guess I'll go around," said the driver. There was a longer way around than the freighters took, not quite so steep. At the top of Beaver Mountain we saw the Wind River Range, stretching white in the distance. The driver rough-locked the back wheels and we started down. It was a scramble for the horses to keep out of the way. There were sudden turns in the road and the furrows cut by the freight wagons, almost threw the careening stage on its side. One of the horses fell, but was dragged along by the others until it finally regained its feet. We finally reached a place where the slope was less steep, the rough-lock was taken off and the driver began again to try to make time down the hills. The little leaders ran like rats, and the heavier wheelers were carried along

23

while the coach swung from side to side in the gullies. So the ride lengthened out for hours apparently. We were due in Hailey at seven. We reached the bottom of the last hill about half past nine.

Finally arrived at Hailey, the driver left the horses in order to help us out. The horses started up again, and we almost had a smash up at the last moment. "Thank God!" said Mrs. Welty. "Before I go with that man again!" We had forgotten our cold and stiffness and hunger, but we were surely thankful to be on solid ground again. We went in to the two-story frame house where the Signors live, and tried to warm ourselves by the fire. Breakfast was made ready, and bright-eyed Mrs. Signor served us with the same monstrous biscuits and black coffee that we had come across at every road house. Edith Signor, after Mrs. Welty had gone on, showed me her album of pictures and we waited for the coming of Mr. Mills to take his new school ma'am the remaining ten miles to Red Bluff Ranch. He put in an appearance about eleven and we waited for dinner at the Signors before taking the ride on.

Mr. Mills, short, dark, of caustic speech, was dressed in corduroy, and brought along a fur overcoat for me to wear outside my own. He had a team of short-maned tough mountain horses, white and sorrel, the sorrel a little lame. The white had rolled in the red mud of the country until it was a peculiar pink all over. We came easily over the ten miles to the Red Bluff Ranch in the spring buckboard. Only one house we passed, a little way beyond Signor's, where it seems the Millers, Samsons and Canoeys had lived. Farther on toward Hailey is a grave, the date of which is eighteen sixty-five, before the first white men came to the country. Six miles along by the red cliffs, six miles along the side of Sheep Mountain is the ranch.

At one place Mr. Mills beguiled the time by telling how he had spent one freezing night there with Whiskers,* tramping up and down in a path cut in the snow, watching

*A hired hand.

Mr. and Mrs. Eli Signor's house at Hailey, Wyoming.

his herd of sheep. He had tried to get them in one night before the storm, but had succeeded only in getting them in a long line, when they refused to move. Five days they had been without food or water. All night he walked up and down the line. In the morning, he made his way to the house, hitched up his horses, head of one to the tail of another, for the snow was too deep for them alone. With their help, he cut a trail to the sheep, turned them loose, when they went back to the barn. He led them to the sheep once more and again turned them loose. At last a path was made, but the sheep would not move. Sandford, his son, came to help. They took a sheep which had been brought up in the house as a lamb, and so was tame. The tame sheep followed them and the others were then willing to follow, and it took the men all day to get them in. Sandford and Whiskers got snow blindness and had to stay in for a week with poultices of potatoes over their eyes.

Whiskers is a Mormon; used to be a deacon in the church, and was on the way to be bishop he said. He cannot read or

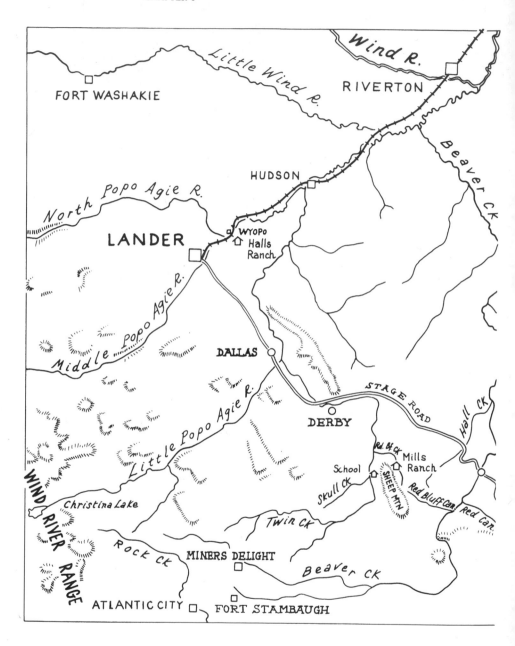

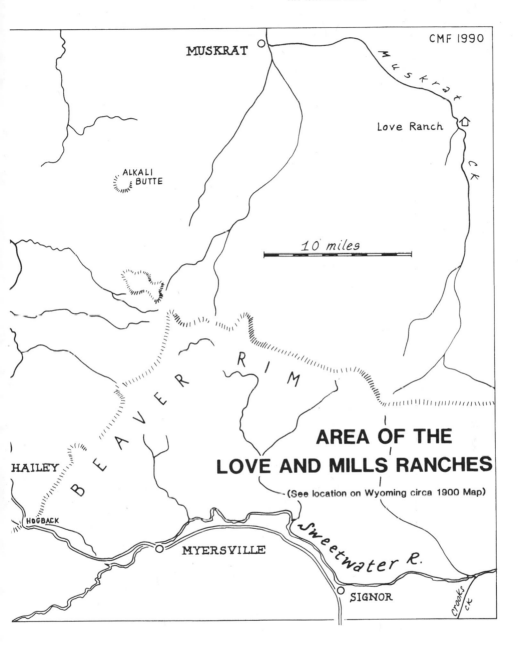

CMF 1990

MUSKRAT

Muskrat Ck

Love Ranch

ALKALI BUTTE

10 miles

BEAVER RIM

HAILEY

HOGBACK

AREA OF THE LOVE AND MILLS RANCHES

(See location on Wyoming circa 1900 Map)

Sweetwater R.

MYERSVILLE

SIGNOR

Crooks Ck

write and is so ignorant that he does not know who is the President of the U.S. His given name is Gottlieb Bregger, but in introducing him once a cowboy could not remember and said the first thing that came into his head.

At last Mr. Mills drove into an open piece of land covered with stubble; over opposite the bluffs was the ranch house, a story and a half high with a background of trees. The corral and bunk house, grain and milk house were log structures off to one side. When we drove up to the gate, two little narrow-chested, large pompadoured girls came out the walk to meet us. All my fears as to the obstreperous pupils were at an end. Mrs. Mills stood at the gate too, motherly, rosy and smiling and all my fears as to the pleasure of the boarding place were at an end too. They took me in to a clean kitchen, a comfortable dining room with plants in the windows, a sitting room well-equipped with books and finally off the sitting room to the room which was to be mine. The bed was not new, but clean. The chiffonier was made of boxes with muslin curtains straight across them. The walls showed unframed Perry pictures of Yellowstone Park, Ethel Barrymore, Sargent's Prophets, Psyche and a portrait of Gainsborough's. There was too—and it's rare in these houses—a wash stand for private individual use and a foot square mirror.

Also on her wall was the following parchmentlike page. It is not known whether Ethel Waxham brought it with her, or whether it was provided by the Mills's as part of the room's decorations.

THE DEEP LOVING CUP

Here's to our better loving!
And here's to our loves outgrown!
Here's to the bitter whirlwind
That reaps what our seeds have sown!

Here's to the friend that loves us
Too deep for tears or word!
And here's to those that love us,

When only the sense is stirred—
Who know not the joy of giving
Is not to dicker and laugh,
Or to taste when the cup is sparkling,
Or only the beading quaff!

Here's to the hearts that touch us,
On only one shining side!
And here's to the soul's real comrade,
Whose compass is deep and wide!

And here's to the one that loves us
And shows it in acts and looks!
And here's to the one that helps us
Through silence or trust or books!

Here's to the friend that graces
His thought with golden speech!
And here's to the mute one, seeking
The words too deep to reach!

But most!—To those that judge us!—
Our peers who do not condemn!—
Our brothers who aid us to balance:—
The gods give a toast to them!

Minne C. Clark
Friend, find yourself herein.

December 1903

29

2

RED BLUFF RANCH: 1905

Nestled in a valley on the east flank of the Wind River Mountains, the log ranch buildings were sheltered by a windbreak of tall cottonwoods, and ringed by bright green fields. Beyond them rose red sandstone bluffs on one side and gray precipitous slopes on the other. It was a verdant setting, with Twin Creek meandering through trees and flowering bushes. The fields were irrigated by "the best spring for 100 miles"—a natural warm spring, whose temperature remained at sixty degrees year-round. Because of the sheltering bluffs and good water, the growing season at Red Bluff Ranch was several weeks longer than at ranches on the open plains, a truly unique situation.[1]

Originally homesteaded by Frank Shedd in 1880 when Wyoming was still a territory, Red Bluff Ranch was proved upon in 1885 by Gardiner Mills. At the time of Ethel Waxham's arrival, the homestead consisted of 160 acres and the buildings. Part of a hotel was moved from South Pass City to make the original log ranch house, which was soon enlarged.[2] Testament to good planning, solid construction, square nails, and possibly the dry climate, many of the original structures and corrals are in use today. Rippled sandstone slabs form a colorful and safe path to the front door.

The Mills household consisted of the parents, Gardiner and Mary, and their three children, Kathryn, Sandford and Margaret. Gardiner Mills originally came from the New York City area before homesteading in Wyoming. He was named for ancestors who had settled Gardiner's Island, at the east end of Long Island. It was important to him and his wife that their children have the best education possible. He and Ethel Waxham corresponded in French for many years after her school "year" at Red Bluff Ranch. Assorted hired men lived in the bunkhouse and

Mary B. Mills.

helped with the ranch chores; some had complete names such as Bill Bruce, others were only known as Smithy, Whiskers, Bowser, Johnson, or Bob. Their stays appeared to be seasonal.[3]

Shortly after her arrival at the Red Bluff Ranch, Ethel received the following letter from one of her parents' friends and contemporaries in Denver. No further letters from Isabel were found.

> ISABEL KELLOGG
> 1454 Williams St., Denver,
> Colo.
> October twenty second—1905

Ethel dear, You are too delicately absurd, 120 miles from the RR—. Shades of the Virginian!

Your "Pater" says you want "the 'xperience." I reckon you're not likely to escape it!

It makes me laugh clear down through my anatomy, but I think it's beautiful! You'll probably practice declining the

Red Bluff Ranch.

noun "man" in the aboriginal language—with fire in its eye hot enough to heat a poker, and bone knives in its belt! Gee-whit-ta-ker!

That elegant 'xclamation proves to you that I'm stirred out of my usual phlegm. But, my lassie I would have liked to say good bye—& held you just a minute.

Of course you're going to have a beautiful time, and ride, ride, ride over the prairies and think, think, think great thoughts, and be obliged to do, do, do small things, mostly.

If anything happens that you do stay there, may I come and visit you? and if anything happens that you don't stay there, will you come and visit me? The "Lark's nest" is small, but there is going to be a room for you; it will be a tiny room, but dear, with just room for you to kneel beside your little bed & say your prayers every night.

Elaine Goodale, the poetess, married a full blooded Indian you know. Who knows what romantic thing may happen to you! May heaven preserve you from anything tragic!

Life has not opened wide enough to you yet for you to truly

33

know how often your chance acquaintances and every day friends have lived through tragedies and bear no outward marks.

Horror, the less reminiscing of this sort the better, unless it is in story books, those safe repositories of human passions, woes & griefs—the mild stimulant that diverts us in a book or play is revolting in real life. There is really no good reason for me to write to you in this strain, and I would much better say goodbye—or I'll be getting stale, but you seem far away—far away.

Of course you had funny 'xperiences going—and probably you had need of your "stiff-upper-lip" when you got there. I hope you won't find it too conventional and up to date; that would be too disappointing! I want you to bring me a real Indian blanket and a snake skin to adorn the "Peep-o-day" cottage at Estes Park.

I took a small bunch of Pink Roses to your little sister, Miss Ruth Eudora Waxham today. Your Father gave me your address, and he said they were all well. Ethel dear, I love you—write to Isabel Kellogg.

October 22. The next day was Sunday. With a back seat in the buckboard, the girls Kathryn and Margaret, Mr. Mills and I went off to clean up the school. They call it a mile along the red road, up hill and down over sagebrush. It has never seemed less than a mile. At last we saw the little school house of logs, standing low in the sage at the foot of Sheep Mountain where Skull Gulch cuts down from the bench to Twin Creek.

The building is fourteen by sixteen with a good roof, almost flat coming low over the sides. Over the logs of the roof and visible from within, are the gunny sacks of the school directors, supporting the sod above them, a pair of Smithy's overalls and a saddle blanket contributed in some reckless moment. "It took all the Schlichting's gunny sacks for that roof," boasted Emmons one day. Round about the door are chips of logs left from putting up the school. A door is in the front, wide cracks in the panels through which the dust blows visibly. Four small fixed windows along the south side afford sunshine, unplanned ventilation, and a view of the road along the creek. Six small panes of glass make up each window. The log walls are mud-daubed without and chinked within so that only the most severe storms leave snow drifts in the corners. There is a coal stove near the door in the place of the old one for wood. A barrel of coal, eight desks of assorted sizes, the table and chair for the teacher and a broken chair complete the furnishings of the school. The whole was put up, I believe, at an original expenditure of seventy-five dollars, and in spite of the tale that old Buffalo Fat scored it as "no good house," is not only comfortable, but good to look upon. We soon had the place swept out and arranged, brought in the books that we had carried over, and set the traps for the mountain rats that had left traces of themselves over the place. Then we locked up again, went along Twin Creek for which the school house is named, and up Skull Gulch for a ride.

Twenty years ago the skeleton of a man was found up the Gulch among the rocks. The marks of his fire can still be seen on the sheltered side of a large rock. A doctor said that the skull was that of a Frenchman, but whether he was right, or it was an Indian, or some prospector, or a man killed by the Indians we shall never know. Mr. Mills had his house up the gulch, then, and kept the skull for some time. Finally he sold the place to an Irishman, and the skull disappeared. Probably the Irishman buried it, superstitiously fearing to be haunted by the ghost of the man.

When we came to the upland we could see the canyon where Fort Stambaugh used to be, halfway between Atlantic City and Miner's Delight, to protect the two towns.[4] It was named for Stambaugh a young officer fresh from West Point who went out soon after his arrival to follow some hostile Indians. The Indians killed Stambaugh not far from the fort, and as it was in the process of construction, it was named for him.

Miner's Delight is a deserted mining town—irony of the god of names! They took out a good deal of ore once, but the process was too expensive and now not a soul lives there. Everything lies just as it was once. Dishes on the tables at the hotel, a billiard table in the saloon, lamps on the shelves and in the houses cans of provisions. As we talked and rode on, Mr. Mills said, "Back in Skull Gulch, a party of Indians went up over the hill, where the school is now. They had stolen a lot of ponies and ten or a dozen White men were after them; but as the Indians went over the hill one by one, the White men counted them as they showed against the sky. There were forty. The White men hurried back along Skull Gulch." There hasn't been any trouble with Indians here since 1879. Then they had the Meeker Massacre in Colorado. The officer Major Thornburgh and all his soldiers were killed; when relief came to Meeker,[5] everyone at the agency was killed and Meeker had a barrel stave driven in his mouth. The Indians said that he talked too much. They almost had trouble at Fort Washakie when the government commanded that rations should be given only to the Indians who would cut off their hair. Of course they would not. They came sullenly for their rations, Washakie, who had always been friendly to the Whites, among them. If there had been any effort to enforce the law, there would have been trouble. But the officers were too wise.

We rode high up on the hills where we could look far away toward Lander. The round yellow splotches on the gray of the sage brush were ranches twenty-five miles away. Beyond Lander we could see the faint outlines of Crowheart Butte, against the Wind River Range behind it. The Crows made a raid against the neighboring Shoshonis once, were pursued and hard pressed. Some climbed the Butte to keep back their enemies while the others went on. For several days they remained without food or water. Then they challenged their enemies to single hand-to-hand combat. Their champion was defeated and every one of them was killed. Their enemies ate the heart of the dead warrior to get his courage.[6]

We travelled on and visited some strangely formed rocks carved by the wind into the shape of giant mushrooms. On the way we had looked over the bluff at Pelon's hay stacks. Pelon is a French Canadian. He and his brother were out once when the Indians surprised them, killing his brother. Pelon hid in the brush. Later when his friends tried to get him to ask for money from the government because his brother was killed by the Indians, Old Pelon answered that he wouldn't. "Him better dead." Pelon used to have a wife whom he spoke of always as "Him." His version of the story is "Him got he so much in debt that he gave him $5,000 and him went." So Pelon has rented his ranch and lives in a dugout. He drives a team of broncs that run away with everyone else and with him when he is drunk. Once Mr. Mills borrowed a team from him and Pelon let him have a bronco and a mare thirty-two years old. He said it was all right. The bronco wouldn't run very far because "Old Ballee, he fall down and then him, he can't run." The ranch Pelon has rented to the Frinks, man and wife, aged twenty-three and seventeen respectively, and their child. (The child is now dead.) Old Pelon doesn't stay near them. "I swear. I can't stay where woman is. I can't talk without I swear." Old French George used to live with Pelon, and the two old men used to quarrel all the time. "Ole French George can' talk French," said Pelon, and French George, "You ole Pelon, you can' talk French."

French George used to be roundup cook, and his biscuits and bread never rose. Finally one day, Smithy, another hand, said, "Next spring is a soda spring, bread will rise when we get there," and he dumped a can of baking powder into the flour. And at the next spring the bread rose marvellously high.

Then we returned by the deserted Ehler place. The Ehlers live now at the Big Bend in Beaver four miles away. Mail and the stage both go there, but Mr. Mills prefers to go six miles farther to Signors. It is safer.

The three Ehler children ought to come to school, but their father may not let them this year. Mrs. Ehler killed her first husband, herself. Recently she tried to hire a man to kill Mr. Ehler, but he told the story on her. Ehler came to the country with one mare. The first summer she had six colts! She must have had calves too, by the way that Ehler's cattle increased. Other mares and cows would come to the corral to try to get the colts and calves there. They are badly in debt—everything mortgaged—but last year Mrs. Ehler bought a parlor organ. Ehler telegraphed to have the order cancelled, but too late.

When the organ came, he had been having his fill of whiskey. He took an axe and chopped the organ to pieces. Having secreted all the weapons in the house except one of his own, he drove his wife and children out to spend the night in the hills. The next day Mrs. Ehler went for the sheriff, who had Ehler arrested and fined. He was sentenced then to imprisonment for contempt of court, but may have escaped sentence somehow, for the next day he and Mrs. Ehler patched up the organ and pasted pictures from the Sunday papers over the cracks, but it could never be used again.

Home we drove by Ehler's old place. Ehler is ostensibly managing his affairs so that he can serve out his term of four months for contempt of court during the organ episode. Still Ehler is at large and prospecting!

We drove back down the hill to the ranch house, and good it was to get in at last out of the cold.

The winter school term lasts from October to April when the boys are called from school to ploughing and other spring ranch needs.

School began next morning and we all walked over the trail on the hills with our ten pound lard pails of lunch.

In later reminiscences about her days at the Twin Creek School, Ethel Waxham added more details about her students and the activities of the school days.

Glad we are [upon arriving at school in the morning] if blue smoke and heat waves rising from the stovepipe show that our masculine advance guard consisting of Sandford, or Bob or Bowser or Johnson came over first to build the fire. From the windows we watch the opposite hill to see three figures coming down in Indian file, swinging bright ten pound lard pails of lunch; we examine the three traps for mountain rats, and sometimes empty them; we consult the sundial and compare it with the watch; someone sweeps the floor, for a dirt roof has disadvantages. Sandford is official monitor of the coal barrel, mountain rat traps and water bucket of our twelve by sixteen foot school. The door has had some passerby's six shooter emptied into it. The ridge pole of the school before they moved it was so low that they advertised for a short teacher—so 'tis said.* All the boys come to school in their overalls, colored shirts, necktie-less, vests unbuttoned. It is etiquette to take off coats as well as hats when the boys come in.

The first fifteen minutes or half hour are given to reading *Uncle Tom's Cabin* or *Kidnapped,* while we all sit about the stove to keep warm. Usually in the middle of the reading the sound of a horse galloping down the frozen road distracts the attention of the boys, until a few moments later six foot George Schlichting opens the door, a sack of oats in one hand, his lunch tied up in a dishrag in the other. Cold from his five mile ride, he sits down on the floor by the stove, unbuckles his spurs, pulls off his leather chaps, drops his hat, unwinds two or three red handkerchiefs from about his neck and ears, takes off one or two coats, according to the temperature, unbuttons his vest and straightening his leather cuffs, is ready for business.

Sanford Mills is the largest scholar, six feet, big, slow in the school room, careful of every move of his big hands and feet. His voice is subdued and full of awe as he calls me "ma'am." Outside, while we play chickens, he is another person—there is room for his bigness.

Next largest of the boys is Otto Schlichting, thin and dark, a strange combination of shrewdness and stupidity.

*Ethel Waxham was about five feet two inches tall.

His problems always prove whether they are right or not! He is a boaster too, tries to make a big impression. But there is something very attractive about him. I was showing his little sister how to add and subtract by making little lines and adding or crossing off others. Later I found on the back of Otto's papers hundreds and hundreds of little lines—trying to add that way as far as a hundred evidently. He is nearly fifteen and is studying short division. He has been through the book so far five times already. Arithmetic is the family failing.

"How many eights in ninety-six," I ask him. He thinks for a long time. Finally he says with such a winsome smile that I wish with all my heart it were true—"Two." "What feeds the cells in your body?" I ask him. He thinks. At last, "I guess it's vinegar," he says. He has no idea of form. His maps of North America on the board are all long turnips. The map of the U.S. I can't make head or tail of, right side up or wrong.

Emmons Schlichting is a little more of an artist and a little more stupid. His face is round and a little brutal. Every expression can be read there—cunning, surprise, absolute ignorance. Yet he has his moments! Once when a teacher had them learn pieces, so that they might go home early on Friday afternoon, he forgot to do so. He gave as substitute an off-hand effusion on a bird, so strange and fearful that the teacher accused him of never having seen the like in a book. He swore, however, that it was in a book at home! Schlichting, père, can neither read nor write, even though he is one of the school directors. Schlichting, mère, has ambitions for the children. She tried to make Otto learn his arithmetic one year with the persuasions of a quirt. This year there is the reward of a saddle.

Schlichting, grand-mère, is the educated one of the family. She reads. When she comes to a large word or one unknown, she exclaims, "Vat a vort! Vat a vort!" and skipping it goes on serenely. Emmons has the family failing in the line of arithmetic. He can't get the tables in his head, but today he had them all written upon the black board, and standing with his back against it, had them all neatly imprinted upon his vest, at any rate.

Ellen Schlichting, the eight-year old girl, learns best of all. She is a shy little thing, light haired and brown eyed with a tanned face. She is just coming face to face with the arithmetic test, and it is exciting to see whether she will stand or fall.

Kathryn and Margaret Mills complete the school population of seven.

From half-past nine until four almost every moment is occupied by hearing some one of the thirty odd recitations, from reading and spelling to chemistry and civil government. For the teacher often the hardest work is self repression, as for instance when she asks, "Where does digestion take place?" Emmons thinks until, a smile of enlightenment dancing over his face, "In the Erie Canal," he answers.

Lesson follows fast upon lesson, question upon question. Once the teacher timed the questions; eight a minute, and all of vast importance.

Twelve thirty is the time for the half hour lunch. We sit in the sun along the side of the school house with our ten pound lard pails between our knees. The Schlichtings feed on pie and cake and tarts, we on bread and jelly and cheese and cookies or cake. Only about five minutes of this precious time is wasted in eating, in spite of the warning of the physiology. "Aw, I don't believe that book," says Emmons, swallowing a tart. I still suspect that he thinks he is solid all though. During the week of the deepest snow when only two or three of the seven are at school, lunches are more elaborate. The beans are heated in a pail cover, and the eggs in the drinking cup—for a cold hard boiled egg can be very cold indeed when the thermometer is at zero. Meanwhile, between bites, the news of the country for twenty-five or fifty miles about is exchanged; what horses and cattle are lost, with what brands; Hanley's luck in trapping, caught a buffalo wolf; the last sheepherder lost in the storm; the dance at the Lucky Strike. George carries out oats to his horse and rides him down to water. Then we have a miniature wild west show of bucking and jumping if the horse is willing. When snow is on the ground a snowball fight follows, or a slide down the steepest spur of the mountain behind the school.

All too soon at the sound of the sheep bell, work begins again. Battles and triumphs are renewed. Ellen masters seven and eight; George spells "picnic" correctly; the troublesome original in geometry is solved; the bookkeeping trial balance is right. But there is only time for a breath of relief before new failures.[7]

The journal continues:

People passing, we call company. Sometimes no one goes by for days. Sometimes many pass. A Mormon boy was the first; he came trailing along over the hills on a horse at recess time, and stopped to talk. The next day at the same time exactly he rode over the same hill, and stopped again. We looked for him on the third day but in vain. Old Hanley was one of the next to appear. While we were peacefully doing lessons in the afternoon the door opened, and old Hanley's head was stuck in. It disappeared at once. Then appeared again. "How far is it to Schlichtings?" he asked, though he knew as well as any of us. Then he went on. The reason he stopped was divulged afterward to Bob. He wanted to come in to light his pipe.

Ted Abra, one of the roustabouts, has rented Ehler's old place and goes by often. He enjoys the reputation of being cattle thief and horse wrangler. Roy McLaughlin is another of the gang. They went by once with about fifty head of horses.

Old man Myers of Myersville passed once. It is said that he will go out of his way fifteen miles to avoid a house in which he may see a woman. Being here of necessity at one time, he spent part of the afternoon collecting flower seeds to plant down at his place.

Deane is the only other so-called visitor who has passed. It is he whom Smithy calls "Assistant Chief of the Pugwash Outfit," because he never pays his bills—a subtle inference which no one else would ever be able to interpret into the name.

When the first Saturday came, we saddled up, Kathryn, Margaret and I, to hunt for a lost cow and incidentally to go down to Hailey for the mail. The day was gray and gloomy when we started out along an imperceptible trail over the mountains. Snow soon began to fall, but after about three hours riding, the sun shone once more, and the sky grew clear. We started for Hall Creek, named for Mr. Hall—and on the way investigated the only two cabins between here and Hailey on the hills. One belonged to old Pete McKay when he used to trap in the neighborhood during the winter. It had one window, one door, and for furniture, one plank bed, stove, two box cupboards and a table, all in an ungodly state of dirt and dilapidation since his departure. Mountain rats had built nests in the cupboards, and left traces everywhere. Outside was a broken-down pen where at some time hay used to be kept.

The dikes on the creek are the only places to get water, and water almost as dirty as the soil. It is either a cloud burst or a drought most of the time, for Hall Creek never has water in it.

Pete McKay used to live up on the cedar ridge during the day and come down to Mr. Mills at night for food—the sheriff was after him for stealing cattle. He said once that he was just catching a calf up on the ridge when he happened to look down into Mr. Mills' field. The men there had stopped their haying and he fancied that they were looking at him. Must have been an evil conscience for they could never have seen so far. Anyway, he drove the calf behind the ridge before he touched it. Mr. Mills was on a jury once to try him for stealing a calf which he had branded in the corral here. It turned out, however, that he had not stolen that one. I think it was he who used to say that the sheriff gave him heaps of free rides into town, but always made him walk back. We rode over his old haunts.

Whenever at the top of a far distant hill we would discern a group of cattle, we would struggle over the draws and up the sides until we could see them all, and be sure that the cow for which we were searching was not there. Then we would see a farther bunch and go to them. Baly always took the worst possible parts of the draws to cross, and the largest jumps, and the lanky bay Mack would go over as awkwardly and as well as a cowpony may. About noon we stopped to eat our bread and cheese. A little later, we found the cow, made sure of the brand, and rode on over the hills to Hailey, where Mrs. Signor made us take a bite to eat. We left about three, getting home about half-past five, and driving the cows into the corral on the way.

The next day, Sunday, there was snow on the ground, and we had the first of a number of "sleigh rides." The sleigh is a sled, less than a foot from the ground, made of four or five heavy planks. The runners are wood planks with a strip of iron on the bottom. "The best sleigh in the country except for an old cutter in Lander," says Mr. Mills. The seat is a carriage seat, balancing itself on the planks. We start out bundled to our ears, the two girls and myself on the seat, Mr. Mills standing behind, *à la charioteer.* There is only a sprinkle of snow, and the horses have to work every foot of the way. The road tips to one side, or has a deep ridge in the middle. We go along on one runner, or plow up the middle of the road with the sled body. The sleigh bells on the tongue clatter away. We go up a side hill to avoid the uneven road. The seat goes off, and all of us in it, into the snow. We fix the seat and go on. A moment later off we go again. After that we stay in the road.

I KNOW A LAND . . .

I know a land where the gray hills lie
Eternally still, under the sky,

Where all the might of suns and moons
That pass in the quiet of nights and noons
Leave never a sign of the flight of time
On the long sublime horizon line—
Where the wide white hush of the falling snow
Rests on the hills and the draws below.
Under the sheen of the cold starlight
The hills lie gleaming and glittering bright
And the crystal silence is shivered by
Wailing of coyotes or wolves' long cry.
Where the silver lyre of summer rain
Is touched by the winds to music again
And the song of the silence wakes and stirs
Like a thing alive in the hearts of the firs.

Ethel Waxham   Red Bluff Ranch, 1905[8]

November 15. The color of the white hills against the pale blue of the sky is most exquisite in the world. The cedars are gray with snow, the sage brush white clumps of crystals. Where a long way off the sun touches the tops of the snow covered hills there shines a streak of silver. A whole white world was there, rising around us, as far as we could see; there did not appear to be such a thing as direction. Everywhere whiteness, everywhere the hills. Where the stubble of the fields of the ranch rose above the snow, there was a shading of yellowgold over the white. That was all. Since the first snow I have seen it so often, and when the full moon shines out of the deep dark night sky, the hills are like shining silver. It is a cruel country as well as a beautiful one. Men seem here only on sufferance. After every severe storm, we hear of people's being lost. Yesterday it was a sheep camp mover who was lost in the Red Desert. People had hunted for him for a week, and found no trace. Mr. Love—Johnny Love—told of a man who had just been lost up in his country, around the Muskrat. "Stranger?" he was asked. "No, born and brought up here." "Old man?" "No, in the prime of life. Left Lost Cabin sober, too."

45

"Lunch at the Twin Creek School before the snow came." From the right, Sandford, Kathryn, Margaret, Ellen, Otto, Emmons.

Mr. Sanderson* has a cabin at the foot of the white chalk cliffs on the way to Hailey. One morning he heard someone calling and went out to find a man almost frozen to death, trying to get down to his cabin. An Englishman it was, who had started from Casper a week before. He had let his horse get away from him, and had had to walk. His boots were leather, tight. For a week he had seen no one, no house. Both his feet were frozen. Mr. Sanderson took him in to Lander where they were cut off. The surgeon did a poor job, and had to cut off more on two other occasions. No wonder that skeletons are found around on the plains and hills. Mr. Love told of two, one of an Indian under some rocks, upon which he had been sitting many a time. The other half a mile away, was of a white man with gold fillings in his teeth.

*Arthur H. Sanderson, stockman and rancher.

Mr. Love came the morning of Sunday November 12th. Of course we did not expect him. He is never expected. In the morning his white-top buggy was there, and his horses in the corral. That was all. He had come in about two in the morning, fed and watered his horses, and turned in with Bob in the bunk house. He had come sixty miles in eleven hours, with "little rats of horses." "Couldn't get any sleep," said Mr. Love, "these horses would have run away or kicked over the pole." Usually he lies down in the buggy and the horses take him where he wants to go. Mr. Love is a Scotchman about thirty-five years old. At first sight he made me think of a hired man, as he lounged stiffly on the couch, in overalls, his feet covered with enormous red and black-striped stockings edged with blue around the top, that reached to his knees. He seemed to wear them instead of house shoes. His face was kindly, with shrewd blue twinkling eyes. A moustache grew over his mouth, like willows bending over a brook. But his voice was most peculiar and characteristic. Close analysis fails to find the charm of it. A little Scotch dialect, a little slow drawl, a little nasal quality, a bit of falsetto once in a while, and a tone as if he were speaking out of doors. There is a kind of twinkle in his voice as well as in his eyes, and he is full of quaint turns of speech, and unusual expressions. For he is not a common sheepherder, but a mutton-aire, or sheep baron, as Mr. Mills said.

Unbeknownst to Ethel, the Mills Ranch was also the informal headquarters of John G. Love. Shortly after her arrival, he appeared suddenly one morning for breakfast. Wrapped in a huge buffalo-hide overcoat against the chill November weather, he had come sixty miles nonstop by team and buggy from his ranch on Muskrat Creek. He arrived as he usually did, in the middle of the night, quietly put his horses in the barn, fed them, and then went to sleep in the bunk house without waking anyone. Whether he came solely to size up the new schoolmarm will never be known, but for him, a lonely bachelor of thirty-five, it was love at first sight. Not so for her.[9] Much later in her short story "Rome Was Not Built in a Day," she wrote:

. . . His resonant Scotch burr sounded through the house before him. Seated, he gave the impression of a large man. However, he was not. His great head, powerful shoulders, and heavy body tapered too soon to his small feet. His skin was fair; his blue eyes under dark brows had the keen, steady look of a sharpshooter. Below his straight nose was a walrus moustache. He had an indifference to clothes, so long as there were enough to keep him warm. He had felt packs under his overshoes. His buffalo hide coat was permanent equipment.

She later told her children that one of the things that had attracted her to him was that he had the look of eagles.

[November 15 continued]

All the gossip of the mountains he told us. The latest news from Scarlet was that he had sent "a bag of game" to some of his friends in Colorado. It contained jackrabbits, cottontails, sagehens—at this season tough as can be—and a few ducks. How Mr. Love roared and chuckled as he told it.

"Madden was arrested a while ago up our way."

"So?"

"Ya-as. He'd killed and sent beef to town, while the hides were hanging over his fence in t'other county. He was at the telephone one day when he heard the sheriff telephoning to somebody else about him. So he called up the sheriff when the other fellow was through. Sheriff asked him if he hadn't killed without sending along the hides. 'Guess you've got me this time,' he said. 'Come to Cheyenne on the next stage,' said the sheriff. 'Alright,' he said, and hung around outside waiting for the stage to come along. Someone else happened along, and he poured forth his troubles. 'I hate to go to prison just now,' said Madden. 'I'm awfully busy and can't spare the time.' 'Tell the sheriff to arrest Woodruff instead. He ain't got nothing to do.' 'Good plan,' said Madden, and

Photograph of John Galloway Love published in
the *Shoshoni Pathfinder*, circa 1904.

acted accordingly. The sheriff did not mind, so they broke
the news to Woodruff. 'That's all right,' said he. 'I ain't busy,
and can go to jail just as well as not for a few days. Might just
as well be down in Cheyenne as here.' So he went."

Johnny Love went on to tell the news up his way. His one
hen had laid an egg every day for six days—out of season too.
Smithy was working for a Dutchman. Swore he would never
do it again, and never move a sheep camp again. "Hear what
Smithy said about Pigot? He had to climb up on the table
when he wanted to spit over his collar."

Then there was the romance of Pigot's daughter. Her
mother said she might take Dutch Ed, and if she didn't like
him, she could get a divorce. Old Pigot would prompt one,
and his wife the other when Ed came to call. Finally the
matter was arranged, and they were married. She went crazy
later and cut up all the clothes she could get into strips. Had

a whole trunk full. Then Ed got a divorce, and old Pigot pocketed his two thousand. He has been swearing at his sons-in-law ever since. One they had to lock up the night after he was married, he was so drunk.

Then Mr. Love remembered the candy and nuts and apples which he had brought along like the veritable Santa Claus that he is. Out he went to get them, remembering always some new thing he had brought.

Later Guy Signor and Mr. Scott, an insurance agent, came to stay for supper and bunk for the night. Guy is really the largest person I ever saw. He wore a loose sweater that showed the tiger-like movements of his body. Then the talk redoubled. They brought some news of Smithy. He would never work for a sheep camp again. Couldn't satisfy anyone. "If the sheep camp were here, it would be all right." He moves it; they want it somewhere else. The wind up there is awful. He was putting up a ridgepole, when the wind was blowing. He looked up and saw the chipmunks blowing over his head. By and by along came some sheep, dead. At last one was flying over who was not quite gone. He turned around and said "Baaa"—and then he was in Montana. Poor Smithy had to hold on to the bedpost with one hand and bedclothes with another to keep from going over into Montana himself. N.B.: Bedpost was probably sagebrush. There's no telling how Smithy will look when he comes. Every time, he has a change in manner of wearing his whiskers; he has tried every style and is still experimenting.

Mr. Scott—tall, broad, big hands, enormous feet, sleek, converses on every possible subject with personal reminiscences. Guy related some of his hunting adventures and showed the teeth of a deer, or elk, the only ivory of America. Mr. Love told of his coming upon a hunter's camp up there, and finding a famously good pie. He ate about half and left a note, "Lead us not into temptation," where the pie should have been. That turned out to be Guy's own pie!

Speaking of Scotchmen, Mrs. Mills accused Mr. Love of being Scotch when Scotchmen were around, but from America when he was with Americans. "That leaves me eligible for the presidency," he drawled.

When Mr. Love intended to go, the tongue of his carriage was found frozen in the ground. He made that an excuse to stay, but sorry we were to find him hitching up the second day, as we were on the way to school.

November 19. Yesterday Kathryn gave me my second lesson in milking. Mrs. Earl in Lander says that you have to learn after you are married, if not before! I do get a little milk, and do better every time. It is good to hear the milk flowing rhythmically into the pail and be regaled by stares of the cows.

After school in the evenings the girls take me around to drive the 18 pigs, and the 32 ducks in for the night, send the hens to roost, feed the calves, and cats and dogs and antelope. At mealtime all the hungry animals gather at the kitchen door, the antelope trying to push their way in, the cats crying.

November 20. A great day. George Ehler came to school. Whether he will stay or not, I do not know. He rode over from the Big Bend on a buckskin horse; his lunch—a quarter of a cake, and a quarter of a pie—done up in a dishrag, and his horse's oats in a sack. He is only thirteen, but taller than Sandford, and fair and handsome. I should like to get him away from his family—kidnap him. To think that it was he who tried to kill his father! His face is as good as can be. Poor boy is in the fifth reader and ought to be in the first. Can't add, can't subtract. "The harvest truly is ripe—"

December 2. The Thanksgiving holidays have come and gone, and as the ever-present snow keeps us indoors and kept company away, I am glad to make the most of a little leisure by putting down a few of the things that have happened. They are very few indeed. The chief event was the drive to Hailey last Sunday in the cold wind which brought snow the next day. It took from eleven to five to go, as the roads were drifted with snow. A few more stories came out. Mr. Mills gives way to reminiscences while he is driving. "See that little hole in Sheep Mountain? Whiskers had a tent there one night when he was herding sheep for me. We had been wet by rain the night before, but Whiskers stayed out with the sheep. When I went to find him, there was only the stove pipe sticking out of a snow drift. No sheep. I dug him out. He had no fire, only a couple of lanterns to keep him warm, and he was still wet from the rain before. There were a few holes in the snow where the sheep's breath came up. We got after them, kicked them, and the whole side of the mountain began to move."

We drove on farther until we came to the end of the canyon where the Harts and Canoeys live now. The Frinks have moved down there in the same "neighborhood," so we have lost our neighbors.

Rosy Hart has come back from town—six feet two of her. She does a man's work in the fields; her mother was like her and died in the harness.

The Millers used to live in the house. Then they sold their sheep, attained sudden wealth, and traded the ranch for a house in Lander. To Denver they went to enjoy themselves, and spent their time riding up and down on the street cars— only five cents a ride. Mr. Miller bought a dozen pair of overalls. Mrs. Miller invested in six silk dresses. Together they bought a $175 music box and a blue painted bedroom set over which sprawled big red roses. Another investment was a green plush lounge.

So they lived on peaches and cream in Lander until the end of the winter, when Mrs. Miller could not borrow ten dollars at the bank. So they traded back for their ranch, and lived there with the bedroom set and music box. Always they left the door to the bedroom open, so that people could see the set. When it rained, they put blankets over the music box and green plush sofa, for red muddy water came in from the roof. Mrs. Miller longed for a door bell—"It would be so nice to hear it ring." The sign of a prosperous family now is a phonograph.

Beyond their place, is the grave of the man found dead in the sixties. The head and footstones are remarkably well-preserved. Over the grave are heavy stones to keep the wolves from digging up the body. The inscription is well-cut. " . . . S. McCaulay. Found Dead. March 7, 1865." Not even the old timers remember about it. Generally a name is more than can be attached to the bones found every winter about the country. A sheepherder found a sock once over toward Lewiston with a man's foot inside; it had been gnawed off by coyotes. Perhaps a mile away he discovered the body. Always more stories of men lost, or bones found. Every snow has its victims.

Mr. Mills started out to Atlantic City last week with some beef that had just been killed. A blizzard came up while he was gone. It reached him about dusk, snow, wind, and cold. He lost the road several times. Finally he drove into a snow drift, from which the horses could not pull the wagon. He hitched them on to the back and tried to draw it out that way, but to no use. So he climbed on Stambaugh and from him to Sorreltop, without a saddle, and started on the six or seven mile ride home. He missed the road often. He could hear the wolves howling after him on his trail. Sometimes he would get off to walk to keep his feet from freezing. He reached home at last, thanks only to Sorreltop, for Mr. Mills was quite lost. The horses' legs were covered with icicles and they were tired out. To say nothing of Mr. Mills.

Our drive to the Signors brought us there in the middle of the afternoon, when as usual, Mrs. Signor gave us dinner and talked as fast as she could. For the first time I appreciated the feeling of the people here toward the Signor house. White boards without and within, neat, clean, vine-covered. "The prettiest thing I ever saw," said Margaret once. There was mail to get—there always is a large sackful for our weekly or semi-monthly visits. Mr. Scarlet was there, making his weekly visit. Also Mr. Alger, "Ede Signor's young man," who has been in the country for ten years and was never known to do anything. He is a man of wealth—supposed to have forty thousand dollars—and spends most of his time trying to avoid spending his money.

Wonder of wonders, an automobile was there. It was broken coming down Beaver Hill, and Mr. Signor had to go after it with horses, and haul it down. The chauffeur, a big fellow with many days' beard, came out while we were examining it, looking at the mud over it, the traps piled high in the back. He was going to have it taken to Lander with four horses. Mr. Signor was to furnish the horses and be paid by the day—he told Mr. Mills that he would make a four days' job of it, when it should take only one.

Edith had had a shampoo, and a hair curl, besides dressing up in a black dress made from something else and blue trimming. She had grown a little too much and the dress opened up the back whenever she bent over. In honor of Alger, I suppose. Guy's "young lady" is one of the Watkins girls, but as Mrs. Mills says, "Guy has a cabbage heart with a leaf for every girl."

But to return to Scarlet. So much I had heard of him that I was more than glad to make his acquaintance. He is a tall, dark young man with a goodsized nose. He talked, as is his reputation. He, his father and mother, used to herd sheep together. They would be in the sheep wagon, and "Mother" would begin a story. "See here, Mother, I want to tell that," from Scarlet or his father. And the father would win at talking every time. Mother is a wonder. Mother loves to work. Mother herds the sheep. Her bed is a hammock of barrel staves slung by the door. Scarlet starts up in the night. "Mother, the sheep are going"; and Mother goes after them because she is nearest the door. Scarlet was almost lynched— so the story goes—when he was at Banis's for his treatment of his mother. She would be herding sheep in winter wearing gum boots, skirts worn in tatters almost to her knees. Mother can fry a hundred sage hens in a condensed milk can of lard; and Mother can cook rabbits so that they are delicious. Foods both despised.

Scarlet was going into horse raising, so he said, but his colt died! He had a dog, however. "Something must be the matter with that dog. I gave him a whole half of a rabbit's leg, and some spuds, which by the way, meant parings—and he is hungry yet. He must be sick." Scarlet has gone to town for Thanksgiving leaving Mother in the cabin ten or twelve miles from anyone, to chop her own wood and haul water, alone. Father stayed only a while. He used to get drunk and lie under the sheep wagon. Scarlet says that he wants his mother to go East, but she cries and says she won't go. She has not long to live and wants to stay here.

And the next day it snowed. At first snow came only once a week; now twice, with wind before and cold after. Often we have to ride to school in the sled, while the Schlichtings come in a wagon with Whiskers. George comes in frosty and snowy from his long ride. When the last day before Thanksgiving came, I asked everyone to write five things for which they were thankful. George's first was for a warm fire; Sandford "would be thankful if it would stop snowing"; Otto and George were both thankful for a horse; everyone was thankful for vacation, and Ellen that school began again on Monday. George, his overalls over his pants, a ragged shirt and shabby coat, a cap with four flaps with some strings attached to tie over his ears, was thankful for plenty to wear; and ye shades of his lunches, for plenty to eat! It's pitiful too, that he was thankful "to be a-live." He is a clean-faced, clean-handed boy, so that I hate to hear the stories of how he stole here and there, and lies. He answers quickly and brightly when spoken to, but is so used to kicks and ill treatment that he is timid and shrinking even in games. For all his size he is not strong. He takes the teasing and blows goodnaturedly. Otto, I like more than ever. When about to read something funny in the reader, he winks at me first over the top. He can see from his seat when people go by, while I at the table cannot.

So when the others crane their necks, he will look out too, then turn to me and shake his head. Nobody there. He is monitor of the blackboard. Ellen is monitor of the dustcloth and Kathryn of the broom stick.

ALICE WELTY
Dubois, Wyo.
Dec. 3, 1905

My dear Miss Waxham,

Your letter received a few days ago.

I was very glad indeed to hear from you. I have thought of you so often, & wondered how you like Ranch life & school teaching. Yes, I was very thankful *not* to have any more *"Wild West"* on my journey home.

I had nice weather & a very pleasant trip all the way, found all well and very glad to have me home once more. Where are you going to spend your Christmas? Can't you come to Dubois? We will all be very glad to have you come. I will turn my *pet* horse over to you all the time you stay.

Soon after my return, my daughter was confined, and now we have a dear little baby, a boy so good & pretty.

I am so glad you like your home and wish you had a horse. There is nothing one enjoys more than a good horse.

We are not quite so isolated here as you are—we have near neighbors & a town *Hall,* where we have dances quite often, and will be sure to have one for Christmas, so you will be sure to see all our people if you can spend the Holidays with us. I have two sons & a young man from Washington D.C. in my family & they say be sure to come.

Yours with love,
Alice A. Welty

<u>December 3.</u> Sledding again today with the team. We did not tip over once, and only lost the driver and the lap robe. A visitor was here when we arrived, judging from a white horse hitched behind the house, a beautiful white—not pink,

according to the custom of the country and influence of red mud. We thought it might be Guy Signor, but as to the man's identity I am yet ignorant, being in my room writing, through disinclination to go out and see. There's many a person I should be glad to meet—the woman called Sour Dough; Three Fingered Bill, or Suffering Jim; Sam O'Mera, Reub Roe, Rode Ealy or Smithy, Pelon or French George.

Pelon and French George lived together one winter. "Pelon, he dirty. Me move out de tab', move out de stove, get the hoe." Then Pelon would not give French George any tobacco, so the old man started out to Lewiston, perhaps eighteen miles away, for some. A storm overtook him, and he had to stop over for some days in a little old cabin where he had wintered once. There was some stale bread, so he did not starve, but alas, "no tobac." French George, however, hit on the expedient of smoking the dish rag, which was pretty good at first, as there was more tobacco in the pipe than dish rag. Later, however, there was more dishrag than pipe, and it was not so pleasant.

Old Pelon doesn't know his name, can't spell it, has to make his mark. Still, there is one man in the country worse off, Indian Dick, because even he doesn't know where he came from. Probably found by the Indians in some emigrant train which they destroyed. Old Pelon's wife died some time ago. Mrs. Mills asked him if he were not sorry. "No, she a dev'." Mrs. Ehler then used to send over cakes and pies to Pelon, and Ehler managed Pelon's affairs so that the old man never had a cent of money. His will was made out leaving everything to Mrs. Ehler, when a distant relative appeared, discovered the state of things, and Mrs. Mills managed to make Pelon write a new will. Now the Ehlers have nothing to do with the old man.

Reub Roe was another interesting old man who used to roam the country, insane but harmless. He used to hold up teams of people and ask them if they belonged to the royal family. Luckily they never did, so they all escaped injury. At last he went into a store in Lander, and dumping his pack saddle on the counter, said to one of the Baldwin girls, "That's all I have!" She did not know what he meant. "It ain't very much, but it's all I have." He was proposing. After that they took him to put in the asylum. "I never did no harm, but to steal a horse of Mr. Mills'." Mr. Mills knew nothing about it, for the horse was so old it had been turned out to die.[10] They put handcuffs on him. "Do they hurt?" asked the man who was taking him away. "I'll take them off when they do," answered Old Reub. Sure enough, he did. They put him to work driving a coal wagon. Small wonder that he deserted and left. He may still possibly be hunting for the royal family.

Sam O'Mera is the man who lives in a stage house on the road to Atlantic City in winter, in the barn in summer. They say he does wash, but more dirt accumulates than leaves him. He used to sleep on top of the boiler—with the chance of rolling off to his death in the night. His hospitality is never accepted when possible not to, for he lives on sour beans and sour bread and honey, dug out of the can with a chisel. He is an old man, almost bald, his little hair combed straight up the back of his head. Johnny Love takes him off to perfection. Speaking of marriage, Sam says, "Them I can get, I do not want. No Sir, I do not. Them that I want, won't have me. No Sir, they will not." Perhaps I may see Sam some day on the way to Miner's Delight.

There's another tale of Smithy going the rounds. He used to have a milk ranch near Salt Lake City. "Why," he says, "I had the world by the tail." A kind heart, has old Smithy, buys freight teams, all skin and bones and sores, fattens them and sells them or trades them for thin ones. "Perhaps the Old Man will lay it up to my account." Wherever he stays, he makes a square box, and puts on a padlock. In it he keeps treasures and cast-off things, which he gives as presents at the next place he stays. Ellen has one of his boxes now for a doll's trunk. Smithy sent a present up from the Big Bend once to Mrs. Mills—whiskey bottles done up in gunny sacks to keep them from breaking. "Thought she might like some pickle bottles," he said. Beer bottles *are* used for jelly here, by dropping a red hot ring around the neck, which falls off.

A letter came last week from Miss Allie Davis[11] in regard to the Institute which opens the day after Christmas. It seems I must have a paper. She may—or may not inspect the Twin Creek school during the winter. They say she will appear driving up with Sunny Jim, "Smiling Allie and Sunny Jim." They were both running for office at the same time in Lander, and agreed that if he lost, she was to marry him; if she was elected he was to marry her. Both were elected, but neither married the other. He is now faro dealer in one of the saloons in Lander. The other county superintendents were cautious. One was an old lady who would not give up her office for years and years. She distributed certificates to anyone who wanted them. Another county superintendent came around to make the yearly visit and went to sleep in the school sitting on the floor.

December 5. Sunday, after Carney of the pretty white horse had gone, a tall dark man drove up with a team, saddle horse attached to the wagon. "Guess it's Bruce come to winter in the bunk house," said Margaret. So it was. "Poor Bill," Smithy calls him. He had brought his bed, gun and dog. Bill is an Irishman; face and head slantwise on his shoulders; hair soft and fine, combed over the top of his head forward to hide slight baldness; narrow between the eyes, long in the cheeks, big of jaw, with fine beard and moustache. He has a childlike gentleness and drollery of manner that is either innocence itself or simulated. He came over to this country and found a five-dollar gold piece on the sidewalk. "Come over, Brothers," he wrote home. "It's all true."

Later he got a job of carrying bricks. "Come over, Brothers," he wrote again. "All I have to do is to carry bricks up to the fourth floor in a hod and the man up there does all the work." He is the mildest man on earth. Was tired one summer and wanted to rest, so he went to the mountains,

Mary Alice Davis, Superintendent of Schools. Photograph from the *Shoshoni Pathfinder*.

turned his horses loose and slept a great deal and fished a little, ate some, and stayed until the water froze. Nothing ever troubles or ruffles him. He turned one conversation at the supper table to bedbugs, their prevalence and swarms all through the country. At Reed's Stage Station, they have three degrees of license in regard to bedbugs—millions in the bunk house, some in the saloon bedrooms, none in the house.

December 7. Playing cards with "Poor Bill" Bruce and the children. Poor Bill so manoeuvered the conversation at the table this evening that it turned once more on bedbugs. He told his experiences illustrating graphically how one fell from the ceiling upon his head at dinner and how and where they bite. Mr. Mills turned the talk to himself—how his aches and pains were worse than anyone else's. "Pit's open," said Bruce, showing a full two inches of teeth up and down in the laugh. Somehow the talk turned to baths. Bruce takes one once or twice a year at the warm spring below. "The dirtiest man was 'Dirty Bill' Collins. He never took a bath in his life. It was that that killed him. He took one at last and began to die right away."

December 8. As usual on Friday evenings, the rug was taken from the dining room, the table moved out and the lamp taken down for our dancing school. Bedroom slippers, fur trimmed are à la mode for dancing. To make the floor a bit slippery, we sprinkle corn meal over it. Tonight Poodles, Bill's ragged black sheep dog, which limps on two legs owing to a fight with Dick immediately after his arrival, watched the corn meal sprinkling seriously, then went out in the middle of the floor and began to lick it up. He accomplished quite a little before we began to dance. Then he growled vigorously. "You'd best put him out," said Bruce. "He'll bite at yer legs."

Mr. Bruce offered to play the mouthharp. For march, we had part of the chorus of "Marching through Georgia"; for waltz "In the Good Old Summertime." The polka was "Little Brown Jug, I Love You," and the Schottisch "Come to the Saviour." It was the first dance with music and kept us up until nearly eleven. Then Mr. Bruce broke in, "Do you's want me to sing for you?" Of course we did, so he drew his lackadaisical feet and hands from where they were idling, braced himself and sang "The Warrior Bold," whereupon he relapsed once more. But his voice was too good for us to be willing to have him stop, so he sang song after song, "Powder Monkey, Little Jim," the Irish song "Sentenced to Death," all death in war or at sea or for a love with golden hair.

"It is going to be a hard winter," Pelon says. The birds have gone south but the ducks have come. No such fall has been for fifteen years. The semi-weekly snow has come, fine and soft over all the hills. When the moon shines full upon it at night, the whiteness of the earth gleams like silver.

December 12. Mr. Bruce is going off for his sheep wagon, which he is going to move up here, for no one knows how long. The reason of his present visit turned out to be that the sheriff was after him to serve on the jury for a couple of murder trials. He did not mind an ordinary jury, but not this! One of the two people to be tried was a woman. So Mr. Bruce cleared out, telling one person that he was going freighting, another another story and so on. Now he is safe.

Sheep wagons are interesting things. Mr. Bruce says you have to sleep with the potatoes—with the bread, too, to keep them from freezing. Luckily they never have much of anything at a time.

More gossip of Reub Roe. He collected pigs' tails, and wove them into his lariat—Another of his proposals: "You can pack your shoes in my war satchel any time you please."

George was away from school today, for his father is in town, trying to get out of his four months' sentence for contempt of court during the organ episode. I quite miss "the worst thief in the state."

December 23. School is over for a week. Otto appeared in the full grandeur of a clean shirt *and* a neck tie! Such a tie! All the colors of the rainbow vied with one another in the space of a few short inches. Perhaps because of the grand clothes, all his arithmetic was right for the only time this month.

Today, Saturday, has been spent preparing for Christmas. Mr. Mills brought home a pine tree—pitch pine—and cut it to the right height. This we exaltingly set up in front of the window in the sitting room, fixing branches below as a covering to the standard. Every year there has been a tree, and every year the same decorations, yet such secrecy as was needed! We hung two sheets in front of the tree so that no one should see it before the proper time. Mrs. Mills dissolved alum in water, which we sprinkled over the needles and branches for mimic frost. Then the ornaments! Blue tarleton stockings, flat, never filled, tinsel decorated; pink, home-made pails for candy; gorgeous paper pictures of Santa Claus, angels, bells and so on, with showers of tinsel falling from them or spreading out like halos in every direction. Then some green and pink and blue rope tinsel and the candles. Lo, the tree is finished! At Mrs. Hall's once, icicles were made for the tree by dipping raisin stems in alum; berries were made of sealing wax; tin foil was taken from tobacco to cover wooden balls; stars had mica glued over them for the glitter. I really had fears lest the tree might not last until Christmas Eve. The antelope began to eat it, while it was yet outside, and the kitten attempted exploration among the branches, which are not too solid.

The tree is not the only sign that Christmas is coming. Mrs. Mills has made thirteen pounds of candy. We are not allowed to see it for fear temptation will be too strong for flesh to resist. We did, however, try to pull some cream candy which had been colored a vivid pink. It sugared in the act, however, and mine for some reason was the only plateful that got even a slight pulling. The rest crumbled to look like strawberry ice cream. In the excitement attendant upon the pulling, Sandford drank a cup of blueing, mistaking it for water. Teeth, tongue and mouth were blue. Mr. Bruce suggested that he drink some starch now, while he was about it. But Sandford's stomach seems to be even blueing-proof.

Eggs! Not having seen an egg since my arrival, imagine the astonishment of Mrs. Mills when Mr. Mills returned one day from Hailey with four eggs in his pocket! They stood the trip well, though they were already a month old. Mrs. Mills went around holding them in her hands, showing them to people. Then the debate as to what should be done with them! Two or three were at last consigned to the making of a momentous plum pudding which will appear tomorrow. The other, I think, is fated for salad dressing, salad to consist of watercress. [12]

The day after Christmas, Institute commences. Mr. Mills is still on the trail of the threshers, [13] so Sandford will take me in. Oh, the excitement attendant upon going! Mrs. Mills, I believe, has written to all her friends that I am coming, and I hope to meet the people I have heard of so often. Since Mrs. Bruce could not accommodate me, I am going to accept Miss Davis' invitation to stay with her. "If Jim Atkins is there," said Mrs. Mills, "Don't be seen on the street with him. Don't have anything to do with him." Then came more advice on all subjects. "Don't get into the saloon by mistake when you are going into the bank." It really seems as if I were going into society instead of to a prosaic Institute in a town of a thousand people. It may not be so prosaic, however. When teachers were scarce in Lander, the janitor's wife went to teaching. A washwoman too, if I remember correctly, was called in also in time of need. But that is nothing to Lander. The barber learned his trade in sheep shearing which he practiced all week until Saturday night. Now he has a chair in one of the saloons. But it is as much as a man's life is worth to be shaved, for several men have been killed in that chair, and there are bullet holes in the wall behind. The blacksmith used to pull teeth for people; his business grew so that he finally could send away for forceps and discard the blacksmith tongs. A man named Johnson came into the country there, making false teeth for those that desired them. He had a little tin furnace that he carted around, and would set up in the dining room, spending weeks making a set of teeth. He made a set for Mrs. Miller, but they did not fit so she wore them only on Sundays.

On Christmas Eve, on Sunday, Mr. Mills went to Hailey for the mail. As he did not return for hours, we began to worry a little as to whether he had been captured by the threshers or entrapped by the court to serve on the jury. But just as supper was put on the table, he was seen making his way slowly across the field with a mammoth sack on the saddle in front of him. No wonder that he had had to travel on a walk all the way from Hailey.

"If I had known that Miss Waxham was to have so much mail, I would have taken the wagon," he said. Most of the presents had not arrived, but the Christmas tree was lighted all the same and the candy and packages that had already come were put under it. "Ohh!" we all said, as if we had not trimmed the tree ourselves, and one and all sat down on the floor to undo our presents. Even Mr. Bruce was remembered, though the gifts were small. The package in which my longed-for pajamas arrived was torn, and I, who suspected what they might be, secreted that parcel in my own room. It was missed, however, and Mrs. Mills and the girls followed me in to open the bundle. My other presents, especially the books, were enjoyed by all. Mr. Bruce insisted on trying to read "Alysoun" and other old English poems aloud, and had a sudden rapture over the Dam Family in the "Bric à Brac." Mr. Mills went to work at once on Kipling, and Mrs. Mills and I looked over Swinburne. When bedtime came we held a council in nightgowns and pajamas besides doing physical culture drill until midnight.

And the next day was Christmas. Mr. Bruce took us out in the sled to get more pine branches to decorate the dining room. We had neither time nor permission to eat anything but toast all day, for all our energies were bent upon dinner. Just before supper the joyful cry went up that Mr. Love was coming, and actually in time for dinner. He had broken his record and arrived by day! A second cry then filled the air.

The table was set and all made ready, when lo and behold Marty Hart, one of the would-be threshers had arrived. Query, would he eat, or had he eaten? Mrs. Mills refused to have him brought in. Mr. Mills refused to go after him. Confusion reigned, during which time linen collars and fried shirts were donned by the men as finishing touches to their toilettes. Mr. Mills broke several buttonholes, and finally threw collar buttons away in disgust, appearing with a festive white handkerchief about his neck, quite as if he had a sore throat. Then we all sat down to peanut soup and celery brought by Mr. Love, while Sandford was caring for Marty Hart. They turned up at last, and to the joy of all, Marty had dined. Marty is a good awkward fellow, larger even than Guy Signor. He can't come in the house without bending over; if he were perfectly straight and not bowed as to the legs, he might measure six feet seven. But supper! Grand style it was, with a Christmas tree lighted in the center, and all of us dressed in our best round about, hungry as bears, but feeling very grand and formal. Small wonder that we were formal. We had never seen peanut soup before; after that came the *pièce de résistance,* three ducks, the ever-present onions, potatoes and so on; later, watercress salad, plum pudding, frozen whipped cream, coffee and nuts. As to the question of dishes, with best clothes on, who could undertake the job? It was shouldered on to Sandford, who with Christmas good will soon finished it. Then immediately, we cleared up the dining room for a dance. Marty Hart developed surprising possibilities. At first he declared that he could neither dance or play the mouth harp, but it soon transpired that he could do both and do them well. Mr. Love had not danced for years and declared that he could never learn—but he tried. Mr. and Mrs. Mills joined in for a Virginia Reel several times. When at last it was midnight we stopped, thinking suddenly of threshers and the trip to Lander next morning.

3

LANDER: 1905

The Teachers' Institute in Lander was an annual affair—an occasion for inspiration and exchange—requiring the attendance of all the teachers of Fremont County, regardless of their teaching experience or skills. Mrs. Mills had casually mentioned it to Ethel in her initial letter. For ranch families and ranch teachers, the trip to Lander was a trip to civilization. For Ethel, accustomed to the refinements of Boston and Denver, it was a chance to see her third Wyoming "city," population approximately one thousand.

December 26. At breakfast, it was discovered that Mr. Love was going to Lander, so to what must have been relief to Sandford and Mr. Mills, it was decided that I should go with him. I rather dreaded it, for I had seen very little of Mr. Love, and I confess was somewhat afraid of him. "You will be more comfortable, so," said Mrs. Mills. The day before had been cold and windy and the top buggy was a protection. So at last Kathryn's little trunk containing my baggage was strapped on the buggy, and a large stone which had been heating was put in. I was wrapped up in a coat of my own with Mrs. Mills' sealskin over it, muffler, fur hat, fur gloves, leggings and overshoes. Then truly, I was so bundled up that it was next to impossible to move. "Absolutely helpless," laughed Mr. Love. There were thirteen layers of blanket in the bottom of the buggy, one heavy lap robe on which we sat, and a lap robe and fur robe over. The chances for getting cold were few indeed. "You will keep warm if the thermometer goes down to forty below," assured Mr. Love.

So we started about eleven in the morning. The wind stopped blowing, and the drive was very comfortable. The road led through the Big Bend, past Derby and Dallas, the Worlins,[1] and into Lander from the east. Mr. Love made the way shorter by stories of all the places which we passed, and it did not seem four hours along the way. We did not stop for dinner, and however Mr. Love may have felt, the cold air had made me ravenous. On getting to Lander, we first tried to find Miss Davis. Here and there through the town we tracked her, gave up once in despair and saw the sights, then went back to rap uselessly on the doors at Mrs. Coalter's.

At last we returned to the school house where Institute should have been going on. Mr. Love boldly invaded one grammar room, and soon appeared triumphantly with Miss Davis under his arm—figuratively speaking. Such an emaciated, delicate woman she appeared, even at the first glance. Dark, thin, carefully dressed, and anxious to be kind and make friends. We shook hands, and she asked whether I would stay for the close of Institute or go to her rooms and get warm. Institute had just then no attractions, so I chose the latter, and she said to make myself at home; she would be back in a few moments. Meanwhile Mr. Love and I had stopped at the hotel to try to get at least a bite to eat. The hotel was being repaired.

When at last we returned to Mrs. Coalter's, and Mr. Love took in my trunk, he looked around. "If she has a chafing dish," he ventured tentatively, "we might make some oyster stew." He had some fine canned oysters in the back of that all-holding buggy. We looked around. No chafing dish, of course. There was one large room with a red curtain half hiding a couple of beds at the back. An open door showed the kitchen beyond. We went into the kitchen. "There is a fire," I suggested. "All right," he answered. Then he took the team to the stable to put them up, and brought back the oysters, while I built up the fire. When Mr. Love returned, the fire was going well. We discovered a saucepan into which we emptied the frozen oysters. "They ought to have milk and butter," said my companion in guilt. It would not do to stop halfway, so we foraged, discovering butter in a glass dish on the table, which was covered with a cloth. Milk we found in a covered jar set apparently to let the cream rise. There were a few crackers in the cupboard, one soup plate and a small bowl, all of which we appropriated. Finally, just as the stew was done and I was filling our two receptacles, the door opened and in came Miss Davis. "You are just in time for dinner, Miss Davis," said I, feeling suddenly conscious of the fact that I had never seen her before. Mr. Love fortunately had been a sheepherder and was accustomed to sheepherder's hospitality. For myself, I felt like a small bad child. Miss Davis was very fond of oysters; she was cold; she was hungry; the stew was hot. In the excess of her courtesy she begged our pardon for not having told us to get a meal. Then we all fell to on the oysters, eating them ravenously.

When they were finished, we began on a five pound box of marshmallows which came likewise from Mr. Love's inexhaustible buggy. The afternoon drew near its early close. "Dear, dear, the evenings do get late so early these days," lamented Miss Davis. "It is almost suppertime now."

Miss MacBride had been asked by Miss Davis to go there for her meals, and before long she appeared. She was well-dressed in a sort of uncomfortable brown that gave an appearance of too evident shyness. Down she sat, murmuring unintelligible sentiments that ran into one another, and stopped anywhere but at the close of sentences. The cause of her embarrassment I learned later. She and Miss Davis both ran for the office of County Superintendent, and she was defeated, taking the defeat badly. When Miss Davis wrote, asking her to prepare a paper for Institute, she refused. Miss Davis insisted. She apologized. Miss Davis took her in when she could not find board in Lander.

Suppertime came and Mr. Love remained. We had a miserable canned goods cold supper. Miss MacBride left, Mr. Love remained. The man who was to conduct the Institute dropped in for a while. It turned out to be of all men the one I most detested, and had thought never to see again, Mr. Tear, teacher of geometry in Hyde Park High School,* now principal of the Keith Grammar School. I recognized him the second minute he was there, when he began to talk about his wife. He had shaved his red beard and was a trifle more bald, but otherwise quite the same—personal, patronizing, didactic, the twenty-year teacher. He had come in to see about a lecture which he had been asked to give; he did not know whether to choose as his subject "Reminiscences of Europe," a pedagogical subject, or "How people live in a large city." Ye gods! I dared not look at Mr. Love. He dared not look at me. Visions of Mr. Tear talking about the milk man and garbage man flitted before my eyes. Miss Davis said, unseeing anything out of the ordinary, that she thought Europe would be more interesting to the ordinary person. Bored to extinction was I as Mr. Tear described the hardships which he had endured and the number of miles he had travelled to come to this place. And every day he missed cost him eleven dollars. He left at last; even Mr. Tear had to leave some time. He went in Lander by the name of Doctor. To be sure, he said that he did not deserve it; and he did not, but it must have been gratifying to one who had worked ten years for a Doctor's degree and had not yet attained his end. So ended the first day.

The next morning began my acquaintance with the teachers of Fremont County. After an early breakfast, when the chickens had been fed and watered, wood and coal brought in for the day, we started the Institute. Miss Countryman, a red faced girl who tried to bear the stamp of convention, we met on the way. She had come sixty-five miles on the stage, and poor child, was frightened badly at the thought of her first Institute. When we three reached the grammar room, a crowd of teachers were huddled about the big stove, while Mr. Johnson, a fine looking young fellow was expatiating to the women on some subject. Mr. Bucher, the principal was

*Ethel Waxham had attended Hyde Park High School in Chicago.

there, too, tall, gloomy, thoughtful. Everyone was well-dressed, very much alive, interested in his or her own problems, however shy about discussing them. They were young, the teachers, with unbeautiful sharp faces, or dull.

A clipping from the Lander newspaper, the *Wind River Mountaineer* dated Friday, December 29, 1905, describes the Teachers' Institute:

> Tuesday morning—opening ceremonies conducted by Dr. Tear. Total enrollment, eleven. First talk by Dr. Tear was an outline of the work for the week. The second period was taken up by a talk on Methods.
> Tuesday afternoon—opening talk by Dr. Tear on Hand Work. Brought out the idea that much of our teaching should be the objective method. The last period of the day was occupied by Miss Lee with a paper on Literature in the Grades. She handled her subject in a masterly way and held the attention of the audience. She is a strong advocate of the theory of teaching literature in all grades by the use of stories and memory's game.
> Wednesday morning—total enrollment 15. Opening exercises by Dr. Tear. The first period was taken up by a talk on Psychology. The leading thought was that Education is a process—a growth—the essence of which is the reconstruction of old experience in the interpretation of new experience. Experience tends on occasion to repeat itself. The next period was occupied by Prof. Johnson with a paper on the Schools of New York. The New York school system was very carefully outlined and some interesting comparisons made with the schools of Wyoming.
> Recess
> The next subject was English and Literature, which was ably discussed by Dr. Tear. The last period was occupied by Miss Weckesser on the subject of "Character Building." Some very good points were brought

out in the paper one of which was that the teacher should first be upright in character before attempting to build an upright character in the children.

Wednesday afternoon—the afternoon session was occupied by a talk on History. The second period of the afternoon was occupied by Miss Waxham on the subject College Life in the East. The last period of the afternoon was occupied by Dr. Tear by a lecture on Geography.

[Journal undated.] Institute began with lectures by Mr. Tear on applied psychology. Alack, it did not meet our needs. I myself longed for light on the subject of the teaching of geography, not a discussion of thought as the process of constructing new coordinations out of old, or of the difference between work and play as the remoteness of the object of activity. Papers were read however, which diversified the program. Mr. Johnson gave one on the New York school system which closed with a peroration on the cause of the fall of Syria and Rome, and the danger to the United States in its "coffers of ill-gotten gain." He teaches general history, needless to say. Miss Weckesser, round and pleasant-faced gave a moral paper on character. "The influence of character is the light that comes from the sun after it is set and guides the pilgrim to his home." Noble sentiments were highly appreciated. It truly surprised me to find here a moral code as rigorous as that in the New Star theatre in New York where the villain was hissed, and the hero applauded in every noble thought.

The paper of the week however, in nobility of sentiments and picturesque in English as she is spoke, was that of Mrs. Hybasha, the wife of the janitor. Her husband came in to hear it, and for me, that alone was worth going to Institute. It began by saying that "man no longer follows the eternal pole star of right, but drinks the Leth (Lethe) of poisonous praise." "In irresolution and cowardice, he cuts, hews and slashes." "What he needs is not so much of the sheep in his hide, but more of the rhinoceros, not too much of the ewe in his forehead, more of the battering ram." "He inherits the religion, dogma and creed of his dad. He gets his politics with the cast off breeches of his dad. He never stops to ask whether they were made by God or the devil, or how his dad got them, or whether they are made of silk or satin or blue jeans."

On this day Miss Carr came. It was she who had been unable to get beyond the eighth or ninth grade so took to teaching. I thought that I would not like her, but I did, immensely. She was a frank, outspoken, clean, wholesome person. The first thing she did on arrival was to wash the dishes that were left from breakfast. A hard time she must have had with Miss Davis' housekeeping when she came to stay with her as she frequently did.

In the afternoon Miss Carr, several of the other teachers and myself, when Institute was over, went to the Court House to hear the beginning of the King vs. Wright trial. A smoky place it was, full of rough men, with a jury of freighters who had probably been throwing rocks at half-starved horses all winter, and had so obtained a state of mind which would harden them to any too womanly feelings of mercy or consideration. The jailer took us through the jail, where the prisoners were cooped up like animals in a freight car. An iron cage was in the room to hold them. Necessary too, for the jailer showed a long rent in the sheet iron of the ceiling where a prisoner had broken through and escaped. The woman convicted of murder had a room to herself; when we were returning to the court room, she looked out from her room and laughed at us.

Thursday evening was the one set for Mr. Tear's lecture. Only two tickets had been sold. Miss Davis was half wild. At the last moment all the lights in Lander went out, so we followed Mr. Tear in and told him that the lecture had to be given up. He was disappointed; we brought him to the house and consoled him with marshmallows. He tried to give the lecture to us, but by a happy chance we escaped. Mr. Foust came to call. Mrs. Mills had written him that I was coming.

73

Friday afternoon, social life reached its culmination. Just after Institute Edith Signor came to call. Mrs. Charlie Hall was next. Mrs. George West was the third, and a charming person she was; Mrs. Bruce followed, and after her, little Mrs. Amoretti, a gay little woman in a velvet suit, elbow sleeves and fine furs. She asked me out to go with them that night to the dance that the "Lander boys" were giving to entertain the Casper boys who had come for the King trial.

Mr. Tear had invited Miss Davis and 'self to dinner at the restaurant. Noticed a masculine way of managing moustache and buttermilk—get the ends milky and then suck them off. As he was to leave next morning, he took an early departure, after giving every good wish under sun and moon and a final God bless you.

The dance was great fun, spite of fact that refreshments could be smelled from the corner. The white-haired, bald-headed; their little boys; maidens and stout matrons, all were there. Nobody danced.

Of course we slept late in the morning, and had breakfast in pajamas and dressing sack. (Miss Davis received Mr. Tear the first evening in a dressing sack.) Miss Davis had examinations to give, so I stayed at home to read and write letters. In the afternoon Mr. Love called. It certainly was a surprise. I explained why Miss Davis was out, but he didn't seem to mind. I said that she would be back soon. He asked if I should not like to take a drive and see the suburbs. Of course I would. It was good to see him, for Miss Davis' ills were beginning to try just a little. We went for a long drive in the reservation* with a box of chocolates between us, and a merry gossip we had of the threshers at home, Institute, Lander and a hundred and one things. He was bemoaning the fact that there is no place for a man to spend the evening in Lander except in a saloon. "Come and toast marshmallows," I said, and he took it as a good suggestion.

*Wind River Indian Reservation where Shoshoni and Arapaho tribes, traditional enemies, were forced to live.

Next morning as we were on the way to church, whom should we see but Mr. Love, apparently bound for the same place. He had told us the night before that he had not been for ten years. "I see Miss Waxham's good influence," laughed Mr. Foust when he saw us all there together. Mr. Fredine, the minister, had frescoed the church himself, and a good frescoer he was, whatever might be said of the preaching. The previous minister had kept a dairy in connection with the church and finally was dismissed for watering the milk of his flock.

Soon after church, my trunk was fastened once more on the back of Mr. Love's buggy and we started back. Mrs. Hall had asked us to dinner there, so we stopped for a cheery meal with her and "Charlie." It was nearly four when we left for the twenty-three mile ride. There had been snow falling since morning, and the road was barely visible. The light faded to a soft whiteness that hardly grew darker when the sun set and the pale outline of the moon showed through the snow. Everywhere was the softly enveloping snow shutting out all sounds and sights. The horses knew the way and travelled on steadily. Fortunately, it was not cold, and the multitudinous rugs and robes with the new footwarmer beneath kept us warm and comfortable. More pleasant it was travelling through the storm than sitting at home by the fire and watching it outside. When the conversation ran low, we travelled on quietly. Mr. Love discovered bags of candy under the robes—he had left Muskrat with twenty-seven pounds only a little while before, of which perhaps four remained— and he fed us both, for I was worse than entangled in wraps and the long sleeves of Mrs. Mills' sealskin. The miles fell away behind us easily and quietly. At last we reached the Mills'. Not a dog barked, though they came frisking to meet us. As Mr. Love was extricating me from the robes, the kitchen door opened and Kathryn and Margaret burst out to overwhelm me with bear hugs. In the door standing in the lamplight were Mrs. Mills and Sandford and Mr. Bruce, waiting with smiles of welcome. "Welcome home, Miss

Waxham," called Mr. Bruce first of all, and truly there was no one happier than I to get there. Inside they were just clearing up after the supper of the threshers. Such a tumultuous New Year's Eve! Supper was made ready for us, the presents in my trunk unpacked, all the news reported, and talk flowed free until nearly midnight when we separated. A din of sheep bells and rifles from the bunk house alone marked the coming of the new year.

The next day we watched the process of threshing, took pictures of the operation, and waited on the hungry beasts at table. In the afternoon, Mr. Love and I went to Hailey for the mail. It was a clear cold night quite unlike the one before when we came from Lander.

Tuesday school began. Mr. Love was an all day visitor. The next morning, after taking me to school, he left. Here shall I cease for a while my record of Mr. Love's doings, and get down to the business of the school again.

4

Red Bluff Ranch: 1906

January 1906. It certainly was cold those first days after vacation. The ink in all seven bottles was frozen as well as the glue, in the morning, and would have to be thawed out daily before the stove. One morning the fire could not be made to burn until quarter after ten, having been smothered prematurely with coal. The water hole in the creek froze, and though chopped for a foot and a half, showed no signs of water. The coal gave out at last. We had to burn wood, until Sandford and Mr. Bruce took the sled to Schlichting's and brought down some large chunks of coal.

The boys have made a coast down the hill behind the school; they slide down most of the way in the slush, and then come in with the seats of their pants sopping wet. All around the stove they will stand for an hour or so, backs to the fire, drying off. Already the nether portion of their overalls has faded several shades, and the color is still going. Otto read, unconscious of error yesterday, about the "partridge of olden time," meaning the patriarch Job, and tripped over "scared harmonies." Since Emmons' asking if digestion went on in the Erie Canal very few such brilliant remarks have been made.

Mr. Bruce and Poodles have escorted me to school almost ever since vacation in the sled or carriage. Sometimes Stockings, Mr. Bruce's saddle pony, will follow along behind with Poodles nipping at his heels.

Almost as soon as the threshers left, Mrs. Hudson, husband and two children came a-visiting for a week or so. There was there no rest for the weary. Georgie and Deane were up to something all the time. Deane's final act before leaving was to pull off my door knob, and slam the door so that the catch caught on the inside. Sandford had to enter taking off the storm window and opening the other.

Christmas presents for the family from Mr. Bruce came a while ago. Pens for every one! Fountain pens for the girls and Sandford, and a gold pearl-handled pen for me. "Them's real gold," said he, "them ain't imitation."[1]

January 15. More impossible weather. Yesterday taking advantage of a little sunshine, though cold sunshine, we all went out for a horseback ride with strict directions not to go faster than a walk. We could not anyway, for the snow and wind. The "diggers" or "knotheads" are still on the mountain so we had to make the most of the horses there were. Margaret rode Mr. Bruce's Stockings, Kathryn had Mack, Sandford put the saddle on lame Sorreltop for himself, I had Buck, and Mr. Bruce took Ed, whom he declared was a fine saddle horse. So we five started out gaily. It did not take long to get cold through leggings and overshoes, but it seemed so good to be on horses again that we rode all afternoon. As we were coming back along the wood road, a solitary horseman galloping behind us, in spite of the roads, attracted all our attention and much guessing. It turned out to be Mr. Love, much wrapped up, riding Sailor, a pretty bay. He had come all the way from the Alkali Butte to spend the night.

January 22. Last week was pretty cold. More frozen ink in the school house. The worst storm ever known in Casper. Thermometer forty-five below. Snow two feet deep in Crooks Gap, and the mails five days late. "This is the weather," said Mr. Bruce, "that puts kinks in the old sheep's backs."

Mr. Love appeared once more, Saturday evening, on the way to town. Sunday he asked me to go to Hailey with him for the mail, and I was glad enough to get out, much bundled up. When we got out to the buggy, the foot warmer had disappeared. "I'll get even with Sandford," said Mr. Love, after hunting through the house and granary and bunk house before finding it. Sandford had asked me to go sleigh riding with him instead of going to Hailey! Perhaps that explains the badness of a good boy. Mr. Mills grumbled and scolded at going out on such a day when the thermometer was not much above zero, and the ground was covered with fresh snow. Perhaps it was foolish.

Perhaps it was foolish, too, to go around by the Big Bend and the stage road instead of by the canyon, making eight miles extra for the horses. "But if I want to be a chuckle-headed fool," Mr. Love says, "it's my own fault and I'll pay the penalty." At the Big Bend, young George Ehler was standing at the door of one of the buildings, and took off his hat as we passed. It was wildly exciting to see three strangers, later to pass a couple of men on horseback, and on the way back to meet the stage laboring along through the snow, and catch glimpses of the muffled faces of a man and woman within.

At Hailey everything was in excitement. A dance had been the night before. "We watched all evening for you," said Mrs. Signor. "Miss Jones was here from Sweetwater with all her pupils and Mr. and Mrs. McKinney and the baby. It was such a nice dance. We had ten women! About midnight I came in and made some coffee and set the lunches out that they had brought in baskets. They had such a good time that they danced until morning."

Our invitation came in the mail. We had not been to Hailey for nearly two weeks, so though rumors of the dance had come to our ears and though we had discussed going, we knew nothing definite. When we opened our invitation, was sprawled on paper. Ach, the consternation and wailing that it produced at the ranch. "They might have let us know," was the universal sentiment. Margaret and Sandford had never been to a dance.

February 9. It is a long time since I have written down the happenings of the days, and they have been many. To begin with when I left off: Whiskers came over some time after the first dance at Hailey to tell us that there would be another on the night of Friday, the second of February. It had taken Guy Signor seven years to persuade his mother to give the first dance, but that was such a success—no one drunk—that the second followed two weeks later. Sandford asked me at once to go. It was generally understood that we were all to go.

Here fate stopped it. Fate that has to manages little things. Colds came out from Lander; they came down the Little Popo Agie River. They reached Twin Creek in good time. On Monday, the twenty-ninth of January, everyone at the ranch had a cold. Mr. Bruce was "on the left," as one speaks of old cows. At school there were seven pupils and a teacher all sneezing and coughing and sniffing, and microbes flying about almost visibly. Tuesday Margaret, Sandford and I managed to struggle to school. The Schlichtings for a wonder did not appear. George did not turn up and has not yet to this day. We three pulled through the lessons and came home early. Wednesday and Thursday Emmons and Ellen came back, but handkerchiefs were still omnipresent—and when a Schlichting blows a nose, something is seriously wrong—and microbes were rife.

On Friday Sandford and I declared ourselves better, but I think it was more to resist Fate than because we were. Still all ideas of the dance had been given up. As we reached the house after school however, Kathryn ran out to meet us, asking whether we were going. Of course we could not resist that challenge. Went inside. Consulted about the advisability of taking a whole cake for lunch, or two pieces; of sandwiches to go around, or enough for two. Immediately we

Sandford Mills.

began to feel better and decided to go. Then we flew around getting ready.

To make more confusion Smithy was there. Smithy utilized every spare moment in telling how he used to walk twice as far to a dance when he was "a kid"; saying that we must dance every dance; that Sandford must drive carefully, that he would be as good looking as any of them in that collar and with those cuffs. "Gee," he said, "I ain't worn a collar since I was at Bent's wedding. We all got drunk that night to celebrate, Bent too. If I was to dress up now, the fellas would think I was going to a masquerade."

Mrs. Mills and Smithy and the people who were not going were as excited as could be. We pretended to be calm, but were ourselves almost too excited to eat. After supper Smithy offered to hook up the horses for Sandford, while we bundled up. I fortified myself with five handkerchiefs and thought of the ginger tea which Mrs. Mills had brought to everyone the night before, and onions innumerable. At last the carriage was ready, with Smithy holding a lantern beside it, arranging the comforters on the seat, and telling the horses how to behave. Everyone went out to see us off. The lunch was stowed away in the back of the buggy, and the mail sack, and hundreds of exhortations were hurled at us through the gate. Sandford tucked me in at last with quite new gallantry, put on the fur overcoat, and climbed in like a big rough bear.

The moon was shining high in the sky when we started about half-past seven. As we drove through the canyon, we watched the moon moving westward, and noticed the position of the dipper. The moonlight was so bright that we could see everything almost as plainly as by day, and Sandford pointed out the tracks of a wolf and coyotes in the snow along the road. Pretty bad the road was, icy and snowy, especially on the hills, but when we crossed the divide it became better. The bluffs loomed large and dark against the moonlit sky; the shadows grew like the silence, crisp and clear cut. The noise of logs falling, as Sandford opened one of the gates, echoed back and forth between the walls of the canyon. I listened, hoping to hear a coyote and wolves, but vainly. Sandford pushed the horses through and we reached the Signor's house in Hailey as the clock struck nine.

The women there for the dance were sitting in the parlor, and the front door was in use. As I came in from the darkness, the light seemed very bright. Five or six women were sitting quietly there with three babies. Their stillness and mournfulness on the threshold of a dance struck me. I did not ask who was dead, but tried to draw them into some weak conversation, after Mrs. Signor introduced me. Rosy Hart was there, the largest woman in the country, tall and strong. Her sister Mrs. Canoey was there, not so large or hopeful looking. On her lap sat the little Canoey baby girl. Across from these two sat Mrs. Johnny Carr tall, thin, in a scant black dress with a pale dirty pink ribbon about her neck. She looked more fit for a funeral than a dance. By the door was Mrs. Frink, about 18, with Frink junior, a large husky baby. Ida Franklin, Mrs. Frink's sister and almost her double was beside her, frivolous even in her silence. Large pompadours, highly curled, abounded. Even the Canoey foundling, a girl about three years old, had her hair frizzed about her head.

Soon the work of the evening was to begin. The men came in and we all travelled up to the schoolhouse. Guy Signor had spent two days taking up the floor and putting it down again so that the dirt would not come up through. Truly it must have been bad before. There were two lanterns on shelves near the ceiling, which gave light to the assembly. The desks were piled up along one side at the back of the room. These were for the women and their babies, who were presently stretched out on shawls on top of the desks for their sleep.

The men lounged along a bench on the other side of the room, and a strange assortment of men they were: the Mexican—silent, dark; Whiskers, gay in a flowered waistcoat and cut away coat, which, rumor said, he traded from a stage driver, who got it from his great grandfather; Scarlet was there with his stories and talk of weather; the Hart boys, big and unwieldy when not dancing; Canoey small, hooknosed; Lem Herold, "would 'a wore a clean collar, but was afraid of getting it dirty"; the "Ferris kid," a kind of black roustabout who acted as if he had had too much, though he hadn't; a few more whom I did not know or care to know; Guy Signor, musician; and Mr. Signor—"the man who killed Sandy McGee"—only it did not happen to be Sandy, but a drunken sheep herder.

Well—we danced. Guy fiddled for a while, then changed off to the guitar, and then the mandolin; then Whiskers offered to relieve him, giving a tune on the mouthharp. He began operations by taking off his coat, but the twelve men sprang on him with a howl and made him put it on again. "This isn't a fight." One dance out of every three was a quadrille. Johnny Carr called the figures. He is a little man, sandy-moustached, scanty-haired, red handkerchief around his neck, dressed up, legs bowed in an irregular semicircle.

"Ladies bow, gentlemen bow wow," he called; "Swing your turtle dove . . . ladies give their lily white hands, gentlemen give their black and tans . . ." The men were all timid about asking anyone to dance; they would nudge and push one another out. When they were on the floor, the dance was one grand frolic. Time flew.

At about half-past one o'clock the men went up to the house for coffee and the basket lunches, which we ate in the school. The ever useful desks were once more called into play, this time as tables. Cake and pie were the favorite refreshments; sandwiches and chicken were rather popular, too.

Soon after eating, Sandford hitched up the horses once more and we started home, notwithstanding Mrs. Signor's earnest invitation to spend the night. Except for a few stars which were pale, there was no light. The canyon was pitch black. I could not see to drive through the gates which Sandford, by a kind of special intuition, always discovered just where they belonged. We could not see the road in front of the horses, so driving was necessarily slow. The moon had set long before; the dipper had travelled halfway around the north star. As we drove, we speculated as to whether it was growing lighter. It really seemed as if it were, at the end of the long drive, for the stars were less bright, and the east was—not gray—but less black—than before. As we finally drove up to the gate, and unloaded the mail and lunch, the alarm went off upstairs at six o'clock. Sandford said goodnight, though it should have been good morning, and went to put away the horses. Truly the bed looked good, though I had some qualms about rumpling it up for so short a time as a couple of hours.

Smithy was off next—or that—morning before I was dressed. I was sorry not to have seen more of him. His brown corduroy overalls were patched in the seat with a checked patch and a big blue one. He is always neat, though things may not match. When we came home from school one day, we knew that Smithy was there, for a wagon was before the bunk house, brightly painted green and the tongue of new pine. A little frightened dog, "Laura," was running about. Smithy had been talking all afternoon with no encouragement or interruption, telling the news of the country. He was, for Smithy, quiet at supper, and his vocabulary, it is said, was limited, for ladies were present.

Sunday Tommy Dunny came to spend the day, and we learned much more gossip. "Hab" was dead. Hab had had a terrible temper. One day he was in the barn down at the Hall's, pitching hay, when a rooster crowed in the stall next to him. "Dry up," said Hab. The rooster crowed again. "Stop crowing at me," said Hab. The rooster crowed a third time. Hab hit it with the pitch fork and knocked its head off. He came into the kitchen holding it by the neck. "Here's your rooster, Mrs. Hall. He crowed at me three times, and I told him not to."

February 13. Another snow is gathering, and the clouds are low on Sheep Mountain. The hills, instead of stretching gray blue and white with sagebrush as they did yesterday, are yellow green from the slight dampness and the red of the soil shows through on the hill sides. The sundial is useless on the window sill once more.

Excitement before school. The "fellows" at the gate are going after horses in the pasture. Rumor says that they will take them to the desert. Roy and Pease and a man in white chaps supposed to be Ted Abra back from his trial about cattle stealing, with—our own George!—were riding hard over the hills and ledges after a bunch of horses. From far away we could hear Roy calling and shouting to the men and horses, though the air was soft and damp. They are still at it with the not unmusical calls, though George did turn up nearly an hour late.

February 19. At last the play has come off. For two months we have been struggling over "Box and Cox,"² shouting it out on the way home from school, rehearsing evenings and any spare time. We have had three dress rehearsals, with makeup. At last the eventful day came. All day we spent preparing as we did on Christmas day for the dinner. Most of the morning I utilized in printing an elaborate poster. The white shirts and collars of the actors had to be laundered by the girls. In the afternoon Sandford and I wrote the posters. Then Sandford had to have his hair cut. There was a penny roll to bake for the performance, and Mr. Bruce's bacon and hat to be borrowed. The stage we arranged before supper, and elaborate the preparations were. No one ate very much, and everyone hurried. The dishes were soon done, and the dressing commenced. [The character] Mrs. Bouncer was never so stout before, nor her nose so red. We put several coats of strong coffee on Margaret's face before making her up, so she had a truly masculine tan under her moustache, and eyebrows and burnt cork villainy. Sandford looked well, like a handsome man of the middle class, age perhaps thirty-two. When all was ready, the audience helped fix the three lamps for footlights; milk pans were behind them braced against pillows, and pretty good reflectors they made.

All hearts went pit-a-pat as the curtain rose. After the first tremble, things went smooth as silk. Sandford was as self contained as one could wish. Then came Margaret as Box. Her first speech was too much for her. She had to stay behind the scenes for a while and giggle. Then she really appeared and did pretty well until it was time to smell of the frying pan, at the front of the stage. Then she was overcome once more, throwing persistent but laughing glances at me. Good Mr. Bruce sat at the very back where the actors could not catch his eye. Mr. Mills sat at the front, more than half the time doubled up with not quite suppressed laughter, while Mrs. Mills tried to keep him quiet with a warning finger. It was a grand success. Never anything like it. The make-up and clothes were all minutely examined and discussed. Everything funny laughed at two or three times.

After the play, we danced until nearly twelve in costume, Margaret trying to dispose of her moustache on my cheek or hand, Mrs. Bouncer fearful of losing her *avoirdupois*. Mr. Bruce played faithfully on the mouth harp never once dancing himself, probably because Margaret was herself a man.

February 26. Went down the canyons yesterday, the whole cavalcade of us, horseback to call on Rosy Hart. We assured our welcome by taking about twenty-five pounds of desired parsnips in a gunny sack. Mr. Bruce played the fool all the way down, asking if his toes were dragging, or his saddle turning, and teasing Kathryn by insisting that Bubsy, her horse, is shortsighted. There at last, we were in twenty quandaries as to which was the front door. This was at last settled by the appearance of aproned Katie Canoey with a smile of welcome at one of the doors. Katie approaches six feet in height, but stoops so that she does not fill doorways as little sister Rosy does. Rosy looks as if the Fates were undecided whether to make of her a Grecian goddess or an Egyptian sphinx—so she turned out only plain Rosy Hart, able to do a man's work in the field with a divine calm about her.

The house is papered with newspapers inside, and everything hangs on the walls, from the clothes of the baby to Canoey's razor strop and somebody's Sunday switch of hair—"scalp," Mr. Bruce called it. To entertain us before time to eat, Marty's fancywork and patchwork quilt were produced, and his pictures. We stayed to a three-thirty dinner and then scampered the six miles back at a pace that made Poodles pant and puff like half a dozen dogs.

March 1. It is truly the day of the lion. For nearly all week the wind has been blowing rude gales, and yesterday in the middle of the afternoon the sun suddenly disappeared and the sky grew dark. A wet snow fell—driven about by the wind. We waited after school a few moments, hoping vainly that Mr. Bruce or Mr. Mills might come after us. Soon, however, the snow seemed less wet, and we started out. The dampness had brought out the darkness of the red soil, and the blackness of the green cedars. The sagebrush too, along the way, was as black about the branches as if a fire had passed over the hills. The bluffs loomed dark and moody against the gray sky, but far away at the Big Bend, the hills were the color of pale straw. The mountain looked yellowish green, softened by a sifting of snow. It is strange how the whole face of the country will be changed by a little dampness, like the face of a person intensified but softened by tears.

The worst snow of the year fell last night, so today the sled had to be patched up to take us to school. The horses had been left out in the corral all night and were icy from head to tip of tail. Along Sorreltop's sides were icicles, reddish and larger than my fingers, hanging like candelabra. Whenever he trotted, they shook and rattled fascinatingly. The snow was so deep that it piled along in front of the sled even to the horses' feet, and we several times narrowly avoided going over with it, all of us. School at last, and no one here.

At lunchtime we built up the fire and cooked our beans in the tops of our lard pails and tried to toast bread on a pointed stick. The bread would persist in falling into the fire, so at last we scraped a clean place on the stove top, and let it burn there. Following Mr. Bruce's example we made a "mulligan" or stew, out of beans, eggs and sandwich, with some of the dirt from the chimney for flavoring, all mixed up in a lard pail cover. "It's like 'stay nut' pudding," Margaret said. "The bread do be the dough-gods." For Mr. Bruce is always talking of his dough gods and dough boys. The other morning he came in and said to Mrs. Mills "You ought to make your flipper dough overnight. The flippers do be lighter. Me flippers dance on me plate."

Before four o'clock, Mr. Mills came for us with the sled. On it he had tied a wagon box, with the seat wired on. Though the weather was colder, straw was in front for our feet, and that kept us very comfortable. True, the wagon box dragged several feet behind the sled, and would have upset had Sandford stood near the back, but it was a great improvement, for the horses no longer threw snow in our faces. No sun, no sky visible, no earth; only fine whirling snow. But that we did not care to see, and kept our noses and chins and eyes carefully covered.

March 15. The fourth day of school this week, and—wonder!—Three children. Kathryn and Sandford and I had thought that we would be the only ones to enjoy the blessing of a public school this week at least.

Last Thursday on top of the heaviest snow of the winter, which fortunately had melted somewhat, a fine light snow began. It continued so until Saturday morning, when it became a true blizzard with a driving wind. All Sunday and Sunday night the hills were obliterated by the storm. On Sunday afternoon however, Mr. Mills hitched the team to the sled, and we started out to break a road to school. The snow on the level was up to the horses' knees, and when we reached the big hill where the wind of Saturday had piled huge drifts, truly, we had doubts of getting through at all. Both of the horses were plunging, and it seemed as if Stambaugh would surely strike over the singletree. Sorreltop was in up to his back. The pole was not to be seen, and the sled sank in so that the seat was on a level with the top of the snow. "A little more of this would kill a horse," said Mr. Mills. He ought to know, having lost one that way. At last we got through and over to the school.

On Monday the snow had stopped, with only intermittent flurries. The wind blew so that our road of Sunday was not to be seen, so we had to break another. The big hill was impassible of course. Only the three of us were at school. "Helbeck of Bannisdale" kept me quiet and busy. After lunch, we amused ourselves by freezing the whipped cream on our cake, and rehearsing the new play.

Tuesday, more snow and more wind, just enough to cover the road; the same Wednesday. On Tuesday we were all in wild excitement. A man appeared on a distant hill, following the trail of some hobbled horses. He wore an overcoat and carried a gun, we ascertained by the aid of Mr. Bruce's telescope. Only an insane man or an outlaw, we thought, could be out in such a snow and such cold. Mr. Mills started after him with the team—the man disappeared. At last Mr. Mills returned, and later the man was seen making his way far off along the tops of the ridges. The other event of the day was the passing of the Harts in a buggy. It was all the horses could do to move. The wheels looked like huge snow balls. It took three quarters of an hour for them to pass through the field.

With the ceasing of the snow it became colder than ever before this winter—twelve below when Mr. Mills came down about seven in the morning. Mr. Bruce moves hardly more than the rabbits who look out of their holes, go out a few yards, turn around and hop back. Once or twice a day he will get down to the house for more magazines or milk. How he hated to go out, Sunday night, the worst. He waited and talked and talked on the miseries of bachelor life. "I tell ye, Mrs. Mills, it ain't what it's cracked up to be, there ain't no pleasure in it. Today a button came off me coat and I lost it in somebody's overshoe in the entry." That was too much for us—not so much the words as the gravity with which he said it. Then he tied one handkerchief over his ears and one or two around his neck, put on overshoes and coat and went to his cold bachelor sheep wagon with Poodles.

There are thousands of tiny little horned larks about the garden and barn and house. They come with every storm, and are tame cosy little things. The cats trouble them somewhat. One dog, Pat, spent the last three days in a nest in the chicken house. He never deigns to go outside even for food in bad storms. The other, Laddie-boy, has been in his element. He loves the snow. I washed his face in it one afternoon. How he was surprised—then seemed to beg me to try it again, and see if he could not stop me.

March 18. News, such news! Two men appeared yesterday, one, a Mr. Harsh, from Derby after oats. To be sure we were at school and did not see him, but it was some connection with the rest of the universe. He said that only two mails have been through this week. The stage was lost once and had to be abandoned. When it was found again, it was covered with snow. Another stage was upset on Beaver Hill and had to be left. The other caller was Roy McLaughlin who rode up for oats.

Truly, the weather is hard on the horses. The three which we have seen for a week on the mountain, hobbled, pressed so against the gate that Mr. Mills let them in and fed them, after taking the hobbles off. One of them was a colt of Polly's, who left the place five or six years ago when he was a three-year old, and has never been back since. Now when he and his two friends were in trouble, being hobbled so that they could not paw away the snow to get feed, he brought them back here. When the little sorrel was set free he could not believe that he was loose, but jumped about as if the hobbles were still tight. Mr. Bruce said that he would throw the hobbles quite off in the ditch, if he had time today! The horses belong to Johnny Burns; he thinks that they have gone to Muskrat, Harsh said.

Last night was the coldest of the winter. This morning it was twenty below by the thermometer, though when the sun rose it grew warmer, so that when we left for school it was only four below. The wires fastening the seat of the sled broke on this special morning as we were going up the hill behind the house. The lunches were upset in the snow, and the poor beans fell out. Kathryn and I would have gone over backwards in one little ball rolled up in the big fur coat if Sandford and Mr. Mills had not caught us just as we were several quarters over. Everything was frozen stiff in the school house, even to the ink, and there were small snow drifts in the corners of the room.

March 19. One day of more snow. Sundogs showing clear, down in the willows. No mail. Mr. Killgore, Mr. Love's campmover, rode over from Sanderson's for oats. That was Saturday. To celebrate St. Patrick's day on Saturday, we gave

91

a masquerade. "You's won't let me in when I come down in me kilties wit' a blanket wrapped around me bare knees. I ain't got no long stockings. I'll have to paint me legs." Bill Bruce declared. That was to lead us on to tell what we were going to be. Even then we suspected that he would not dress up.

Kathryn planned to be a squaw, and she really made a natural one, in two gray blankets, her ankles wound in white, red bedroom slippers simulating moccasins, blue beads, hair in two braids tied with red, and a papoose slung over her shoulder by a light blue cheesecloth square. Her face and arms were covered by dry red paint, and her eyebrows blackened so that even Poodles did not recognize her. Margaret was Little Lord Fauntleroy, in knee pants, blouse, collar ties and red worsted sash. Sandford was a cowboy, booted and spurred, chaps and six shooter and cartridge belt, hat, gloves and cigarette. I was a Japanese lady, in Mrs. Mills' silk crazy quilt, and the lining for a sash pinned in a butterfly bow behind; over shoulders a Japanese scarf, and in hair four little fans.

Truly the masquerade was a great success. Mr. Bruce never once demurred about playing. Poor unobtrusive Mr. Killgore was all eyes, mild, but still eyes. He sat in the kitchen most of the time chewing tobacco and spitting into the coal scuttle or rather coal pail. The dance continued until midnight exactly, when Kathryn began to scrub her face, and the rest of us went to bed.

Sunday Kathryn had a bad headache. "She shouldn't ha' washed her face so hard," said Mr. Bruce. "Gee, it's lucky she didn't wash all over. 'Twould have killed her sure, like it did Dirty Bill." No mail. It is three weeks since I have had a letter. Mr. Mills says that he will go over "in a day or two," which probably means a week. Sandford took Margaret and myself out in the sled in the afternoon in spite of the snow, so we had a little air on Sunday. The last days have certainly dragged; no communication with the outside world, nothing to do outside or, apparently, inside the house. It is hard to keep contented with a hundred energies within that have no outlet whatever. For two weeks now it has been nothing but sitting down all the time. My spirit has a chair sore.

March 20. My sister Vera's 25th birthday. For many days the thermometer has not been above twenty-eight, but today begins better. Think of wanting the snow to melt, this lovely snow. I never knew before what beauty there was in whiteness, all whiteness under a delicate sky. In the afternoon the blue is deeper in the east, and pale in the west; everywhere else white, except for the scraggly green-black cedars. My pet cedar has been piled with snow even to the branches close beside the trunk. One day it was exquisite with frost. Again its shadow on the snow was bluer than the sky.

Even Dante will pall! I've been going through "Hell" lately, for diversion. One evening thought I would trust to Providence, went to the bookshelves, shut eyes and pulled out a large old volume, fully expecting to have at last an interesting book. Boswell's life of Johnson, it turned out. What could one expect after that?

March 21. Tommy Dunny spent the night at the ranch. He rode over to tell Schlichting that the feed was gone from the pasture. Hay is twenty-five dollars a ton, and can't be found for that price. Cattle are sold for seven dollars a head. Snow is two feet deep, and the thermometer forty below, about Lander.

Today it is warmer here. The threatening clouds brought no more snow, and the wind has ceased. Already at ten o'clock the thermometer is above freezing. How much that means perhaps only the cattle and sheep could tell better than their owners.

George got through to school, and there was this odd western child-exchange of news, reserved, curious, mature. Margaret—for the life of her she can't keep a thing to herself, though she tries—told George of Tom Dunny's jokes. He must have his joke, he told me. Tell truth I didn't

93

want at all to talk to Tommy so I stayed in my room, chilly too, for more than an hour before supper. Tommy it seems, said that he came to see me, and wanted me to come see company. Then asked which was the best man Mr. Bruce or Mr. Love. Said the water was better up here than down at Halls. Bruce had better stay. Johnny Love had found it so, too.

March 26. Warmer and warmer still. Rain and damp snow. Streams of water running off the mountain and down the field, piling up banks of foam where they broaden out, cutting their way through slush in narrow places. No stable earth, only red mud and yellow water. The ducks are in their element. They can swim almost anywhere on the ranch without having to make for a ditch.

The sled of course was out of the question and we had to go to school in the buggy. The horses could barely crawl along. We noticed as we came, seeing the road for the first time in weeks, that only for a few yards had we followed it at all in the sled, that is to say crossing the gulch. When we came near the top of the big hill we noticed a fresh trail crossing the road, that of a coyote dragging a heavy stick. Here and there drops and splashes and blurs of blood. Of course we turned off the road and followed the trail, down the hill. Across the gulch we could see a small gray coyote hopping painfully along up the opposite side. When he saw us he tried to hurry, but could not. Mr. Mills got out, crossed the little stream, and killed him with a heavy monkey wrench. He had almost escaped from the trap by chewing off his foot. Only one screw held him there. We left him bedraggled and still warm, lying by the bank. Poor "four-footed friar in orders of gray"—couldn't help being born an outcast.

"By the time school is over, the fleas will all have hopped off," said Sandford. "That's the beauty of skinning them when they are cold."

All the country to the south up by the three buttes is white, white with snow. To the north the sky shows dark and threatening over the black hills, and red looming bluffs. The dampness brings out the black of the cedars and sagebrush and the keen sage smell in the moist air.

Once at school it transpired that for the first time we had forgotten the key. Mr. Mills put his foot up against the door and kicked it in, breaking the lock. Sandford had brought in no wood; all outside was water logged. We began to break up the barrel for coal. None of the little wretches have turned up yet, and probably will not as it is now eleven o'clock. The new sun dial that Sandford and I made for the window seems to be working well. The motto for it is to be, "*Abundat dulcibus vitiis,*"* which no one here can translate *sans* dictionary. It certainly does abound in faults.

Mail came last Friday night after three weeks without any. Mr. Mills brought two flour sacks of it up in the wagon, and how we did paw over the contents when emptied on the floor, papers, letters, packages, postal cards. The dance was postponed for we were all too eager for mail. We could hardly eat, and the evening was spent looking over the mail. Bittersweet it was to me, however.

In the mail was the following letter from Ethel's stepmother, Alice Waxham:

Denver, Colo.
March 21, 1906
Ethel P. Waxham
Hailey, Wyo.

My Dear Ethel!
While your sister Faith sent a letter to you last evening, I am going to write, too. Faith looks better than I ever saw her & weighs more than I do, by a number of pounds. Papa dear is well though worried because everything is dull! Miss Schultz & Baby Sister Ruth Eudora are getting on fine. Ruth is now in short dresses & looks so sweet. She is looking more

*"It abounds in sweet faults."

like Ethel which is so pleasing. We have been having a splendid visit from Doctor Quince. He is one of the *most elegant* gentlemen I ever, ever met. He & myself had two dear visits alone together. He told me all about his own life from a boy up. He is devoted to his wife's memory, yet he hopes to again marry & wants a girl wife! He is a man *any* girl could simply love to death, it seems to me. He is so neat & in every way elegant! His position in life is high indeed. His little housekeeper marries soon, & he says he is at a perfect loss. He grows disheartened & sad because there is no one in his life to love (so he told me). While he is not a young man, yet he is not old! I would give anything to see you, Ethel come for him. Well, I do not mind telling you, dearie, everything & anything. We all love Doctor Quince & we love you, & well, I'll not say more. Doctor Quince told me he would not think of any girl until *after* he saw our Ethel. Keep this secret Ethel. I told him you were the most perfect little woman I ever had known. He felt your little story, "On being a Doctor's daughter," was the sweetest ever was, filled with bright thoughts.

We have been having much snow. How we do long to hear from you & to learn whether you are comfortable or no. Saturday evening the Boulder boys give their glee club concert. I am one of the entertaining ladies. After the concert a reception and dance. How I do wish that you were here to help me in my part. Do write & tell me everything dearie. Papa dear & I send heaps of love for our dear girlie.

Lovingly, Alice

April 2. More snow and wind. We barely got to school, walking in slickers, wet to the knees. No one else has appeared.

The play came off Saturday night, "Her Picture." How we did work to get ready for it, pressing clothes, writing posters and programs and this time tickets, too. It was some trouble to arrange a studio; Sandford was carpenter, and as he had never seen easels or palettes had to have constant supervision.

The fireplace was also rather difficult of construction, but at last two boxes, red lights and firewood made a pretty good imitation. The tea table was a cheese box on a pickle keg. When everything was arranged the room looked better than it ever did before. Sandford in a white flannel suit did pretty well as the artist; Kathryn made a rather slim and girlish widow in her white dress, black belt and black and white hat. Margaret as Tom the bashful lover did better than she knew, sitting on the edge of her chair, knees together, feet out, toes in, and choking on her tea. The reason for her choking was the sight of the audience. Mrs. Mills had fashioned two cabbage heads into roses, with colored paper about them, and Mr. Mills was feasting off the top of our bouquet. When the dishes rattled, as I poured the tea, Poodles made a break for the stage for refreshments, and it took all the united efforts of the audience to restrain him. When Sandford went to sleep, Mr. Bruce helped on the action by snores, when Margaret leaned over the back of my chair to kiss me, Mr. Bruce made the appropriate noises. When we rang the bell for the curtain at the end, the curtain boy, Poor Bill, could not manage it alone. Mr. Mills tried to help, and finally only Mrs. Mills saved the day by pulling it without the aid of the cords. After the play we danced until midnight, and next day most of us had headaches.

Mr. Bruce and I took pictures of the studio and play, and Mr. Bruce developed his. They were really the best he has taken. One was a portrait of me. When he printed it, he cried out to Mrs. Mills, "There's the white-haired kid. She do be natural."

April 9. Another play, Saturday night. We had been practising Pyramus and Thisby from "Midsummer Night's Dream" all week at school, much to the amusement of the Schlichtings, but never a word did we breathe of it at the house. It was only a week since the last play, so when secretly Saturday noon we took the poster from my room window and nailed it to the back door, and Mr. Mills came out not long

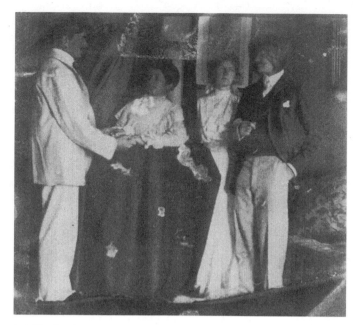

Sandford Mills, Kathryn Mills, Ethel Waxham, and Margaret Mills in the play "Her Picture."

after, the shock of the surprise was heard through the whole house "What does this sign mean? Mummy did you see this?"

The play was a grand success, winning more applause than we have had yet. Pyramus is always funny.

Sunday we took a walk over to the gate to see if the bridge was still in, for all the bridges are out on Little Popo Agie except the one at Worlins. The water had carried away some poles at the end and undermined it badly, but it still stood. The county bridge is substantial enough. We went on to see that, and back over the hills. In the evening there was the most glorious of round yellow misty moons rising slowly over the cedar ridge before the red sunset clouds turned ashen gray. We all went out once more for a walk toward the bluff where, when the stars came out, we made a sagebrush fire and danced around it. Oh, the good strong smell of the burning sage and the crackle of the leaves, and the flame

Mr. Bruce's portrait of Ethel Waxham.

shadows! "The sheep are all bedded down," said Mr. Bruce. "They won't move until morning except to say Baa-aa. They are never quiet all night long."

April 10. Mr. Mills went for mail yesterday to bring the seeds. They came by pounds and pounds. Ploughing will begin tomorrow, probably in the garden, and Sandford will have to stay at home to plough. Mr. Bruce, living on duck eggs, he says, has attained so much energy that yesterday he went out to Burn's sheep camp to look for a job, "but pray God I don't find it," he added. Back he came at night without one, but is to return in three days to see Burns.

Gossip says that Tommy Dunny was flooded out of his house and had to move into the dance hall on the hill—the Kings' daughters' possession! A neighbor lost three thousand ewes and lambs by the sudden rise of water into his pens. A few were saved by being thrown on the roofs or on haystacks, but his total loss is calculated at thirty thousand dollars.

Meadowlarks and robins are here. Prairie dogs sit and chatter on their holes as we go by to school. "Wood ticks,"

said Mr. Bruce several days ago, "will be here in two days."
—and so they were. He is an authority on bedbugs and wood
ticks. The antidote for their bite he says is horse liniment.
The solid ground is a pleasure to our feet, though in places it
is not yet solid. Twin Creek is three times as wide as ever
before, at the ford near the school. All day long we hear the
water roaring down the gulch.

April 11. Mysteries manifold. Two tracks on the way home
from school yesterday, one going up, one down. Try as we
could, the only solution was that someone tried to go over
the bridge, found it out and returned. As we went down to
the house, the horses were in the corral, four harnesses on the
fence, but no wagon. Mr. Mills had started out in the
morning with four horses and a load of oats for Harts. "Stuck
in the mud," was our verdict, and correct it turned out. Six
horses, for Mr. Mills came back for Bill and his team, could
not get the wagon up the second hill. As for the other
mystery, Pelon and the Chief of the Pugwash had been
through.

We went down to look at the bridge. Sure enough, for the
first time since '99, the bridge was out. The water had risen
in the night nearly up to the shed in Ehler's corral, and had
floated off the bridge, though it was wired down. Some
willows held it not more than six feet from its proper position but it is useless, of course, and much dilapidated.

Ellen came to school today in her Easter millinery—a sun
bonnet! Little old woman, her hair tight to her head, brown
face and bent shoulders. Otto and Emmons come by fits and
starts on half days, for they have to help haul hay and go after
cattle.

April 12. Mr. Bruce left this morning with sheepwagon and
horse family to go to work for Burns herding sheep. Poodles
was overjoyed to see the sheep once more when Mr. Bruce
went to the Big Bend to look for work. Mr. Bruce himself
recognized many of the sheep and lambs, one in particu-

lar born the tenth of July last summer in the mountains. "Many's the mile I've packed that little lamb," he said. His work is a snap—only eight hundred yearling ewes to herd, in the cedar draw. All evening the thought of the work seemed to be in his eyes, memories of other long days in the open air, so that he seemed only half sorry to go, and I found myself envying him. To be sure he pretended to snivel and weep at the last, but all for Margaret's sake.

Yesterday for the first time these six months, we saw men whom we did not know. As we were trudging up the first hill with lunch pails, two men appeared over the crest so suddenly as to take our breath away. We thought for a moment they were tramps, but when we reached the top of the hills discovered a wagon and four-horse team following. A Mexican on a heavy stallion was trailing slowly behind. Of course, we were not in ignorance longer than the walk to the house, for Mr. Bruce had seen the same outfit on the road, and said it was Dick Barnes with his men—which made our minds easier. Kathryn knew the Mexican in Lander, Eline Orango his name.

April 18. For three of four days, sunshine before another storm. Margaret and I rode out to hunt for the horses Saturday, from half-past one until seven. All over the Hall Creek country, to wood canyon and over the mountain we rode, but in vain. Sunday, Kathryn and I went to Hailey for mail, by way of Bull Springs and the stage road, where we found the diggers.

We had to have eggs for Easter, and dyed them with diamond dyes, turkey red and fast black. They made quite a show with the few white ones to set them off. The day before I had found some tiny white moss flowers which I presented to Mrs. Mills in the one egg cup. Sandford brought me some too, from Beaver where he spent the day fishing. In the evening we had two large bonfires of the raspberry bushes, which were cut down after the garden was ploughed. Such great pale flower flames! High in the air they flew and blossomed out in the wind. When the fire died down to the pile of dry grass beneath, we brought the old Christmas tree and set it upright on the pile. The flames crept up the trunk, and suddenly it all caught from the side in one sheet of flame. Poor tree, it was like burning a friend at the stake.

On this morning came a heavy wet snow that lay upon the branches of the trees and fence posts, quiet and white. The netting of wire about the chicken house was one fine piece of lace work. Of course the Schlichtings did not turn up at school and we had the day to ourselves. It is just as well perhaps that school will be over Friday. The broom is little but handle. The barrel has gone for kindling, perhaps half of it, so that the little coal in the bottom falls through. For weeks we have been melting snow for water so that even the water bucket is in sad condition.

April 20. Last day of school. Ellen appeared in a red dress and hat with a pink sash tied around it. The boys wore clean shirts—though the sleeves of Otto's were not far from his elbows, and both wore ties, Emmon's being red and blue, Otto's green and yellow in general effect. Nothing was done all day but prepare for the exercises. Kathryn had stayed at home to practice reading her essay. We at school swept out four times with the broom brought from the house, that all might be clean, washed the windows, scrubbed the desks, and wiped the blackboard with a damp cloth. These operations took up all the lunch and recess time. About two o'clock Sandford came over on horseback. No overalls today. He too, was dressed up in best trousers and coat. Mrs. Mills, Kathryn and Mr. Mills drove over in the buggy.

The boys and Ellen spoke first, and how lamely they did hobble through. Margaret read her paper on common Wyoming birds, and only the awe of ceremony kept Sandford and Mr. Mills from contradicting her, when she spoke of the number of eggs a magpie laid, and so on. Last of all Kathryn read her essay. She looked very pretty in her white dress, and read well, though embarrassed. After she had finished I presented her grandly with a bogus diploma tied with pink ribbon, a few flowers, and a medal which Sandford had labored on—a round leather panel, "Kathryn Mills, 20 April, 1906" scratched upon it, *and* a motto "In God We Trust!" The whole was to be hung by braided horsehair from her belt.

Then it was over. The pictures came down from the walls, the books were packed away in the buggy, the papers burned, everybody said goodbye to everybody else, and we all drove back to the ranch.

September, 1906. Now that I am at home again [in Denver] and have leisure to read and dream over the record of the year, I have realized how incomplete and inadequate it is. There is no part of the seven months that I would forget, and none of the stories that I would want to slip away from my memory. Here and there, on bits of lesson paper are jotted down some of the sayings of Otto and Ellen, or trifles of gossip; these I have gathered together as too precious to be lost. So I shall try to fill out a little what was lacking before.

There are dozens of school doings or sayings which I might have recorded, from Otto's first "Aw now, listen, would ye!" when he thought he had made a mistake to Margaret's "I savez" over her arithmetic.

Why did I never make mention of our Halloween party, and the shadow pantomime of Paul Revere's ride which Kathryn and Margaret and I arranged fifteen minutes before it was given? That should never have been omitted, nor the games we played afterwards with candles, and flour. Sandford was too much afraid of the new teacher to join in heartily and even the girls were a little shy at first. Then there was Cinderella. We practiced several weeks on that shadow play, and gave it at Thanksgiving time. Kathryn was leading lady; Margaret played proud sister—we dispensed with the other—with a fine artificial nose which in spite of being tied on with tape, changed its position during the play. Sandford made a gala prince in the knee bicycle trousers, which appeared in every one of our plays, I believe, golf cape, tam o'shanter with a turkey feather and a sash. His shadow was really impressive. I was fairy godmother, and fortunately had little to do. The white-nosed kitten, behind the scenes to be used as a rat in the scene of metamorphosis, nearly sent me into hysterics.

As to what has happened since I left Wyoming, my letters from the ranch and elsewhere will show better than I am able.

5

DENVER/BOULDER: 1906–1907

It's an interesting question—what one tries to do,
in writing a letter—partly of course to give back a re-
flection of the other person.
                    —Virginia Woolf, *The Letters of Virginia Woolf*

Because of a four-way misunderstanding between the Mills family,
Ethel Waxham, some neighbors, and John Love, concerning an invitation to visit the Hall family after the Teachers' Institute, John Love
didn't come to the Mills ranch during the last months that Ethel was
there. He gradually deduced that Mrs. Mills wanted Ethel to marry her
son Sandford, despite the age disparity, and had fabricated the misunderstanding to keep John away.

Ethel left the Mills ranch to return to Denver. John arrived only an
hour after she left, having ridden seventy miles from his ranch to the
Mills'. She had left no message for him and no address. Stunned and
disheartened, he rode home. Months went by with no letter from her
and no address to write to. He telegraphed Western Union in Denver for
Ethel's address, and on August 6, 1906, a collect wire (costing forty
cents) to Casper gave it as 1901 East Colfax Avenue. At that time there
was no reliable telegraph service between Casper and Lander. John
promptly wrote her and received a cool reply on August 11, 1906. Thus
began their 1906–1910 series of letters.

It should be noted that John Love had a horseback or buggy ride of a
minimum of 30 miles round trip from his ranch to Moneta, 30 miles to
Muskrat, 40 to Wolton, and a maximum of 140 miles for the letters
postmarked Hailey or Lander. The mere posting or receiving of mail in
winter was frequently accompanied by risk, hardship, and danger.

Apparently on one of the long wintry buggy rides between the Mills
Ranch and Lander, John Love had proposed to Ethel and had been
rejected. The likely reason for her refusal was that she was already
engaged and had been for five years to someone whose identity to this
day remains unknown. [1] No mention of this is made in her diary, but she
may allude to it in the poem "My Garden of Wishes" written in 1906.
At the time of John Love's proposal, he had known her only six weeks,
but his mind was firmly made up. Years later she wrote in her story
"Rome Was Not Built in a Day":

> A pretty blue dress I wore, he explained, was the rea-
> son for his determination to marry me. But he kept
> the idea longer than I did the dress. "No" was "no" to
> other men, but not to him. His letters followed me
> to Denver; again to the University of Colorado; to an
> Anglican convent; to a high school in Pueblo. I was
> nearly as stubborn in refusing as he was in insisting.

Form No. 168.

THE WESTERN UNION TELEGRAPH COMPANY.
─── INCORPORATED ───
23,000 OFFICES, IN AMERICA.   CABLE SERVICE TO ALL THE WORLD.

This Company TRANSMITS and DELIVERS messages only on conditions limiting its liability, which have been assented to by the sender of the following message.
Errors can be guarded against only by repeating a message back to the sending station for comparison, and the Company will not hold itself liable for errors or delays
in transmission or delivery of Unrepeated Messages, beyond the amount of tolls paid thereon, nor in any case where the claim is not presented in writing within sixty days
after the message is filed with the Company for transmission.
This is an UNREPEATED MESSAGE, and is delivered by request of the sender, under the conditions named above.
ROBERT C. CLOWRY, President and General Manager.

RECEIVED at

14 D OH NX 9 Collect

Denver Colo Aug 6th

J G Love,

Casper Wyo.

Redience nineteen hundred and one

east colfax avenue.

E U Combs.
110pm.

John G. Love's first letter to Ethel P. Waxham, once he had obtained her address, has been lost, but the following, written on her twenty-fourth birthday, is her reply:

ETHEL P. WAXHAM
1901 E. Colfax Ave.,
Denver, Colo.
8/11/06

JOHN G. LOVE
Muskrat, Wyo.

Dear Mr. Love,

Your letter reached me this morning and threw light on several things which were beyond my understanding. No word of any trouble, no reason or explanation of your absence was given me. The only hint I had was in a chance remark made by Mr. Mills that he had "read the riot act" to you. That was too vague for any definite meaning, except that your long friendship with the family was in some way broken, and the thought that I might be the cause of the trouble was anything but pleasant.

"On the square," as you asked, it certainly was the part of the [R. H.] Halls to have called on me in Lander, as Mrs. Charlie Hall did, if it was at all possible. You offered to stop on the way back, or go on as I chose, and my choice was less a decision than a whim, though in it were the reasons which I did not then put in words. The invitation was not so cordial that I felt it made any difference to them whether we stayed or not; you did not want to stop, I knew; I was tired and did not feel like meeting new people; I liked to travel in the storm, selfishly, and cared more to get back to the Mills people. Even now, I fail to see that, according to the commonly accepted social code, the occurrance was of enough importance to cause such trouble. I only wish that Mrs. Hall or Claire or the one who felt that it was "mean," had written directly to me, instead of making another person pay the penalty of what was my fault, if any fault at all, while I, the guilty one, knew nothing of the matter. If any word of mine can help to settle the misunderstanding, I shall be glad to write it.

To be sure the social code differs in different places. Never before December 26 did I ever help make oyster stew in a stranger's kitchen, yet then it seemed quite the right and proper thing to do, and Miss Davis, instead of taking it amiss, enjoyed it. I think it all depends upon the intention, which was innocent in both cases. I am sorry both to have offended the Halls, unwittingly, and to have made trouble in three places. When we did go down to the Hall's to visit later, it was, I understood from Mrs. Mills, at a renewed invitation from Mrs. Hall. They were all kind to us, and we stayed for a week.

As for the reason that you did not come to the ranch while I was there—I did not know. Sometimes I was afraid that it had been my words to you. I knew that whatever it was, you had some reason for not coming. I trusted too, that it was a good and worthy reason, for I had come to think of you as one of the most true gentlemen that it has ever been my good fortune to know.

I shall be glad to be "best friends" with you, if it does not cause more trouble between you and other friends of longer standing and stronger claims. The social code—to which you appealed—says as I knew very well eight months ago, that since I cannot say "yes" to you, I must say "no," and nothing between. It is harsh, that code. Perhaps that is the reason that for the first time in years, while I was reading the last three pages of your letter, I disgraced myself by crying.

Often I am homesick for Wyoming, and want to go back. The summer has passed in miserably futile attempts to persuade the family and myself that we are contented, if not happy. My fever—though not even the doctors knew it, poor troubled souls—was only a desperate attack of the blue devils that got the upper hand for a while.

If you come to Denver in the fall, you must come to see me. Write or let me know beforehand, for I might not be here. I will take you for an automobile ride, though a long gallop on little "Papoose" would be more to my taste. I did want to see "Punch" and "Merino," too.

Please, I am very sorry to have brought misunderstanding, and trouble to you, of all people, who have been and are so good to me.

Sincerely yours,
Ethel P. Waxham

JOHN G. LOVE
Muskrat, Wyo, Sept. 12/06

[Forwarded to the Delta Gamma House, Boulder, Colorado.]

Dear Miss Waxham,

Yours of the 11th received on the 25th as I passed Muskrat on my way up to Mills'. I lay awake that night out in the sagebrush curled up in my buggy robes and thought and studied astronomy. I am going to Wolton tomorrow, so will have a chance to mail letters. I must ask your indulgence for using pencil and tablet. You have no idea how pleased I was to hear from you and it is beyond my pencil to express the satisfaction I felt. Thank you very much for the picture. It does not flatter you any, but at the same time it is very life-like.

Your letter confirmed my suspicion that you were left in blissful ignorance regarding the grievous sin that we had committed by not going to R. H. Hall's on Dec. 31st last. You were to blame me and I was to blame you for some imaginary grievance. We were never supposed to meet or to write to each other in order to explain matters. The social code would prevent you from writing first even had you been so inclined. The one thing lacking is the motive. Why did Mrs. Mills change front and want you and me to be strangers to each other?

I left there in blissful ignorance as to what I had done to so grievously offend them. When Mr. Mills said that he "read

109

the riot act", to me, he lied. Furthermore he was hardly in a position to do so. He owed me money that he would have found very inconvenient to pay just then, had I demanded it. I did not ask it from him, but on the contrary, I loaned him $255 more without interest and without a scratch of the pen to show for it.

Of course it will cause many a sharp twinge and heartache to have to take "no" for an answer, but I will never blame you for it in the least and I will never be sorry that I met you. I will be better for having known you. Not one of your friends will appreciate your friendship, or value it more highly than I. I believe that it is almost as true of the human race as it is of water that it will seek its own level. I know the folly of hoping that your "no" is not final, but in spite of that knowledge, in spite of my better judgement, and in spite of all I can do to the contrary, I know that I will hope until the day that you are married. Only then I will know that the sentence is irrevocable.

I have often wondered what sort of a fellow your fiancé is. That he is a fine fellow and far my superior, I have no doubt. How he could content himself wherever he is, with you way up here in Wyoming is beyond my comprehension. I wish him the best of good fortune and every joy that I could wish myself were I in his place.

You say that if any word of yours can help settle the misunderstanding, you will be glad to write it. Never at my request or with my consent. Some day perhaps I will know the whys and wherefores and the motive, but at present the whole Mills family, even Kathryn, shut up like clams whenever I undertake to delve into the past. I have always considered Mrs. Mills the peer of any woman on earth and have valued her friendship above that of anyone that I have ever met in the state, yourself excepted. To be compelled to believe that she of all people would stoop to deceit is certainly hard lines. The case is so plain that I will never be able to think quite the same of her again. I am lots better, however, for having known her, for in all these years I have never been guilty of any act that I was ashamed for her to know. I must still give her the credit for making me live up to somewhere near the high standard set me by my sisters in the years gone by.

I have been out of luck with my horses this summer. When I got back from Mills' after I found out you were gone, I felt so sore that I turned out all of the driving and saddle horses I had taken so many pains with. Punch was stolen and I probably will never see him again. Reno got cut on a wire fence and now goes on three legs. My other driving team I last heard of on Beaver Creek. Babe and Papoose (ladies' horses) and Pilot and Red I have not seen since. Fortunately I have plenty more that won't remind me of my folly every time I look at them.

Now "little girl," should you care to waste a few minutes' time in writing to me, I can assure you that it will be more than appreciated by me here on earth and who knows, but perhaps in the Great Beyond, it will be booked to your credit as a sort of missionary labor.

Yours Sincerely,

John G. Love

A brief journal written while she taught at Kemper Hall and letters to and from friends and family provide the only records of Ethel Waxham's life during the period 1906–1910. These letters, although many have been lost or destroyed, reflect the choices that she and her friends made, some leaning towards Apollo, some towards the shepherd, as Mr. Hyde had said they would. Some friends' letters indicate vivid but transitory friendships, but their words are included to give an indication of Ethel's broad scope of interests and talents. Other letters are from friends with whom she continued to correspond for the remainder of her life. Amy and Will Wattles were long-time friends. Nora Dunn was a classmate from Hyde Park High School in Chicago, where she was lauded by the school paper for her outstanding creativity. Donald McLean and Ethel taught Sunday School together in Denver. Only two of Donald's letters from this period remain, but Ethel's address book shows that they maintained contact through at least seven of his address changes in later years.

While at Wellesley, Ethel was one of four very close friends who, partly based on their physical sizes, called themselves the Three Bears and Goldylocks. Big Bear, the tallest, was Florence Risley; Middle Bear was Winifred Hawkridge, none of whose letters remain; Ethel Waxham was Little Bear, and Caroline Maude Holt was Goldylocks. Adrienne Muzzy was affectionately known as "Muzzer" Bear. Their friendships and lively correspondence lasted through their lives. While at Wellesley, they and other classmates formed a writers' club called "Scribblers." Other Wellesley friends were Ethel Vaughan, Marian Berry, Laura Hibbard, Maud Thompson, and Helen Watson.

While in graduate school at the University of Colorado in Boulder, Ethel shared an apartment with Marcia Chipman and her mother, but took her meals across the street at the Delta Gamma House. Probably the difficult circumstances at the Waxham family home, which were only alluded to, but never described, combined with Marcia's fond memories of her own student years at Kemper Hall [K.H.], influenced Ethel to accept a teaching position there. Her difficult term as a classics teacher at K.H. was made more bearable by her friendship with Louise Dudley, a graduate student from Bryn Mawr; Elizabeth "Billy" Williams, the "science department"; her former Wellesley classmate Laura Hibbard, and by Big Bear's proximity as a teacher in Chicago. All were very much involved with Apollo initially, but since at that time married women were not usually allowed to teach, gradually some chose to exchange "Greek roots for potatoes, French verbs for scrubbing brushes and Latin prose for making bread," [p. 347] and marry.

The constant voice during this time, even as Ethel worked on her master's degree in literature and accepted other teaching jobs, was her own shepherd's, hoping she would choose him.

WILL AND AMY WATTLES
Los Angeles, Cal., Stam.
September 12, 1906

My dear Ethel—

It is very hard to tell who was the most pleased over your letter—probably I showed it the most, but anyone knowing Will could see that his pleasure was as great as mine. And when the music came,* we were doubly pleased. Thank you so much for remembering us. Indeed, we felt it quite an honor to have something of your own originality in print, for

*None of Ethel Waxham's musical compositions was found among her papers.

often we have wished that others besides ourselves might enjoy parts of your letters—they were so good. The words are well chosen and the thought is good—and very characteristic of our dear friend—so Will says.

As for housekeeping—"The little wife" has two advantages over most wives—one is that she knew pretty well how to cook before she married and the other is that she has a hubby who is very easy to please in the cooking line, so she does not have any sad experiences to relate like the young things in the *Ladies Home Journal* do.

Are you going back again to Hailey to teach as soon as school is opened? I wish you could get a school in Los Angeles but as they are very hard to get, I suppose there is no use in wishing.

We went to San Diego on the 21st of July—and took our vacation and had a most delightful time, taking in all the points of interest and especially a bullfight—over the border line in Tia Juana, Mexico. The location of San Diego is beautiful and the climate is perfect, but such a quiet dead place. It is a place where millionnaires go to luxuriate and not a place of business, although some of the residents proudly informed us that their city was growing. We are so we hope to always be

> your loving friends,
> Will and Amy

Ethel Vaughan
Kansas City, Kan.
September 16, 1906

My dear Ethel—

On my return from a little visit in the country the other day, I found your song waiting for me. I think it is beautiful. The poem itself is lovely, both in thought and expression. A man here to whom I showed it, is going to use it as an encore at an approaching recital.

Are you devoting all your time to writing? I expect someday to "point with pride" to my acquaintance with the gifted authoress Ethel Waxham.

How much of your Salem fortune has come true? I have forgotten mine, but yours you wrote down, I remember, so perhaps you keep better watch than I can do. Several of us had ours told by a clairvoyante this summer. It wasn't nearly so complex as the Salem one, so I hope to remember it better.

Write to me, Ethel. I shall be so glad to hear what you are doing.

Sincerely your friend,
Ethel Vaughan

MY GARDEN OF WISHES

In the garden of my wishes by the sea
  There have grown a thousand blossoms
Since the day I first met thee,
Since the day I heard thee singing
Where the road leads down to the sea.

In the garden of my wishes, buds so sweet
  Never come to fragrant blossom
Where the trees and grasses meet,
I bring thee tribute of wishes
A spray of flowers at thy feet.

There is long silence through my garden fair,
  Far away the sea is dreaming,
No bird songs thrill the air.
  My garden of wishes is waiting
The spell of thy singing there.

Come be my lady of wishes,
Come pluck my rose for me
Before the wind of the right time
Blows cold from the sea.

Ethel Waxham   1906

MARY B. MILLS
September 30, 1906
Red Bluff Ranch

[Ethel P. Waxham, Boulder, Colo.]

After working on the jump all day, dear little girl, making pickles and pickles and more pickles, I feel that I must write just a wee little bit for the girls to take over to mail tomorrow.

They came home quite heartbroken with your letter and we were all in the same condition after reading it.

We don't wonder your pater is delighted at having you no farther away, but is there no hope of your reconsidering the matter of teaching here again?

It almost seems as though we could even offer a fine winter if the present weather is an indication—such glorious days!

I am going to enclose you the recipe for the "peppery chopped cucumber kind of pickle" so your big sister can make some if she has a jar or a cucumber left. She must be having lots of fun—her first experience—I know just how she feels—likes to fill all the shelves and then hates to take a single jar out of its place. Must not write more although my heart says many things.

> Yours most aff'y,
> Mary B. Mills

P.S. I had forgotten to ask you if, during the summer, you received Kathryn's diploma from Miss Davis to sign. I wrote her about it a week or two ago and she told me she had sent it to you and thought Kathryn had it long ago. However, I did not think it had ever reached you. Let me know and I will tell Allie Davis—you saw by the paper she was "running" again for the position of Superintendent of Schools—no one else would take it.

ETHEL P. WAXHAM
Boulder, Colo.,
28 October, 1906

Muskrat, Wyo.

Dear Mr. Love,

I was very much pleased to hear from you, although your letter troubled me in several ways.

In the first place, I cannot believe that there was any evil plot in the misunderstanding that arose because we did not stop at Mr. Hall's. When Mrs. Mills wrote that I said I expected to stop over there, she certainly wrote my words. Perhaps I did not make my whole meaning clear. The fact is that I thought very little of the affair, and as nothing was said of it, it soon slipped from my memory entirely.

Whatever Mrs. Mills did I am sure could have been from no other motive than to put an end to any ill feeling that may have arisen. You who have known her so much longer than I must agree to that. You cannot think too highly of Mrs. Mills. You will make me sorry that I ever went to them, if your opinion of her is in any way less than before.

The "riot act" I thought might refer to your all-day visit at school. Make allowance for the expression, Mr. Love, and what is left need not amount to much.

When I wrote that I did not wish to interfere with your friendships of long standing, I meant that if any friendship we may have might interfere with your friendly relations to the Mills people and to the Halls—I ought not to accept your friendship. The good will of the people one meets with most means a great deal. Claire Hall, I admire for her ability to do easily the things that I have never done, and know nothing about—baking and brewing, and cooking and sewing, butter making and turkey raising. Will you not, please, treat the whole affair as a misunderstanding? I believe that the solution cannot be found by questioning or looking for motives, but by waiting, trusting in the good intentions of those concerned to come at last of their own free will to the truth.

Kathryn writes in her way of your visits. I know that you

brought an antelope to the ranch, and once went fishing and hunting with Sandford, taking a sack for game.

I am very sorry about Punch and Reno and especially Papoose. Since you first spoke of Papoose, I have felt a special interest in his welfare, even more than for Polly and Buck. Since leaving Wyoming, I have not had the pleasure of a single ride, and I certainly miss it during these fine fall days when I want so much to be out of doors among the hills instead of studying out of books indoors.

When the University of Colorado here at Boulder opened in the fall, I came up to visit some of my friends. I was offered the position of English assistant, for which I had applied last year. I had only two hours to think the matter over, and decided to accept it. The teaching that I do is not very hard; a class of twenty-five girls, and their themes to correct. Beside that I am doing some studying in Greek and Literature that takes up almost all of my time. I do get off sometimes over Saturday and Sunday to go home, but the work is generally so hard that I quite long for the easy happy times I had last year. In fact I miss Wyoming and my friends there more than I ever dreamed that I would. Only the thought of returning at some yet-undetermined time to see my friends and the Yellowstone Park is consoling.

Edith Signor sent me a *Shoshoni Pathfinder* some time ago,[2] which had, beside the reading matter, pictures of places that I knew well or had heard of, and of people. Among these was a picture of you which was, I thought, pretty good.

May I be frank with you still, as I always have been? I told you that I was engaged to be married. I had been engaged for five years, and a little longer. During the last year or so a trouble arose which reached its culmination last summer. Now I am not looking forward to any wedding day. What you say of people seeking their own level seems to me to be very true. One's friends, too, are one's chief pleasure. It is so with me, anyway. If we are to be friends—if it does not interfere with your other friendships—I shall hope to hear from you again.

Sincerely yours,

Ethel P. Waxham

117

John G. Love
Muskrat, Wyo.,
November 12, 1906

Dear Miss Waxham,

I just got back today from Omaha and found your letter awaiting me at the ranch. I will not try to tell you the pleasure it gave me to hear from you again. I have tried hard not to expect a letter from you amongst my mail and not be disappointed when there was none. Last month, though it was wasted energy, for I *was* disappointed and the mild attack of the "blues" that you had this summer was a mere nothing to the dose I had. I tried hard work and failed; I herded for fourteen days; I next tried the excitement of the old life in the saddle. I got in my fastest saddlehorses and for the first time in ten years, donned my high-heeled riding boots, spurs and "chaps." I got along at that for a week. Besides the excitement of the chase, I got together *all* of my work, driving and saddle horses, even Punch, and also twenty-seven of my "broncs." I then went up to Mills', Halls', Lander, etc. I came back past Muskrat, still no letter. I then went to Casper and got transportation for Denver, changed my mind and came home, went to Muskrat for the mail, still no letter and next day I started for Omaha. I went to the theatre every night, bummed around and spent a lot of money foolishly, got disgusted and started for home, stopped at Casper on the way back and invested over ten thousand dollars of hard cash[3] in more sheep and cattle. Tonight I am happy and contented and soaring along up somewhere in the vicinity of the "seventh heaven."

"Little girl," do not think that I desire you to forego any pleasure or enjoyment for the sake of writing to me. Neither do I desire you to let it interfere with your much needed rest. Now that I have got peace established with the Mills and Halls families, I am going to take your advice and let the "dead past bury its dead," and drop the whole thing. Mrs.

Mills, I have no doubt, will tell me sometime all of the whys and wherefores.

Papoose, the little sinner, is fat and glossy and always ready to eat oats. He is almost a black with white stockings behind and only four years old.

Yes, we will be the best of friends and I will be honored by your friendship. I can get along somehow with just friendship when I am this far away from you with most of my money tied up in this ranch, sheep, cattle and horses. How long I can manage to exist here without seeing you remains to be seen. The next time that I get the "blues," I will most assuredly come to Denver, unless you absolutely forbid it. In that event your word is law and your wishes will be respected. "Little girl," you and I have exactly changed places. You say that you are not looking forward to any wedding day. I was not but now I am. I will do my level best to get you to do likewise.

I know that you have not been brought up to cook and labor. I have never been on the lookout for a slave and would not utter a word of censure if you never learned or if you got ambitious and made a "batch" of biscuits that proved fatal to my favorite dog. I honestly believe that I could idolize you to such an extent as to not utter a harsh word. "Little girl," I will do my level best to win you and will be the happiest mortal on earth if I can see the ring that I wear on my watchchain flash on your finger. It has never been worn by or offered to another. If I fail, I will still want your friendship just the same.

We had one very hard storm and several herders lost their lives but that I think was their own fault.

They have a new teacher at the Mills' now, but I have not been up there since she arrived. Mills says that the picture of me in the *Pathfinder* makes me look like a road agent. I am tired and sleepy so will close before my writing is entirely unreadable. With best wishes, I remain

Yours Sincerely,
John G. Love

CAROLINE MAUDE HOLT
[GOLDYLOCKS][4]
Wellesley, Mass.,
Nov. 20, 1906

Ethel P. Waxham, Boulder, Colo.

Dearest Little Bear,

I have looked sharply at the postman each morning to see if his pockets bulged suspiciously, but so far not a trace of a letter from Denver have I found. I am very lonely and very homesick for my Bear family. Big Bear sends me little notes very often—like the five minute calls just before class or luncheon and Win [Winifred Hawkridge][5] comes over and sleeps in the trundle bed whenever anything happens she wants to attend, but there are never any tracks on the back of the Morris Chair anymore and never anyone curled up in the corner of the couch when I come home at night.

Julia Hewitt and I are keeping house this year. Julia has the room I had last year and I have the big front room with the big closet with a window and the cunning little kitchen with its little gas range and cupboards and shelves and such a lot of pots and pans as you can't imagine. Why, when dishwashing day comes—twice a week—I am just overcome with wonder that there are so many different kinds of cooking dishes.

Poor dear Muzzer Bear* has been very very ill with typhoid fever ever since the middle of September. She is going to begin to sit up this week. For a long long time even the doctor thought she could not possibly get well again and she was very bad and wouldn't do as the nurses wanted her to— that is she would not swallow her food because she thought they put medicine in it and she had all sorts of dreadful fancies about everything and everybody and we were terribly worried for fear she was not going to be well in her mind again. This last week that, too, has come right and the nurse

*Adrienne Muzzy

reads letters to her and she sees people a little. Send her a postal card with [bear] tracks on it to give her something new to think about.

Gertrude Schoepperle is coming out to read to Scribblers next week and Scribblers appointed me a committee of one to ask Little Bear to "please, please, please write us or send us something already written." Won't you dear? It is a great inspiration when something comes from "Those who have gone before."

Typhoid scare is nearly over. There have been no new cases for about a month now so we feel safe once more. Some of the people are already back at work again.

Are you all over your fever and what are you doing? Did you get a "job?" and if so where is it? How much do you weigh? I could not wear your clothes any more for I weigh 113¼ and I look just like the Freshman who used to have to pay two carriage fares or at least as if I were her little sister.

Miss Lockwood and Miss Hubbard still sleep out of doors.[6] Even the snow storm did not drive them in. Miss Lockwood is as dear as ever. I helped tie a quilt to keep her warm this winter.

College Hall is so splendid this year with two electric elevators running nearly every day it scarcely seems like College at all. I think the Trustees should have considered carefully before they put such speedy affairs into the girls' lives.

I am always correcting books and papers just as usual. Today I corrected the results of the girls' experiments on living crayfish—we gave each girl a crayfish this year to take home and see how much she could find out about it. Some of the papers were very, very funny. One girl said she found that the crayfish preferred cold to heat for she put her crayfish on the radiator in a jar of water and he died. While one girl left hers in the window and the water in the jar froze, but after it thawed, the crayfish revived.

We have just had supper and I have persuaded Julia we don't need to do dishes tonight 'cause I have to work hard, so

I suppose I must go and work hard and not talk any more to Little Bear specially since she refuses to talk to me.

> Lots of love,
> Goldylocks

ETHEL P. WAXHAM
Boulder, Colo.,
December 8, 1906

Muskrat, Wyo.

Dear Mr. Love,

Your letter reached me some time ago, and needless to say, I was glad to hear from you again. I am writing now in hopes that this letter will be with you in time to say, "Merry Christmas and Happy New Year." Will you spend Christmas Day at the Mills' ranch in your capacity of Santa Claus?

Work closes at the University in two weeks, and then we shall scatter to our respective homes for the holidays. If the vacation is only as pleasant this year as it was last, I have nothing more to ask. The two weeks before it comes will be full enough to make me appreciate the rest, if nothing more—hundreds of themes to scratch over with red ink, Latin hymns and musty old books to bother my head; we have a new system of Greek philosophy to study. I get very tired sometimes of this confining indoor work, and long to be trudging to the Little Twin Creek school, Kathryn on one side of me and Margaret on the other.

I hope that your attack of the "blues" is over for good. If you come down, I shall be very glad to see you. I do not forbid your coming, but on the other hand, I have no hope to give you if you come. Our friendship I value, and value highly for its own sake. I should have answered your letter before if I had known that it made such a difference to you. For what should a person have time, if not for her friends, whether absent or present?

I read in the Denver paper about several storms in central

Wyoming. We had a record breaker wind storm here in Boulder several weeks ago. The tiles and cornices blew off of the library roof, the old rickety Main Building shivered and shook in its shoes, screen doors blew away with chicken houses and roofs of barns. The telegraph and telephone poles, many of them, fell, cutting off the electric light supply so that the whole town was in darkness. Chimneys were overthrown on every street and window panes blown in. For a whole day the town was in confusion. People were blown off the walks on the campus, and tried often to make their way against the wind backward or on their hands and knees. Only one person kept a straight and steady course between the Main Building and the Library—that was the Professor of Literature, a little man in height, but great in *avoirdupois*. He weighs perhaps two hundred and fifty pounds. The trees were bending, and everything seemed to be in motion—but he went his way with hardly a quiver of the coat tails to show that the wind was blowing.

Since then our snows and muds have been prosaic enough. The chimneys stay where they belong, and no one is blown off the sidewalks. The wind made me think of Smithy's story of the high wind in Wyoming, when the sheep blew over his head.

Wish you Merry Christmas once more and many Happy New Years to follow. From your friend,

Ethel Waxham

MARY B. MILLS
Red Bluff Ranch,
December 9, 1906

My dear "Miss Waxham,"

I hardly know how to address a dignified university teacher of English even if she is the dearest little girl in the world.

Your letters are always so good, we would like to find one in every mail. Our individual mail service has not improved with the advent of the railroad, although it reaches Lander in better shape. The mail for the mines* which goes from Lander, brings our mail to Dallas and it is brought from there to Myersville *twice* a week—it is rather of a nuisance.

It does seem fine to have the railroad though. Now it takes just twenty-five hours to get to Chicago and they expect to shorten the time and also lower the freight rates. Since the road started, they have shipped out two hundred car loads of cattle and sheep a week. Sandford went into town yesterday and came out this afternoon—he says they are building a larger roundhouse and depot.

They are as busy as bees at school and Miss Bancroft* is busy too. Of the nine scholars, no two are in the same class entirely, some recite one or two lessons together, so there are the twenty-seven classes just as you had there. *Otto is adding fractions*—don't you feel proud that he did not have to go back to *reading numbers*—Emmons, from all accounts is rather hopeless. Miss Bancroft does not seem to have a happy knack for getting along with some of them, although she seems to be very conscientious in her work. Is very pleasant around the house, but does use such a dreadful amount of slang—college girl-like, I suppose, but I don't like it.

Yes, dear, she has your room and your place at table, but no one can ever have your place in our hearts. The first morning, without thinking, I asked Kathryn to take in some warm water and call Miss Bancroft. "Oh Mama," she said, "Don't ask me to do *that*." So I do it now. I knew how she missed you, but I think we will get along very nicely. We are expecting Mr. Bruce this week with his phonograph, so I suppose they will have a dance some Friday night.

Court commences tomorrow. We will probably know before long what Mr. Ehler's fate will be—although most people think the trial will be put off. Mrs. Ehler has sold the

*Hard rock gold mines at South Pass City. (J. D. Love, personal communication, 1989.)
*Elizabeth Bancroft, originally from Denver, was the new teacher at the Twin Creek school.

lower place, and they expect to sell the upper place, too. She went into town yesterday and is to live in a tent on old "Uncle Jimmy Carr's" place. I don't know what will become of young George. He was drunk half the time this summer, and did everything else bad he could.

Your account of "Coming to Lander" makes me think of a funny thing I heard the other day. Before we became so cosmopolitan [as to have the railroad], a travelling man was coming up on the stage. He said, "I didn't mind paying sixteen dollars and walking most of the way, even taking a pole along and getting the coach out of the mud, but what I *did* mind was having the driver 'cuss' me for not keeping up."

Don't I wish Kathryn was at the university with you. Wonder will you be there another year. I dread sending her off all alone.

Baby [Margaret] doesn't seem quite well lately, although she declares she feels well. She wails to go to bed right after supper—something unusual for her—and doesn't eat very well. You remember hearing of Dr. A. C. Godfrey of Lander. He felt the work was so hard for him he must get away and expected to go to Arizona, but I see by the paper he has an appointment in one of the Denver hospitals, St. Joseph's, I believe. There is a fine opening for a good doctor here—one who really knows something and doesn't drink.

We had the same snow storm you had in Denver the middle of October or rather the latter part, but the snow went so quickly, and we have had beautiful days until last Tuesday, when it snowed again.

It was lovely today and the girls went for a little ride. I will leave it to them to tell you what a time they later had teaching Miss Bancroft to ride. It is surely funny. She has no idea how to ride, and each time they go out they go on a little farther. She hopes to be able to go as far as the P.O. next week.

The children will be writing soon.

Do you get lonesome, dearie, with just Marcia [Chipman] and Marcia's mother? She must be a dear little lady.

We are always looking forward to the time we are to see you again. Do write often dear. With very much love,

Mary B. Mills

JOHN G. LOVE
Wolton, Wyo., Dec. 19th/06

[Forwarded to Delta Gamma House, Boulder, Colorado.]

Dear Miss Waxham,

Your letter just received and read with pleasure. Yes, I expect to spend Christmas at the Mills' ranch as usual if the weather permits. I do not expect to enjoy the holidays as much as last year, but still I expect to have a good time.

So you did not realize that it would make any material difference to me just when you wrote. If you had been a week later in writing, I would have had the notes and mortgages signed, and would have been thirty thousand dollars in debt for more sheep. I did try hard to make myself see how foolish it was for me to be such a fool over a mite of humanity like you with no encouragement from you whatever. I had made up my mind to invest in sheep and make an idol of the almighty dollar and see how many of them I could get together in the next ten years. It was an unworthy object I admit, but I had to do something. As I neither drink nor gamble, that was the only thing left to do. I was still out of debt and had a little money left. After I got your letter, I dropped that idea and went the other way. I sold an un-divided third interest in my livestock for $10,760.00 and a two-thirds interest in 24 mares. I reserved as my individual property my ranch, with its 15 miles of fence and buildings, my dogs, cats, ducks, chickens and all 21 of my favorite horses.

I am going to try hard to content myself here all winter for much as I would like to see you, I realize that it would probably be better for me not to until I become reconciled to the inevitable. I found out to my sorrow last winter that there is far more truth than poetry in Will Carleton's saying, "If you want a man to get the full bitterness of hell, give him a taste of heaven."

We have had some heavy windstorms and also some heavy snows here already this winter, but my livestock are in good condition and I can't complain. Several herders lost their lives, one within a few miles of Hailey.

I am writing this letter under difficulties. I have only the glow of a lantern for a light and my right hand is badly swollen from being kicked by a horse. I would have liked very much to send you a Christmas present, but the ones I got for you and would like to send, I dare not. The social code says that under existing circumstances you should not accept them, it would surely hurt me to have them returned. I did order some of the best candy to be had in Denver sent to your house so you will know that I have not forgotten you.

"Baby" Mills told me one day, "Just think of it, Mr. Love, Miss Waxham did not know what a leveler or a marker was."* I told her that might well be, but you knew what a wax image was and she laughed and blushed. Kathryn said that she knew "Baby" was green, but she had no idea that she was *that* bad.

I can just imagine how you and those who are with you looked when you were watching the professor plod stoically along against the wind. There is very little snow here on the ground at present and the weather is nice and warm. The hour is late—or rather early—so I will close by wishing you a Merry Christmas and a Happy New Year.

Yours sincerely,
John G. Love

---

*Used in determining slope when building irrigation ditches. (J. D. Love, personal communication, 1989.)

ETHEL P. WAXHAM
1901 Colfax Ave.,
Denver, Colo.

JOHN G. LOVE
2 January, 1907

Dear Mr. Love,

It was a delightful surprise that you prepared for me on Christmas morning. Not only myself, but my family and my friends have been enjoying the candy, which is delicious. When it is gone—which is fortunately not yet—the box will still be a pleasure. Besides its prettiness, it is just the right size for the gloves or handkerchiefs which I will keep in it. Truly, it would not have been much more of a surprise to me to have seen you yourself at the door.

A letter came to me from Mrs. Mills yesterday, telling of their Christmas celebration at the ranch. She did not speak of you, and I wondered if you were there.

We had a tiny little tree on a table in the parlor Christmas morning, with our presents about it. Our pet dog, Kippy, a small black and tan, was wild with excitement and sat up and begged for every package as it was taken from the tree. She had only one present this year, however, a box of candy which was empty in no time, although it was quite as large for her as the one you sent was for me. The cook sat in the corner with her apron on and whenever there was anything for her, she jumped up and down clapping her hands and crying, "Oh goody, oh goody!" Poor girl.

In a few days, it will be time to go back to work at Boulder and I shall not be sorry. I have been away from Denver so long that I have not many friends here and the vacation has dragged by. Some days I spent reading for my thesis in the library. Yesterday the program consisted of two banquets—first the Wellesley Club annual banquet at one o'clock, and second, when that was barely over, the University of Colorado banquet at seven. One a year is enough for me. I would rather eat bread and cheese out of doors when I am hungry or candy from a paper bag.

It is the hour for New Year resolutions again. I suppose they are being made by the hundreds and thousands all over the country. Mine, if I made any, would be like Thoreau's, I am afraid: "Rescue the drowning, and keep your shoestrings tied." Instead of making little resolutions, I have been trying to write a few letters that might still carry with them the date "1906."

May 1907 be more kind to you than 1906 has been—and may that be very kind indeed. Thanking you once more for your Christmas remembrance,

Sincerely yours,
Ethel P. Waxham

John Love's reply is missing. Ethel continues in a letter dated January 6, 1907:

Your letter instead of coming to me in Denver was forwarded by mistake to Boulder where I found it waiting for me two days ago when I returned. I must plead guilty to the charge of inconsistency. I should have known that it would make a difference to you whether I wrote or not, if I had only for a moment considered what pleasure it gives me to hear from you. Now I should like to give you pleasure—so I am writing. Consistency incarnate, this time, isn't it?

And why, after reading my letter did you decide to sell the interest in the livestock? I cannot recall anything that I said which might bear on the conditions! Have you tried again to get water on the ranch by the plan that you were telling me of a year ago? Is the old man still caretaker when you are not there? Every Monday on the third page of the paper I look for Wyoming news, although it never is satisfactory. It gives the weather perhaps, and then an accident on the railroad, or some murder in one of the mining towns.

Lately I have rejoiced in about eight letters from the Mills people, telling of the Christmas celebration, and the good

129

times they are having riding and teaching Miss Bancroft how to ride. It was not very good riding a year ago, I remember. Wasn't it about this time that we were all out on Sunday afternoon, when the roads were so bad that Mrs. Mills tried to make us promise not to go faster than a walk and you rode up behind us on Pilot? We planned many more rides than the weather allowed in the spring. Where I wanted to go most of all was to Miner's Delight, but when I left, the roads were still impassible. Since then I seem to have heard that the town was sold and is being torn down, but I hate to give up the hope of seeing it.

Thank you for your Christmas wishes. When my father asked what I wanted for Christmas, I told him that my supreme desires were a trip abroad, a ranch in the country, a horse, a dog, and a pair of slippers, and with any of these I would be more than content. But Santa Claus evidently thought that he knew better, and dropped none of them down the chimney. I did think that he might have been lenient about the slippers. But no! as my Freshmen say in their themes. Still he was very generous, bringing me a fine new red cloak, books, writing paper and pretty things. Tell me how you fared. It was very thoughtful of you to send me the only candy that I received during the vacation. But you make me curious about the gifts that you didn't send.

Now that the holidays are over, work begins again tomorrow. I came back a little early to visit Marcia Chipman and her mother. I wrote to you, did I not, that I was staying with them, and eating with the Delta Gamma girls? They are dear people, and the girls are pleasant, too. I have decided to work as hard as I can, and play as hard as I can. I have fortified myself with a pair of dumbbells, and the resolve to be strenuous and not to hate it.

But this first evening I have not yet begun. It is a late, cold, foggy Sunday evening, when one wants to write a letter for company's sake, and for no other reason. The only drawback is that one has to do all the talking, instead of half, which is pleasanter. But you may have heard the little rhyme:

> *"The dog is in the pantry,*
> *The cat is in the cake,*
> *The cow is in the hammock,*
> *But what difference does it make?"*

What difference *does* it make if I write too much? You may stop reading, and never tell me. Somehow, this year more than ever, I like to feel that I have good, strong, close friends; and I trust you because it seems as if you really do care for me.*

It is time for this long, dreary Sunday evening to come to a close, since work begins tomorrow. With best wishes for a good winter for you,

> Your friend,
> Ethel Waxham

JOHN G. LOVE
Wolton, Wyo, Jan 12th/07

Delta Gamma House, Boulder, Colo.

Dear Miss Waxham,

Your ever welcome letter just received and as I expect to go to Wolton tomorrow, I will write a few lines in reply. Yes, I was at Mills' on Christmas as usual and had a pretty good time. I took the children their usual quota of candy, nuts and popcorn. I also took up enough photographic supplies to last them a year and did not forget to give the girls their "brass nickel" as of yore. There was only one thing lacking and that was your presence, for with that I would have been absolutely contented. I met Miss Bancroft for the first time and she is indeed a very nice girl. I understand that she is a friend of yours and you will know her far better than I, so I will omit description.

Thank you for your good wishes for 1907. I, however, do not expect the year to be much kinder to me than was 1906. I have only one complaint to make against 1906: I was denied

---

*Her father's divorce from her stepmother was imminent.

the one thing that I most wanted. It is still the same thing that I most want in 1907. While sitting here at home in solitary state on New Years' Eve, I thought back exactly one year to the time when I spent a few of the happiest hours of my life and a few of the most miserable minutes.

Kathryn is the only one of the Mills family who mentioned your name during the three days that I was there and she did not mention your name when anyone else was present. So you see, if it was not for your kindness in writing to me yourself, I would have practically lost track of you entirely. Never will I do that of my own free will. I sincerely hope that Fate has in store for you nothing but kindness. Still, perhaps in the dim distance of the future, the time may come when you need a friend and if that time ever should come, remember this: I *never* forget.

Taken all in all, we have had a very pleasant winter here so far. Miss Bancroft is making famous progress in learning the art of horseback riding, but poor little Polly must notice the difference in the weight that she has to carry compared with last winter. It has been trying to snow here for the last two days, but there is only about an inch on the ground at present and it is getting too cold to snow.

With best wishes I am sincerely yours,

John G. Love

MARIAN BERRY*
Wellesley, Mass., 15 Jan., 1907

My own dear "Little Bear,"

My letter to you I have left until the very last, so that I could have a nice long talk with you, as I have intended for a long, long time. How I should love to see you!

I was glad to get your very interesting letter some weeks ago, telling me about your work in Boulder. How I should like to be one of those Freshmen under you!

---

*Wellesley friend of the Three Bears and Goldylocks.

Are you wanting to take your M.A. this year or are you expecting to spend another year at the University?

Margaret Dungan received the most startling letter last Thursday from the Albert Teacher's Agency in Chicago and addressed to the President of AKX, reading to this effect: "Can you give us any information in regard to Miss Risley?* We have written to her but can receive no reply. In a recent interview with a Wellesley 1890 graduate, we were informed that Miss Florence Risley had been lost in the late tidal wave while cruising with friends in the Gulf of Mexico." Now I lost flesh, color and ambition at thoughts of such a thing. I couldn't believe it, and yet I felt uneasy and troubled to such a degree that I couldn't eat or think of anything else. Finally I got hold of Carrie Holt,† in fact, went to the village in the evening to see her. And when I told Carrie of the report of Florence's being lost in a tidal wave, she sat down bursting with laughter and exclaimed, "Well, I guess she swam out then, for I had a letter from her today." How do you suppose they could spread such a report without surer grounds for it? I am going to tell Florence the most recent news in regard to herself.

Did you have a pleasant Christmas, Ethel? Did you go home?

Well, dear, I am going ahead on my special topic for Eng. Lit 10 for next Wednesday.

Much love to you—Let me hear from "Little Bear" when she has time to write.

As ever affectionately,
Marian Berry

JOHN G. LOVE
Wolton, Wyo., 30 Jan., 1907

[Postmark: Shoshoni, Wyoming, February 5, 1907.]

*Big Bear of the Bear family.
†Goldilocks of the Bear family.

Dear Miss Waxham,

Your letter just received yesterday. It has probably been lying at Shoshoni for over two weeks as we now have no regular mail service to Muskrat. I am getting my mail changed to Wolton* as fast as I can.

You ask what there was in that long looked-for letter that made me decide to sell an interest in my livestock. I can readily understand why you cannot remember having said anything that would cause me to change my plans in any way. You know "a drowning man will clutch at straws." In that line toward the close of your letter, you gave me to understand that your engagement was at an end. I had just sunk almost all of my ready cash, over $10,000, in more sheep. I knew that if I got another attack of the blues, I would most assuredly hunt you up, even if it caused me to lose half of them. By selling an interest in the sheep, I could feel assured that they would be well cared for no matter where I was. I got no cash whatever on the deal—simply a note and mortgage and the undivided 2/3 interest in the 23 mares. I will plunge and either die a millionaire or a pauper.

I have grave doubts yet as to my ability to exist without seeing you until July. Trying to content myself here is not living; it is simply existing.

I was too busy this fall hauling posts and putting up fence to do anything towards the irrigating proposition, but I intend to go at it in the spring. I bought two new plows and five scrapers and am feeding 12 work horses oats so that I will be ready to begin just as soon as the frost goes out of the ground. Yes, the little old Irishman is still here and looks after things when I am gone.

So you look over the papers for the Wyoming news. Well, I look over the Denver papers for the Boulder items as industriously as I used to look for the Denver items.

You missed it by one day, for it was on the seventh of January that I caught up with you and the children that time

*Wolton was a distance of forty miles from John Love's ranch.

horseback riding. The 14th of January was the last time that I had the pleasure of your company; and the morning of the 15th of January, when you started for school, was the last time that I saw you. I remember it as well as if it were yesterday, but it certainly seems ages ago.

Your Christmas desires were not so extravagant but what even I could have granted them *all* and even thrown in an extra pair of slippers. I will live in hope that yourself and Fate will someday give me the chance to do so. I would like to see you in your red cloak. You always looked nice in everything I ever saw you wearing except that corduroy suit. I hated, yes, I absolutely loathed that suit and always wished that some serious accident would befall it, but not you.

Christmas presents as far as I was concerned, were practically a minus quantity. I am pleased to think that you enjoyed the candy. I was going to send you some genuine Wyoming buffalo horns polished and mounted, but I did not have them yet. The two practically useless baubles that I got for you and wanted to send, I dared not. After I thought it over, I well knew that not even at Christmastime would you accept them from "only a friend," not even to please me. They won't spoil and I will keep them for you, hoping . . .

I am indeed glad that you have such nice people to stay with. You never mentioned who you were staying with before. I hope that your dumbbells are light ones, so that you will not be tempted to go in for the strenuous life too strongly.

I never heard that little rhyme, but whoever wrote it was a sensible individual who did not believe in worrying over trifles. You propound the query "what difference does it make if I write too much" to me, understood. That is unanswerable as it belongs in the category of the impossible. In closing you say: ". . . it seems as if you really do care for me." Well, "little girl," even if Longfellow says in his poem, "Things are not what they seem," I can assure you, at least in this instance, that they are exactly what they seem, only "more so."

The weather here so far this winter has been all that could be desired. The livestock are all in good condition, but still there is plenty of time yet for a heavy loss, although I am hoping for the best and not expecting one. I also, would rather eat bread and cheese out of doors than go to a banquet, but for an entirely different reason from you. I have been out here in the wilderness so long that I would be like a fish out of water and you know "a man canna baith grand and comfortable."

Mr. Hall was elected to the legislature last fall and is now down at Cheyenne. Allie and Mrs. Hall are visiting in California.

I have not been able to figure out just why Kathryn Mills has stopped going to school. Miss Bancroft certainly has the educational qualifications to teach her for many a year to come. Miss Bancroft dons a big apron and helps with the dishes every night. When I was first introduced to her, she was industriously basting the turkey. Mrs. Mills was practically on the sick list Christmas day. Miss Bancroft makes "fudge" for the children, sings and dances well; in fact she is a very capable and a very pleasant girl. Fortunately the phonograph was not in running order while I was there, so I had a good excuse for not trying to dance. I had to promise them that the next time I came, I would try and dance if the phonograph was working. I hope that it breaks down again on the day before I go, and I do not know when that will be. Christmas is the only time that I have been there since October.

Mr. Mills is not on speaking terms at present with Guy Signor. I understand that it was on account of some remark he overheard him make about Miss Bancroft. I am inwardly rejoicing over the quarrel, for as long as that lasts, I can feel assured that the girls will go to no dances at Hailey. I would hate to hear them talked about as I heard you talked about by the scum that were at the "Hailey Ball," when you deigned to honor them with your presence. That was certainly a case in real life of "casting pearls before swine." I would have liked to have tried to learn to dance last winter for I believe that you could have taught me to do so fairly well, considering that it is hard to learn an old dog new tricks. I have no yearning to learn now. I told Miss Bancroft that I was willing to pop corn, play any game or eat mud pies, but when it came to singing or dancing, I would have to be excused.

You told me a year ago on the first of this month that I would soon forget you. I held a different opinion at that time and still have not changed that opinion one iota. I will be better by remembering you, will be better through having known you.

Yours sincerely,
John G. Love

MISS ALLIE DAVIS
County Superintendent of
Schools
Lander, Wyoming
Feb. 7, 1907

Boulder, Colo.

Dear Miss Waxham,

How pleased I was, on my return to Lander to find you had remembered me. I appreciate so much the pretty little handkerchief. It brings pleasant memories of one happy week and of friendship which I prize very much. I would be so pleased to have you visit me. I am going to live in Shoshoni this winter and do light housekeeping and I would be so glad if you could spend at least part of your vacation with me.

I have had such a delightful vacation and a most pleasant visit East with my people and home folks. I wish I had time to talk with you tonight; it is so much better than writing, as I have so much writing to do my friends are often neglected tho I love them just the same. Write me,

Very Sincerely,
Allie Davis

ETHEL P. WAXHAM
Boulder, Colo.,
February 15, 1907

Wolton, Wyo.

Dear Mr. Love,

I am fortunate in having two letters from you to answer in one, so as you suggested, I am saying to myself, "What difference *does* it make?"

Edith Signor sent me a note, a short time ago, in which she said that she meant to visit Denver before long and hoped to see me there. I shall certainly go down from Boulder, if I know when she is coming, for it will be good to get the Wyoming gossip first hand. She said that the [Mills] girls were looking forward to my visiting them during the summer. I remember saying that I would surely come someday— is my writing so poor that they might read, "next summer?" How I should enjoy a summer with them!

It may be, however, that my father will need me more, very soon, than he ever needed me before; if that is so, I must stay with him. [7]

We had a great excitement here at the house last week. The family consists of Mrs. Chipman, a gentle little lady who always wears her white hair piled high on her head, and dresses in black silk, with white lace at her wrists and throat; Marcia, her daughter, who is a few years older than I, but who, on account of travelling and ill health has not yet finished college; Mr. Perkins, a very long-legged New England boy who has a room off the kitchen, takes care of the furnace, and protects us all with his masculine presence; and myself, Ethel Waxham, the poor English assistant in the university. A little after four o'clock on Friday morning, Mr. Perkins came running upstairs—at least six steps at a time— and pounded on the doors hard enough to wake the seven sleepers, calling out that the house was on fire, "Hurry!" The halls were full of suffocating smoke. It did not take long to

138

snatch a few clothes, and run for the front door, you may be sure. Mrs. Chipman took her most valued possession—her husband's watch. For my part, I rescued a thesis on which I had been losing flesh and rest and temper for a hundred solid hours of work. It was finished—thirty large pages—only the night before, when I said that I would not rewrite it to save my soul. So I took that, carried it safely across the street, put it down in a corner of the Delta Gamma porch with my red cloak over it, and went cheerfully back, prepared to dance on the ruins of the house and all my other possessions.

We could not go into the house again, for the smoke, but fortunately Mr. Perkins had telephoned to the fire department. An engine with three lusty firemen soon came clanging up the street. An entrance into the cellar was made. We watched the blaze from without while the firemen sprayed it first with chemicals and then with water. It was out before long, although the chief said that if they had come fifteen minutes later, the whole house would have burned—and ourselves in it, I suppose. We had to stay outside for several hours while the house was being cleared of smoke; we saw the new moon rise, and then the sun. We shivered, but rejoiced to be still in the land of the living. Poor Mrs. Chipman had not quite recovered from the shock of the earthquake in Berkeley last spring. The thought of the narrow escape of all the things that she has treasured for so long, her grandfather's portrait, the silver tea set which was a wedding present, and all the heirlooms which mean so much to a woman whose life is behind her, still troubles her. Marcia and I did not feel that—I confess I had a gay little thrill of excitement when the fire engine dashed up.

Since then, the days have been comparatively dull. Sunday would have done credit to a day in June, it was so warm and beautiful. I wandered away with one of the girls and spent the whole day until evening climbing the hills. What do you think I found? A single little yellow rock flower, that must have been deceived like us, in taking February for June. I wondered if the moss flowers were in bloom in Wyoming. If they are, it will be a month earlier than we found them last year. I can hardly stay within doors during these warm days, the hills are so enticing.

Miss Bancroft must be enjoying the spring with Polly. I am glad that you wrote me of her. Although I used to know her pretty well, we never write to one another, and the girls do not speak of her very often. I hope for their sakes that she gets along well with the work and good times.

I am too busy for dances here, if I cared to go, which I do not. They are prosaic affairs in the boys' fraternity houses—not at all like the "Hailey Ball!"

You do not understand why I went to that with Sandford; how could you?* It was the same impulse that led me to go to Wyoming in the first place, and the year before made me spend a vacation in a settlement house in the slums of New York. I do not want to see one side of life only, but many. A person cannot expect to run the whole gamut of human experience; what you cannot have or do not wish for, may be had from sharing the lives of other people, in reality, on the stage, or in books. It was this desire not to miss anything that might enrich or complete experience that made me wish to see a Wyoming dance. I am not sorry that I went, although I should never go again. The "scum" must have been indifferent; I was introduced only to the "Hart" boys, and danced only with them and with Sandford. Just as you did not like my going there, my friends were scandalized at my going to the "unknown wilderness" of Wyoming to teach in a district school and live among strange and therefore unpleasant people! But the seven months I spent at the ranch I would not exchange for any other seven months in my life. They seem shorter than seven weeks, even seven days, here.

I am glad that you loathed that corduroy suit—so did I! It was a relic of high school days that had been long cast aside, but when I left so suddenly for Wyoming, it was the only

*At the time of the Hailey Ball, Ethel was twenty-three; Sandford was seventeen.

140

thing I could find for riding. It must have been hatred at sight, on your part, for you saw it only once, I believe. In May it will be a year since I have ridden horseback. Such a thing has not happened since I was nine years old. I sincerely hope that it never will again.

Spring vacation begins the twenty-fourth of March, and lasts for a week. Already we are looking forward to it as a break in the routine. It will not be too late then to plant seeds at home, will it? No one seems to plant anything here, while my fingers are itching for the feeling of the seeds. I may not have known a "marker" by reputation, but always in the spring I plan innumerable gardens of flowers and of vegetables, gardens that never are planted. Still I care for them nonetheless, and if ever I have a real one of my very own, I think that I shall love it for all the others that have gone before. My imaginary garden this year is a very extravagant one: lettuce and radishes and celery and onions and other vegetables, but every single kind of flower in the very largest catalogue to be found. Last year it was a small, neat garden, chiefly of vegetables. Next year remains to be seen.

Is not this a good long letter like your last ones to me?

Sincerely yours,
Ethel P. Waxham

JOHN G. LOVE
Wolton, Wyo, Feb. 24/07

Dear Miss Waxham,

Your ever-welcome letter just received and read with pleasure. I am indeed glad that you, your thesis, and worldly possessions escaped the fire. Who but a sensible little mortal like yourself would ever have thought of rescuing a few sheets of paper as one of their most valuable possessions during the excitement of a fire! What was the theme of the thesis?

I do not suppose that the Mills girls really read in your

letter that you expected to visit them "next summer," but I know that they would like for you to do so. K. certainly appreciated you, "Why, Mr. Love, she can just do anything." I know someone else who would like to see you fully as well, if not better than they. They have to wait for you to come to them, whereas I can go to you. It is indeed a wonder that I have not done so 'ere this, for I can be in Denver less than 24 hours from the time that I leave the ranch. My driving horses are fat and sleek and can take me to the R.R. station in a little over an hour. Reno has not had the harness on for two months and Punch has not been harnessed for over six months. It has been over thirteen months now since I asked one of the fair sex to honor me by occupying the seat beside me in the buggy. You were the last one and you only got to ride behind two work horses.

We have been having delightful weather all through February, just like summer. The prairie dogs and badgers are out, likewise the ants, grasshoppers, and flies. I've just come back from an eight-day outing, but not one taken solely for pleasure. I was bringing a little bunch of sheep from the camps to the ranch so that in case it should be stormy and muddy in March, I would have them where I could feed them hay and grain. I got a letter from my partner, Jack Guinard, telling me that he thought that we ought to bring about 150 of the sheep to the ranch. The next day I spent cooking. I stuffed and roasted two chickens, did some baking and packed a box of eggs, butter, salt and pepper, etc. Next morning I got my robes and blankets, hitched up and put "Dorris," my favorite dog, in the buggy seat beside me and started out. I drove the sheep and the team also, camped wherever night overtook me, and suffered no discomfort whatever. The grass is starting in some places already, but there is still quite a lot of frost in the ground yet.

There were several who wanted an introduction to you at the "Hailey Ball," but Sandford assured them and also the one styled "floor manager" (John Carr) that you did not care for any introduction. Your most grievous error, however, was when you and Sandford got your supper and "went off in a corner and *devoured* it all by theirselves." Of course, I see wherein you were wise in so doing (you knew then what you were eating) but you know that when in Rome, you are expected to "do what the Romans do."

I for one am glad that your curiosity led you to drift up here to Wyoming and now my supreme desire in life is to persuade you to come back. If I can only persuade you to come as I want you to come, I will be more than willing to contentedly and happily drift anywhere on the earth.

The twenty-fourth of March will be too early, I think, for planting even vegetable seeds, to say nothing about garden work for flowers.

Papoose has been getting into the bad habit of shying here of late and if I can't get him broken of the habit, he will no longer be safe for an inexperienced lady to ride. I have in five three-year old colts that I want to break to the saddle this spring. Papoose is hard to beat; he is pretty, fast and sure-footed.

I am in Wolton with a four-horse team and my wagon loaded with 3,500 lbs. of oats, ready to start home in the morning. There are a dance and party here tonight, but I am more than willing to leave that pleasure to others.

The roads have been very good here all winter and I have been busy with a four-horse team hauling posts, grain, lumber, etc. I have done less reading this winter than I have for years, but still I have managed to keep up with the news of the day. It is too noisy to write so I will have to close for the present.

Yours sincerely,
John G. Love

MARY B. MILLS
Red Bluff Ranch,
March 3, 1907

Boulder, Colo.

My dear little Girl—

If you only knew under what difficulties I am writing. Mr. Bruce has the phonograph going and I can't always shut it out of my ears—some of the records I should like to send in the letter—they are really beautiful—others, well—. I turn the crank and change the music, so Mr. Bruce is free to dance. We are expecting Allie and Claire Hall over the 15th and are going to have a grand ball—do you remember the 17th of March last year—wasn't there heaps and heaps of snow? And how little we have had this year—since the first of February it has been more like spring than winter. The girls make the most of Saturdays and Sundays, and wish every time they start out on their horses that you were with them.

It does seem such a long, long time since I wrote, but Kathryn has written and I believe Sandford has. Poor boy has been having rather a hard time—both he and Mr. Mills had the grippe in January, and just as Sandford was about well, he had a relapse—dragged himself to school when he shouldn't have gone—a week ago Friday he came home a perfect wreck and has been home ever since, but I am happy to say very, very much better—lost twenty-five pounds and still looks a ghost.

Poor child, you are working hard—too hard, I'm afraid. When the end of school comes you will be ill.

The other day Miss Bancroft and Kathryn were coming from Hailey over the trail (Margaret was sick) and they ran onto ten head of deer. They were surely excited when they got home. We had seen the tracks all winter, out in the cedars. Today, they found a freshly shed horn. We expect some morning to get up and find them in the fields.

My, but we had the greatest excitement on the Creek the other day. Mr. Mills had started to Mr. Hall's on horseback. About 10 o'clock a man rushed over from the Pelon ranch and said Mrs. Barnes had fallen to the floor and he thought she was dead. Her husband and daughter had just started for Lander and just two little ones were left with her—I ran for a bottle of brandy and one of camphor. Then I surely had the wild ride of my life—it seemed as though the horses had wings and never touched their feet to the ground. The woman had had a heart seizure. By the time the clans had gathered from up and down the creek, I had her conscious again—it was certainly a close call. "Old Buck" brought Mr. Mills back from the Bend in about half an hour. He knew I would be worn out. Wasn't tired when night came. Whiskers laughed; he said the neighbors had never gathered so quickly before—record time.

You know Mr. Ehler is to spend the rest of his life making brooms. Young George is in Denver, so perhaps he will come under Judge Leisday's eye after all. We are going to have a good neighbor. Mr. Vaughan is moving all the buildings at the gate down to the middle ranch and is fixing up that house—he is not to live there himself—has a man and his wife, but Arthur Vaughan will be out all the time—a nice boy—so at last Sandford will have a friend of his own age.

Everyone sends oceans of love.

Most aff'y,
Mary B. Mills

ETHEL P. WAXHAM
Denver, Colo., March 19, 1907

Wolton, Wyo.

Dear Mr. Love,

Your letter has been waiting for some time for an hour in which I might answer it. Now on the outer edge of our spring vacation, it seems almost "now or never."

Vacation came a week sooner than I expected, but I did not

complain. Vacation never comes amiss. Instead of working on my thesis—my M.A. thesis—as I expected to do all week, I have put in almost every moment of the time in acquiring knowledge of quite a different kind from that of Mæterlinck and the static theatre. The cook had left, Lily had left, and I have been trying to take the places of both of them. My father and I are alone at home, so that the cooking is not much of an ordeal, but keeping everything spic and span, even with the occasional help of a scrub lady, takes time. I, a vegetarian, have been so false to my colors as to learn to broil steak, make pot roast, veal cutlet and beef loaf—though not to eat them. My chief joy is in the inventing of new dishes, which to my utter amazement always turn out well. You would not believe it unless you tasted them, but there is often not a scrap left for the dog or cat. "Eggs à la Chinois" was my noon invention today and Pater pronounced it capital and ate every bit. One of my friends said that it is at some time in her life the ambition of every woman to write a cookbook—but I will try not to turn this letter into one.

Mrs. Hall and "Allie" passed through Denver on their way from California several weeks ago. I was sorry to have to leave for Boulder just an hour or so before their train arrived. Mrs. Hall wrote me a good letter saying that she was sorry not to be able to come to dinner—I had invited her through her friend Miss Dilley. In a postscript she added, "The girls join me in sending love and good wishes." Is that "finis" to our story, I wonder, or the beginning of chapter three? Whenever I think of our escapade, I want someone with whom to laugh at it, now. It seems so ridiculously trivial. You would laugh at it, too.

Your buggy trip after the bunch of sheep must have been good fun. Have you been troubled by the cattlemen in your part of the state? You see, I, too, have been reading the newspapers. It is time for flowers now at Twin Creek. I remember little moss flowers. The anemones have blossomed on Anemone Hill near Boulder, but I could find never a

146

moment—or rather an hour—to go so far to pick the furry little things. Marcia and I are going to have a garden, a real garden, not imaginary, or on paper, but made of water and earth and plants. The man was to have come two weeks ago to do the ploughing; Marcia said that she would not plant anything until I came back, which was dear of her. The New England Mr. Perkins will do the hard work.

The only trouble is that there is not land enough to plant everything that we want. Marcia does not believe that the pictures in the catalogue are true, or that things are as the seed men say. It does not matter to me—I only want to try and see. My sentiments are the same that Kipling expresses somewhere:

> *"For to admire, and for to see,*
> *For to be'old this world so wide,*
> *It never done no good to me,*
> *But I couldn't help it if I tried."*

I do want to "be'old" Yellowstone Park, and have been urging my father to take the trip this next summer—with me, of course—if he can spare the time. It seems impossible, however. He is planning now to go to Chicago and New York perhaps, if affairs go as he wishes. Little sister Faith is staying with Vera and her husband. I don't know what will become of me, then, unless I live under a gourd vine somewhere like Elijah, and get a raven to bring me bread and butter.

But I have not answered your only questions, yet. The valuable thesis that I saved was a ponderous and stupid thirty or forty-page paper on "the Latin Hymns as a Source of the Mystery Plays." The Professor told me afterwards that I have found some things that no man on earth knew—not even himself. And he used my paper in some work he was doing. But I have been happier when I found the first flower in spring.

Sincerely yours,
Ethel Waxham

John Love paid his first visit to Ethel in Denver between March 24 and
April 5, 1907.

JOHN G. LOVE
Wolton, Wyo., April 5/07

Dear Miss Waxham,

I will just write a few lines to let you know that "I arrived
here safe and sound." I encountered no earthquake, no strike
or no wreck. I am in very good spirits considering that I had
to take charge of the two white elephants and leave you
behind. I do not think that you realize the amount of will
power that it took for me to start, or the amount it is going
to take to keep myself here for a while.

I am writing this on my knee amidst a chatter of voices, so
I had better close and write at length from the ranch.

Yours sincerely,
John G. Love

ETHEL P. WAXHAM
Boulder, Colo., April 12, 1907

Wolton, Wyo.

Dear Mr. Love,

Your letter arrived not long after you left—you took the
wrong road to meet with disaster. All the trains from the
south have been delayed this week.

I have made several inquiries regarding Boulder Falls, and
regret to tell you that I fear we did not see them. They say
that the Falls no longer exist. Others say that some nine
miles up the canyon, you leave the road and climb over the
hills several miles farther, on foot, and then, if they are there,
you see them. It is almost certain, however, that we went
beyond the Falls to what is called "Castle Rock."

My thesis is progressing slowly at the rate of five or ten
pages a day. It will have to hurry before long. The sweet peas

and the radishes are up in the garden, and no frost has yet hurt the apple blossoms. That is all the news except that I interrupted packing my suitcase to write this note to you. I am going to take the six o'clock train to Denver.

Sincerely yours,
Ethel P. Waxham

JOHN G. LOVE
Wolton, Wyo., April 13, 1907

[Postmark: Wolton, Wyoming, April 21, 1907.]

Dear Miss Waxham,

Here I am once more seated at my desk in my own private den. I found things in rather bad shape when I got home, but "What difference does it make?" I enjoyed myself to the limit while I was gone, thanks to you. I know that you gave me all the time that you could spare and I most assuredly appreciated your kindness.

So you yearn to see Yellowstone Park. I also would like to see it. I extend to you, your father and Miss Faith a cordial invitation to come to Wyoming as my guests. I will take a four-horse team and one of my new camp wagons and we will see the Park and lots of scenery besides. I will furnish you all with saddle horses and go along as teamster, general roustabout and assistant cook and personally guarantee your safety and comfort. Of course, if your father cannot spare the time, that plan will have to be abandoned. I would still like to take you there, but alas—there is only one way in which I can do it. Unfortunately, I have not the say so regarding that. I am going to try to exist without seeing you until the last of June. I really think that I can, if you will only please write often. If you cannot spare the time to write, but yet do not absolutely forbid my coming, I will surely come again.

You say, "the cook had left, Lily had left." You never spoke of Lily and never wrote about her so I have not the faintest idea who she is. You and Miss Faith certainly seemed to be getting along famously with the cooking when I was there.

We have no trouble with cattlemen in this part of the state.

Your mention of anemones being in blossom reminds me of the fact that we never gathered any of them on our way down the creek that evening. Between the hat, the elephants, and my anxiety to catch the train, they entirely slipped my memory. If your father goes East and Miss Faith stays with your sister, take my advice and do not depend on the ravens feeding you, or you will most assuredly get small by degrees.

You are correct in sticking unflinchingly to what you believe to be right. You know that those baubles were real "white elephants" to me; you knew that I really did want you to take them. I respect you for sticking to what you believe to be right and which from your standpoint and the social code unquestionably was right. On the kissing question, you were also correct, but I do not really think that you have the faintest idea just how badly I did want to kiss you. I will live in hope of yet seeing the time that I can kiss you not just once but times without number, but if that time never comes, I will always remember the only kiss that I ever wanted and did not get.

When I started to write this there were two ladies and three children chattering like magpies in the adjoining bedroom, and I stopped writing for a while. Now along in the wee sma' hours they seem to be all snoring. Truly, I believe such noise would drive a man to strong drink or morphine.

I forgot while in Colorado to try and bribe you to have your picture taken. I was so absolutely contented with the original that the matter entirely slipped my memory. If it is not asking too much, please get a good picture of yourself taken and send it to me.

I have not yet had time to go to Mills' after the currant bushes, but will go before long. I am going to Wolton in the morning so I must close and get to bed. Give my best regards to your father and Miss Faith, also to Mrs. Chipman and Miss Marcia. For yourself, I could in all sincerity repeat Mrs. Hall's "P.S." with an addition or two understood.

Yours sincerely,
John G. Love

ETHEL P. WAXHAM
Boulder, Colo., May 7, 1907

Wolton, Wyo.

Dear Mr. Love,

Your letter reached me several weeks ago, and I should have answered it before, except for that thesis. Did your partner reach home safe and sound? And how were the sheep? Have you been to see the Mills people? I have not heard from them for more than a month. I meant, too, to telephone to Miss Bancroft while I was at home, or at least to her family, to see if she had returned. But for a week I have done nothing at home, or in Boulder, but peg away at the thesis which is yet unfinished.

Even now I am writing on the train to Boulder while a gray rain is drizzling down. Pater told me more than a week ago to write to you at once to thank you for your Yellowstone Park invitation. He says that nothing would give him more pleasure than to accept it; just now, however, it does not look as though he might. But if it is possible, he says that we will be glad to come. Little Sister is delighted at the thought of going. I think once more that you are "too good."

During the last few weeks, spring has come and gone almost regularly every three days. Snow and sunshine have been alternating with rain for a change. The fruit blossoms are gone, but not all of the crop is lost. The weather seems to be trying to console Boulder for having gone dry, and the dry farmers will be false to their names this spring. I have not seen our garden except from a distance when it was too muddy to venture from the sidewalk.

The Delta Gamma convention began on the twenty-fourth of April. There were about a hundred and twenty of us "sisters" together in Boulder. With business, getting acquainted and giving the delegates a good time, the week flew. We had several snow storms, but in spite of that, took an all-day trip to Glacier Lake on the train. The other entertainments were two teas, one party, one dance, four receptions, an automobile ride in Denver, luncheon, dance, and banquet. All of this chapter—the Boulder girls—who entertained the delegates, have been having their pictures taken for the next issue of our Delta Gamma magazine. Perhaps you will have a "birthday present" from me before very long.

Monday

The trip from Denver was too short to finish the letter which I began yesterday. Last evening I sat down to work at my thesis, determined to finish the last part of it. I did. But not having heard the clock strike while I was working, and thinking that I had spent a long time on it, I went downstairs to make sure. It was halfpast one! I have not worked so late since I left Wellesley. Now I must hunt around to find someone to typewrite the thesis, and make me a masters' hood— for the faculty to present, and get ready for the oral examination. I say "the cow is in the hammock" every day for consolation.

Big sister Vera has a new baby, and I am now the aunt of Robert Waxham Shattuc, an enterprising youngster with the record for lung power on the third floor of St. Joseph's. Her pride is only slightly hurt by the fact that everyone calls the child "the Waxham baby," instead of "the Shattuc baby."* There were eleven there, at once, eleven babies. Grandmother Shattuc has been very much worried lest Robert should be lost and another child put in his place. So she examined every baby very carefully until she considered

---

*The baby's grandfather, Dr. Frank E. Waxham, was associated with St. Joseph's Hospital.

herself able to identify Robert under any circumstances. They are all equally homely, but Robert has more hair and more wrinkles.

Lily was the girl at home who helped with the work, although she seemed as much bother as help. Still, she was not as bad as the cook. That poor girl had a "stiddy" who was unappreciative—she sent him three valentines, and he did not even think of her.

It is still raining, in spite of the imprecations that have been cast upon the weather for the last three weeks. Such a steady rain always makes me think of the child verses of Stevenson:

> *"The rain is raining all around,*
> *It falls on field and tree;*
> *It rains on the umbrellas here*
> *And on the ships at sea."*

It certainly does rain, not only on, but under the umbrellas. I must even now go out into it for supper.

Best regards to the third "white elephant."

Sincerely yours,
Ethel P. Waxham

MARY B. MILLS
Red Bluff Ranch, May 8, 1907

Dear Little Girl—

I looked it all up in the little calendar and think a letter is way way overdue, don't you, dear? And you have been working so hard, too. Everyone is seeing you and bringing words of you back to us. As Edith Signor says, "just the same little Miss Waxham." She enjoyed her little visit very much and had so much to tell about "Kippy."

Friday the girls and Miss Bancroft went down to the Hall ranch, and Saturday morning Sandford drove them all down to the train at Hudson. Quite different, isn't it dear, than when you left for Denver? Miss B. took the 7 o'clock train, would have to stay all night in Cheyenne and get to Denver at noon today. The girls went down on horseback. Sandford had to go into Lander so he took the trunk etc. and checked them there.

I had quite a shock the other day. I was looking over my plates to find some to print for Miss Bancroft. I came across a package of your films, done up ready for mailing, which I supposed had reached you ages ago. I had not done anything all winter, but what could you have thought? As they are here, I will keep them a week longer and print some, that is, if the sun ever comes out.[8] I have some new paper I am quite in love with, and will send you some samples.

The spring started early enough but it has been wretchedly cold the last two weeks. Everything is stationary. The leaves are just waiting for a warm day. We had about an inch of snow the day you had your big storm in Denver. Are you still going back and forth every day? Of course "Pater" is delighted to have you with him, but it must be very tiresome. And is the thesis finished yet? Your name will look very strange and grand on the sheepskin. How fortunate none of your papers were destroyed by the fire. It truly must have been exciting, but I know you saw heaps of funny things that happened.

Mr. Love was full of his visit to Denver when he got back. Poor child, you must have had about as hard a time getting rid of him as you did the day at school. If a girl will look at him, he quite loses his head. So that is the price you have to pay for always being so considerate of other people's feelings. If you were otherwise, dear, we wouldn't all love you so much.

If you knew under what difficulties I was writing! A man from Popo Agie is here and at present tuning Kathryn's violin for her, so you can imagine the confused noise in my head.

This man told something pretty good. He was down at Burnett's store at the "Int."* and an Indian was asking what this and that was. The clerk said, "canned corn, canned

*Another term for Wind River Indian Reservation.

beans," etc. The Indian turned to the phonograph and said "Ugh! Canned white man!"

I must tell you a good joke on Miss Bancroft. We had had an unusual amount of wind, and Miss B. complained a good deal and said it *never* blew in Denver. When Allie Hall was over, she asked her how she liked Denver. "Well," Allie said, "pretty well, but it was blowing such a gale I didn't see much of it." I said, "One on you, Miss Bancroft." When Edith came home, she said she would like Denver, too, but the wind blew so. Of course, that was too much for us. We knew the wind had been unusual there, too, but that was our bye word. "Is it like Denver wind?"

Dearie, I think I'd better stop my rambling, but you know unless my letters ramble they're not like me.

Tell me all about your gardens, yours and Pater's and yours and Marcia's. Did that horrid man finally plow it? Indeed you *are* a garden authority. The girls have missed you so much this spring. No one with which to watch the buds swell and count the stalks of asparagus.

I have some necessary sewing to do. Then I must go to house-cleaning, such delightful work.

Dearie, do write when you can find the time. It is always a happy day when the mail brings one of your letters.

> Yours, most aff'y
> Mary B. Mills

SANDFORD MILLS
Hailey, Wyo., May 11, 1907

[Postmarked: Hailey, Wyoming, May 22, 1907.]

Dear Miss Waxham—

It is snowing now at the Mills ranch, the first storm to amount to anything. It snowed the day Miss Bancroft was to start for home, so she had to wait until the next day. We took her down to Hudson. Miss Bancroft, Kathryn and Margaret rode down to Mr. Hall's on horseback. I went to town and got Miss Bancroft's ticket, then we stayed at Mr. Hall's all night and went to Hudson in the morning. Kathryn and Margaret saw the train. They said it did not make as much noise as they thought it would.

I suppose you have seen Miss Bancroft since she was home.

I want to thank you for the nice stamps you sent me.

We have about all the plowing done and some oats sowed, father was sowing oats this morning before it started to rain. Yesterday we planted most of the garden. Thursday we planted forty apple trees. We have moved the berry bushes and made the rows go up and down the garden. We did not get the garden planted as early as last year, I guess it was because you were not here to help. Have you planted anything yet?

I must tell you about some of the dances we had this winter. Simon Herrol and the Ferris kid (they were at the dance that we went to at Hailey) were here some of the time, and Alice and Claire Hall were here for one dance. We invited Charlie and Marty Hart and Arthur Vaughan but they did not come. At another dance Smithy was here, he danced in the old way and went around in a circle, then we got him to sing for us. The next day he was going to the mountains, he had his horses harnessed and came down to the house, and the girls told him that they were going to dance that night, so he stayed. Father went up to the barn, and said Smithy was talking to his horses and telling them "he would not go today, that he had to stay and dance with those girls."

We haven't given but one play this winter—a shadow play, given Thanksgiving night. We have all the musical instruments we need, so we wouldn't have to make any. It must be because the president of the company is not here to superintend it.

Did you see many plays this winter? Were they as good as the ones we gave? Did you color any Easter eggs this year? Have the wild flowers come in Colorado yet? They are almost all out here, and the leaves are coming on the trees. The antelope likes the flowers in the yard better than the grass, we have to keep it shut up most of the time so they can grow.

Polly and the rest of the diggers are all right. Kathryn's bay filly has a colt. Kathryn thinks the world of it, she gave it some long Indian name that nobody can remember half the time, and I don't think she can remember it either. Have you ridden horseback much since you went to Denver?

Did anybody tell you that Old Dick died this winter? He was sick most of the time and died sometime in March, it doesn't seem natural not to have him in the way. Laddie is big but he can't take the place of two dogs.

Today I was riding after horses and saw seven head of deer just this side of Hall Creek. When I first saw them, I was about two hundred yards from them; they looked at me a while and then went on eating. I went around on top of the hill and was about fifty yards from them when they ran down the hill and came over towards the ranch. Then I ate dinner with Mr. Bruce at his sheep-wagon. It is after nine o'clock so I will say good night.

From your friend
Sandford Mills

JOHN G. LOVE
Wolton, Wyo., May 14, 1907

Dear Miss Waxham,

Yours of the 6th just received. I did try to find time to answer your letter before this, but absolutely could not. I had the letters going once more just the way I wanted them, and now through my fault, they are wrong again. I am writing this one on a book sitting in the sheep wagon listening to the snow and rain patter on the canvas. We have been having delightful weather until the last three days, and now right in the heaviest of the lambing season, we are getting a heavy dose of rain, hail, sleet and snow. This is the third day of it and every day means a loss of two hundred lambs to me.

Perhaps at some future time we may search for the Boulder Falls until we do find them, for I understand that they are really worth seeing. They have not moved, but are away back off the road.

My partner got back all right, but is not able as yet to take the brunt of the work through the lambing season, so I had to get out once more myself. I keep three saddle horses tied up to a load of hay and feed them plenty of oats. I keep one of them on the go from half-past three in the morning until ten at night. I found the sheep all right when I got home, but things at the ranch were at a standstill and I paid off three men that day. I have eight men at present and it is hard work getting them to earn their fifty dollars per month.

I went up to the Mills' ranch about the 27th of April after some currant bushes. I stayed there one night, stayed one night at Signors' and one at Sandersons'. For the first time in over a year and a half, your name was mentioned in the Mills' house, but not very much was said. "Baby" asked me point blank, "Did you see Miss Waxham?" Edith, of course, told her mother, and Mrs. Signor had been at the Mills' ranch, so I well knew that they knew I had seen you. Miss Bancroft was then counting the days until she would be free to hustle to Denver, and I think we have seen the last of her up here in the sagebrush. K. said she is very nice and very thoughtful of others, but she is not "Miss Waxham." I, of course, agreed with her. No doubt you have seen Miss Bancroft by this time and heard all the news. She and the girls were going down to the Halls'. Sandford was to take her trunk into Lander and get her ticket and the big start was to be made from Hudson on May 3rd. I heard the whole plan discussed pro and con as to whether the Halls really wanted her to do that, etc. Candidly, I was amused and decided once more that I would never make a shining light "in society." I am out and out just what I am and am never ashamed of my likes and dislikes. If I have a reasonable doubt about being welcome at a place, I do not bother going there; if I do not like anyone, I do not care how soon they know it.

I am glad that your thesis is almost finished. Someday I

will take pleasure in reading it even if I have to go to the library and hunt it up. After all your labor, I do hope that you will get your M.A., as I have no doubt you will. There is nothing in the course, is there, bearing on "elephant" training? Do you really think that it would be much harder work to be trainer for a very docile "elephant" than it would be to be "dream interpreter?"

It would indeed be terrible if that hopeful youngster, Robert, should be accidentally exchanged for another. They should have tatooed a mark on him to avoid all mistakes.

I laughed until I was sore over the poor girl's unappreciative "stiddy." I had not heard the word used for years and had never seen it written.

It has cleared up and I must stop for the present and go see how the lambs are getting along. It is now almost dark and the prospects are good for a very cold night.

May 16th

The weather is once more clear and pleasant and lambing is progressing nicely, lambs arriving at the rate of about two hundred and fifty a day and most of them live. The foreman of my other lambing crew came to tell me that the men were having trouble amongst themselves and wanted me to go and see about it. I told him that I had all that I could do without riding twenty miles extra, and that if they could not get along with each other to send them down to me. So far none of them have shown up.

I can't see just how the delegates to the Delta Gamma convention could get away at that time in the college year. I hope that your father will see his way clear to take a holiday this summer and go to "the Park." If he can not go this year, he probably will be able to get away some other time.

I have an unexpected chance to mail this, so I will have to close. With best regards for you all (you know what is to be added for yourself), I remain

Sincerely yours,
John G. Love

On June 7, he adds:

> The lamb crop is going to be very slim this year—only about three thousand. I have not yet been able to locate all the cattle, but I found some of them and branded thirty calves. I have not been out to run horses, but have seen about a dozen young colts. Six young ducks, *two* chickens and four kittens complete the list of the increase in livestock to date.

ETHEL P. WAXHAM
Boulder, Colo., June 12, 1907

Wolton, Wyo.

Dear Mr. Love,

Your letters were received some time ago, but not answered because examinations and Commencement and affairs at home gave wings to time.

Commencement exercises[9] were held a few weeks ago in the large yellow Chautauqua building, which looks as if it were put up to accommodate a circus instead of a sedate lot of professors and pupils. A gorgeous yellow and gray and black hood was ceremoniously put about my neck—I fancy that I must have resembled a gigantic black and yellow gold finch.

Marcia and I have been making plans for the summer. Pater has sold our house in Denver, and has gone away for a while. My sister Faith is going East, probably, in about two weeks to visit relatives. Marcia's mother starts for Chicago tomorrow. The altitude is too much for her here. So this house is rented for the summer months, and Marcia and I are going to camp out in a tent on the Chautauqua grounds [on the outskirts of Boulder]—the very highest tent there, which has the best view, i.e. most secluded, and is to be furnished with a small porch for our especial benefit. Marcia will attend the summer school, while I shall have all my time free. There are many places described in the Chautauqua booklet, which have names and must be explored: the tomb of the Titans, Kit Carson's Chimney, the Devil's Staircase,

Mixey Glen, Crockett's Bear Cave, and the Royal Arch, for instance. Marcia and I plan to have at least one picnic every day, and just as many meals out of doors as can be arranged. Summer school is only in the morning, and never on Saturdays, so we shall have a good deal of time together. Marcia is going to join her mother in Chicago when the summer school is over, about the last of July. My own plans are entirely unformulated from that time on.

It seems that we must thank you for your invitation to the Park, and decline it for this year at least. Pater will not be back in time to go, and Faith will be away.

Miss Bancroft came to dinner one day in Denver, and brought pictures and gossip from the Mills' ranch. I certainly did enjoy talking over with her our respective good times in Wyoming. She was glad to be back again, however, she said.

The garden that Marcia and I call ours produces radishes abundantly, and nothing else in season, except weeds. Flowers are appearing, sweet peas, nasturtiums, morning glories and Japanese hop among others, but they are so slow that we shall not be here to enjoy them, since we leave the last of this week for our tent.

The pictures that had to be taken because of the Delta Gamma Convention were so poor that I have not ordered any of them and I have given up hope of getting a satisfactory one until I become more 'andsome.

Best wishes for the sheep, the partner, and the currant bushes.

Sincerely yours,
Ethel P. Waxham

FLORENCE RISLEY
[BIG BEAR OR B.B.][10]
Rosehill, Ontario, July 3, 1907

[Forwarded to Boulder, Colorado.]

Belovedest Little Bear, what I hope is an M.A.

For one long year B.B. did what he used to pity other

161

people for doing; he ground off his nose to earn his daily bread. But now he is paying up for such bad actions by sleeping as long as he likes and eating whenever he wanders into the pantry, for it must be known that he is in the loveliest place for a bear. There is a cottage which is two thirds piazza and one third fireplace and the rest B.B. lets the family occupy. Down below the piazza is a whole ocean of sand with a row of poplar trees and below them, a long smooth beach. The sail boat is the only means of transportation except a deadly old train that goes by twice in a sun. When the wind is favorable, as it is not today, B.B. screws up his hair tighter than ever and sails over to Buffalo [New York] to get his mail, because it is easier to sail five or six miles to Buffalo and back than to walk a mile and a half to the nearest post office and back.

When B.B. is not sailing or fishing or eating all kinds of country things, he is reading to know enough to look wise next winter. So far he has read *Pamela* and a pretty French book by Zola and two or three books that he ought to have known long ago. Some essays by Augustine Birrell which he likes pretty well and some more by A. Dobson, which he likes better. The rest of the summer he has to spend reading more novels, wading through *Clarissa* and *Tom Jones* and *Pendennis* and Miss Edgeworth and Miss Burney and H. Walpole so there will be no miseries when his children ask him questions.

No, Little Bear, no journeys to Paris this year, although I have found a cheap but respectable line to go on and although I have a very good friend who could tell me all about Paris and how to live there. In fact, it is most strange why, but B.B. came home with just twenty-five dollars in his pocket to last him until the first of November and pay his summer expenses. If it is a good thing to do, B.B. may stay in Chicago next summer and see how it feels to study, but he is yet too poor to stop teaching—Poor Big Bear!

Please, Little Bear, tell me some very loveliest and favoritest books to read, because although I have so many others, yet I am much behind the times because it has been all of a day's work to prepare for the next day.

[*Signed two paw prints*]
Big Bear

MARY B. MILLS
Red Bluff Ranch, July 7, 1907

My dear little Girl,

You don't know how excited your letter made us. I had hesitated asking you to come to us for your vacation, thinking "Pater" needed you this summer, but now that little sister has gone, and little nephew takes so much room and the Denver house is sold, may we beg for you? I think it would be the vacation you need—plenty of rest and mountain air.

It has been cool until the last week; now the girls are begging for their sleeping tent. Mr. Mills says he will put one up for you, too. Of course, Mr. Mills and Sandford will be more or less busy, but I think we can take some of the trips we wanted to before, and you know there is always horseback riding.

We will be so impatient for your reply—No stage ride this time.

By the way, I see they have just found near Myersville two sacks of mail which were taken from the coach Feb. 19, 1906—someone will get their mail rather late—about seven hundred letters.

I had been busy with sewing so had put off papering the house. Now if you will only come, I can put it off until cooler weather. We will take up rugs etc. and not have any more inside work to do than possible.

Do let us know as soon as possible. With ever and ever so much love from us all—

Most aff'y
Mary B. Mills

NORA DUNN*
Mobeetie, Texas, July 23, 1907

Dearest Ethel,

Your letter came just as I was leaving California for Texas and I planned to answer it on the train, but I reckoned without my fellow travellers! For two days and nights I was the only girl—or woman—on the entire train, and half the men were intoxicated—no they weren't, they were drunk! In my coach there was a drunken artilleryman on his way home for a furlough, and also a consumptive who, I found out afterwards, was one of the San Francisco car strikers. When he was noisy, the artilleryman—whom I nicknamed "Tillie," for short—was sleeping his latest off; and only once did they both celebrate together, so you see I had something exciting all the time. When "Connie" found I had to get off and lay over in Trinidad, he started to get off, too, but I eluded his vigilance, so don't know what finally became of him.

When Tillie first got on at Ferry Point, just out of Oakland, he was decidedly tipsy, and when the conductor made some objection to his ticket, he—Tillie—pointed to me with a shakey finger and said, "G--you, my tickit ish all right. I'm going shame plashe, zhat ghirl ish—I'm on my way to Chicago, but I'm ghoing by way of H--L" You understand now why I didn't stop by Denver! I really did want to see you so much. At best the trip is a hard one and I wanted to break it in Denver, but I had to come straight on, and by the end of the week that it took me to get here, I was ready to stop for good. I am going back to dear old school in less than two weeks, and, though I love California, I hate to go back to the drudgery of forty-two weeks of "fifty little demons." Then I have had such a glorious time this summer, that I fear school teaching will not seem as great a boon as it did last year.

It has been one round of dances, dinners—not course dinners, but dinners served on oilcloth tablecloths, every

*A classmate from Hyde Park High School in Chicago.

thing at once—fried chicken, hot thin biscuits, cream string beans, potatoes, and things that make one hungry to see them. Then there are card parties, flinch parties, and as sister Agnes has begun to call them "sessions"—really "calls."

Then this coming week, "Aunt" Hum, is going to give a dance for all the young people of the town. Papa went out to the Grove Ranch, where the dance is to be held, to see about building the dancing platform, out in the middle of the cottonwood grove, so we can dance by moonlight. Isn't that lovely,—no walls to decorate, no lamps to smoke, no heated rooms to suffocate in, but instead, leafy walls of Nature's own making, the soft light of a beautiful Texas moon, and the cool breezes of rolling prairie lands.

After the dance, Saturday morning, eleven of us, including "Sister" Agnes, as chaperone, are going in a couple of covered wagons, over to the Washita—a creek full of fish some eighteen miles from here, where we are to camp four or five days, before I go back home.

I have met some very interesting men this summer; men without much culture; with no polish save such as Nature itself gives to its own; but frank, sincere, simple, true.

Yesterday I was "talking over the back fence" to one of the town girls, when her brother dared me to throw a "pail" of water I had over him. I did it, and now I must "pay the piper." He is one of the fishing party, and he promises me a ducking in the creek, but I am going prepared with a bathing suit and an extra suit of clothing throughout, so I shall not mind if I am made to pay my debt.

I wish you could be with us, under the stars, beside the little rushing brook, joyously happy.

Good bye, my girlie,—I hope your summer in the tent has been a lovely one; I have longed to be with you, or to have you here, "In Texas down by the Rio Grande." (That is just merely a quotation—not truth—as Mobeetie is, alas, up in the Panhandle.)

With a heart full of love to you, dear,

from

Nora K. Dunn

John Love paid another visit to Ethel.

ADRIENNE MUZZY[11]
Minneapolis, Minn.,

[Forwarded to Hailey, Wyoming and received August 7, 1907.]

Dear Ethel,

Would I had words to express my thoughts! Would I might cuss aloud! Why did I not get off at the University station? Why did I not sit me down in your tent and wait until someone turned up? I weep to think of the tea party which might have been. I was sorely tempted to spend the night in Boulder anyway—why oh why didn't I? I yearned to camp out in that tent—sez I to myself, Let's stay here anyway, nobody knows me from Adam, nobody cares whether I break into this 'ere tent or not. Sez myself to I, Begorre, thou gosling—suppose this isn't Ethel's tent, suppose some stranger should come and find me encamped on the front veranda, suppose a stray policeman should take me for a sneak thief. Whereupon I tore myself away. I was somewhat consoled by calling the Vallecito postmistress names, and after all, the poor critter didn't deserve it. Since that poor consolation is taken from me, I can only hasten East. Until then, 'scuse me while I go out on the fire escape and swear.

Yours
Adrienne Muzzy

BIG BEAR
[B.B., Florence Risley]
Rosehill, Ont.

[Envelope missing.]

Belovedest Little Bear,

If Big Bear were not in the Canada hunting grounds where the berries and trains and other things come late, this would have been a birthday letter to give Little Bear a hug next Sunday morning.

The nice warm comfy spot is still there where Little Bear's 'licious letter settled and made B.B. as joyful. It would surely take the weary of the world if B.B. could have a corner of Little Bear's tent even if he might feel cramped. For it must be known that B.B. is as fat as a banana. All that besides sewing like mad to make himself respectable and cover up the mangy spots next winter. One skirt of many gores, one tailor suit that nearly annihilated the neighborhood during the strenuous time of its manufacture, and three or four sundries more useful than ornamental.

Please get a job in Chicago, Little Bear, and sit with me in the peanut gallery to hear the opera and see the shows, and afterward to go to Dago eating house which is perfectly respectable for unknown females, that look sedate.

These days, when even the poplar leaves hang limp, and the windmill goes to sleep, there is nothing to do but sit very still in the door of the hollow tree and read until it is time to gather a few berries and a little honey for dinner. Every morning early there is a neighbor horse to exercise because his owner is over in Buffalo watching for the stork. It is a great pity that the horse is not the kind to be ridden; but then it is pleasant enough to race up and down the beach, so I think I'll not scold.

Please, Little Brother, have somebody snap a kodak of you for to let your Bear family know how you look since you have riz to be an M.A. For either you ought to be prodigious fat to support the dignity or else prodigious lean to show the process and its effect.

A big bear hug from B.B.

John G. Love
Moneta, Wyo., July 23, 1907

Dear Miss Waxham,

I arrived here at home safe and sound and am once more seated at my own desk in my den.

You will never know how sorely tempted I was to say the

cow is in the hammock" and contentedly stay where I would be near you. The main reason that I did not was not one of finance or business, but I was afraid to trust myself to be contented with seeing you just once in a while. It is certainly hard lines to be compelled to stay this distance away from you, but perhaps Fate will not always be so unkind.

I have been busy all day. I helped haul two loads of hay until it got too windy to do any more. Then I worked a while in the garden. While I was away, the men did not water the currants and gooseberries, and over half of them are dead, as are the strawberries. The weather has been very dry and hot, and today was a scorcher. I went out this evening to hunt up Punch and did not get in to the ranch until after dark, but I found him and now have him in the pasture, waiting to hear whether you are coming to Wyoming or not.

It will take me a day or two to get things running smoothly again. Then I will drive over to Moneta and get my suitcases, etc. The elephants are both in one of my coat pockets and may be gone, but I hope not. It is not so much the intrinsic value (I was offered one hundred twenty-five dollars), but I want you to have those particular ones. If those little hands of yours do not grow, I will have to get that one re-set.

While hunting for Punch, I found two new colts and five new calves. I will have to brand them as soon as I get time. I do hope that your father does not locate so very far off, if that is where you are going to be. But no matter where it is, I will surely come.

Your last letter was dated June 12th and the one before that May 5th. Just think, "little girl," the ages that seemed to me. Please do not forget about the picture. I know it is asking a good deal but I really do want one so much. Give my best regards to your father, Miss Faith and Miss Chipman. Hoping to hear from you soon and also to see you before long, I remain with love and kisses—the former you have and the latter I would like to give you.

Ever yours,
John G. Love

ETHEL P. WAXHAM
Boulder, Colo., July 26, 1907

Wolton, Wyo.

Dear Mr. Love,

It really must be time—even in the eyes of an unprejudiced observer—that I answered your last letter.

Fate was with you for your visit here, even as you remarked, and cut the visit short at exactly the right time. Sudden company, sudden heat, sudden illness of Marcia, and then a night and a day of drenching rain followed your departure. There is only one improvement since, in camp. The stove has developed a conscience and works steadily and smokelessly for hours together. The two baby deer in the pasture ran away, and while Mr. Fox was spending two days hunting for them, in agony of mind, they slipped back through the fence and calmly took up their existence where it had stopped. And if this were the Lander paper,[12] I could find no more local items of news to insert.

My visit to Wyoming is still only in "the all-encircling good." Pater's plans are still unsettled, like my own. I do wish that they would precipitate themselves, and send me, bag and baggage, to Wyoming next week.

Marcia and I are going to the entertainment in the auditorium tonight. The Pierces, who are called "society entertainers," give a few little plays—the two of them. I hope that they will be better than Mr. Perstead. Tomorrow is Farmers' Day, but I have not the curiosity to read the program of events.

This damp weather has brought out the mosquitoes, like one of the plagues of Egypt. There are eight bites on my face already, and it is not very big.

Daylight has left me only time to finish, so goodbye to you
from
Ethel P. Waxham

In a letter dated July 30, she continues:

Your letter reached me today, but I will not try to answer because it is so dark that I can barely see whether my pen writes or not. I expect to leave for Wyoming next Monday evening and reach Lander Tuesday night.

Hoping to see you soon, I remain hastily, blindly, and sincerely yours,

Ethel P. Waxham

6

KENOSHA: 1907–1908

There is a gap in the correspondence between August 9 and October 11. Summer school in Boulder had ended; the tent in Chautauqua was vacated. Marcia went East to join her mother. The Waxham family home had been sold, and Dr. Waxham was traveling in the East. Ethel's sister Vera was happily ensconsed in her own little family; Faith was with relatives in Rockford, Illinois. Pressed by the Mills family's renewed invitations to come for a visit, Ethel went to Wyoming. There was no opportunity to tell John Love that she was going from there directly to Kenosha, Wisconsin, to be the Latin Department at Kemper Hall. She boarded the train in Lander and disappeared for the second time. Undaunted, he obtained her address from a mutual friend, and resumed his courtship. Aware that Kemper Hall was to be another unique experience, Ethel began another journal.

> Kemper Hall, September 29, 1907. The lake is pounding away at the breakwater on the shore, and the good people are singing in the chapel. There is still an hour before Sunday dinnertime, enough to begin my record of the year. I have been here four days and a half, but the days in the land of the midnight sun are not so long. It seems as if there should be a vacation, or as if spring should come.
>
> Tuesday morning the Northwestern brought me to Chicago, and I took the first train out, to be in time for the classification of scholars here, the arrangement of work, settling, and all the business of the opening year. The train was well-filled with new Kemper Hall girls, and those who were conditioned, and obliged to return one day early. I felt

171

very young and simple among those worldly young ladies and wondered if I should have to teach them Latin verbs. One child, I afterward discovered, boasts that she has broken up ten schools, and now she is going to break up Kemper Hall. She is in my Latin class. The girls with whom I came up in the cab were also new girls. One of them was away from home for the first time, but declared that she "would stick it through if it killed her," and another wanted a roommate to "cry her heart out to when she was homesick." They took me for a new girl, too, and I tried to efface myself as much as possible, which was a very good thing to do, considering that I did not know that it was to be policy for the teachers here.

The front porch was easily to be recognized from the pictures of it. We rang the bell—somewhat dubious as to whether we should walk in or not. Visions of the ease with which one enters Wellesley disturbed me when the maid asked for our cards. That was a flank movement for which fully half of us were not prepared. I hung about the drawing room door for a few moments, then stopped a Sister, introduced myself, and asked for the Mother Superior. The Mother Superior came after many more moments—a bent figure in black, with a keen hawk-like face under the white fluted cap, a trembling but hard voice, and thin hands. She spoke to me, and then handed me over to Sister Flora Thérèse to be taken to the Teachers' Cottage. That was my first shock: to learn that I was to live without the pale. But I picked up my umbrella and rug frame and started after Sister Flora Thérèse, wondering how far away "The Cottage" might be. It was, however, only across the street, an unprepossessing place sometimes known as the "Farmers' Cottage." Whether once inhabited by or built for farmers or fit for farmers, it is still beyond me to tell. I wondered vaguely what it seemed to need most of all, and decided upon a coat of paint. Sister Flora Thérèse was very pleasant, was sorry that my room was not ready, and hoped that I could be comfortable in a room downstairs for the present. I was then put into the parlor and told that I would be called for in time for lunch. The parlor was the second shock—I wondered whether Marcia Chipman had seen it when she spoke of Kemper Hall as the loveliest of places—and supposed that since I was new and young, I had been put into the poorest lodgings. The room was dark, papered with dark, hideous paper, the woodwork was marred, the rug and furniture old and apparently selected for the nondescript and idiosyncratic qualities which each piece possessed.

When I had washed and written several safe-arrival notes, time hung heavy on my hands as I prepared to wait for two hours until lunchtime. Then Miss Thumb came to my rescue for the first time. Her name is spelled without the "b," but should be with; it is the most appropriate name that ever mortal had. She is a square, prunes-and-prisms lady with a mouth like a buttonhole, which she purses up on every occasion. She told me that she had charge of all the teachers, and my heart fell. But she took me over to "The Pines" to meet Miss Williams,* another new teacher. Someone came running lightly downstairs in answer to her call. I was surprised that anyone here should run so, until I saw a little, slim, curly-haired girl who is the whole Science Department here. I liked her before I saw her, and still more afterward. She took me to her room before we went out to look around, and I immediately ceased to pity myself. Hers is a tiny room without a closet, and with only two very diminutive windows close together. The heat of the apartment is dependent upon a stove; one gas burner furnishes the light. My own room had a register and electricity. Little Miss Williams was half-dead of loneliness, and glad to have someone to share her discoveries regarding Kemper Hall. She showed me her laboratories, the classrooms and the lake before lunchtime and told me that teachers were expected to use the side door entirely, and to keep out of the front of the house, where alone the rooms seemed made to live in. She must have noticed my surprise, for she said, "There is more than one spider in this dumpling," and told me about the mail.

*Elizabeth "Billy" Williams.

Letters and papers are not delivered directly to the teachers even. The Mother looks over everything for Kemper Hall, when she finds time, and puts it forth in public to be overhauled until seized upon by the owner with all the newness rubbed off. The Mother Superior is very frail, for all her duties, and the teachers are supposed to keep out of her way as much as possible, efface themselves, become a part of the walls when she appears.

After lunch, my room was ready, and a pleasant surprise it was, a northwest corner room, balconied, in a neat cream color. The sun shone in cheerily over the cleanliness and ugliness of it, and I took heart. Someone called from below, and going out, I fell into Laura Hibbard's arms.[1] I could hardly believe that she too was to be here, as the English department. It was too good to be true. "Your face is the only thing that has given me joy so far," she said, and we knew, each one, how the other felt toward Kemper Hall. We went out by the lake, sat under the willows, and wondered what our future was to be.

Laura was given, temporarily, the best rooms on the place, the Priests' apartments in "The Pines." But scarcely had she unpacked her suitcase, when she was obliged by "Thumb" to move into the guestroom. It is very cold and damp. We sat about the black stove until the fourth new teacher came, Louise Dudley,[2] a Kentucky girl from Bryn Mawr. It is through her room that Laura has to pass to her own, when the varnish dries sufficiently for her to move in. Work was to begin the next day, and only Miss Williams had any directions for work or schedule. Laura and I had waited coldly without the hall for supper, and had been thoroughly chilled; then we had gone in to wait, but had no place to stand; the Sisters were passing about with distant looks for us; still more chilled we had passed out again and waited on the porch. And still in the evening, our teeth chattered from Kemper Hall's reception. "Thumb" interrupted us to tell how much was done for the teachers here.

The next morning I "floated about" as one of my youngsters said, for three hours around the reference library, waiting for the amiable Miss Braislin, director of studies, to tell me a bit about my classes. But the schedule which she did give me took my breath away: twenty-four hours of recitation a week and one study period, out of a possible thirty. Twenty is supposed to be as much as a teacher should have, I have found out since. Sister Flora Thérèse took me to the book press to fit me out for the work, and said that she thought the textbooks today too attractive, almost. She is the jolliest of the Sisters, for all that, and we are going to try to read Greek together. I dug away all afternoon at the Latin grammar, wondering why it did not rain.

And the next day it did rain, not in a brisk fashion, but sadly and hopelessly. Miss Williams told us that we were going to be victims of something called "inside and outside inspection"—fortunately only for the children, we discovered later. "Thumb" told us, too, that the Mother was going to stop giving luxuries to the teachers. We thought of our rooms and Miss Williams gasped out when we were alone, " 'What next?' said the tadpole when his tail dropped off."

Tables were assigned to us that day. I have the head of a table of "Intermediates"; Miss St. George has the tea and coffee end. The first formal meal was a terrible experience. The teachers marched in first, we new ones ignorant of the fact that we should have bowed to the Sister at the head table. Then we stood behind our chairs while the children advanced in a long procession toward the door where they halted, bowed to the Sister and passed on, hand in hand. The little ones came first, then the larger ones. When we were all standing behind our chairs, a Senior standing by the door started a chant to which those of us who knew, responded:

> *"The eyes of all wait upon thee, O Lord*
> *And thou givest them thy meat in due season.*
> *Thou openest Thy hand and fillest all things living with*
> *plenteousness.*
> *Glory be to the Father, and to the Son and to the Holy*
> *Ghost."*

The Sister then said Grace and we were seated, but not yet ready for a social time. Silence was the rule until the Sister rang her bell. It was awkward and uncomfortable, the girls told me, because one of the Sisters often forgot to ring the bell. At the end of the meal, prayer, song and march were repeated. But another tap of the bell, before finishing dinner, was a sound bringing consternation to the ignorant—what to do? Half a dozen girls rose and passed out. We waited, hesitating. A question to an "old girl" brought the answer that those who left were Sacristans. "Indeed?" was the only answer of the still unenlightened. Later, it transpired that these girls had charge of the veils and preparations for chapel which succeeded breakfast and dinner. The pupils marched from the dining room, put on white veils and entered chapel, bowing two by two as they passed the altar. The Sisters cross themselves like Catholics. We teachers were not allowed to enter, uncovered. The Sisters made little frilly caps for us to use—twenty-five cents apiece. These must be worn far forward, for some reason, or the line will be stopped to change their position. The march through the corridor, closed doors and windows of stained glass on each side, and pictures of the Christ were the first thing that gave me the thrill of mystery. A curtain of tapestry blown outward, but still covering a large door-opening within which burned a lamp or candle, marked the Sisters' chapel. And an antique bell of intricately beaten metal hung by the curtain on which its shadow flickered strangely. This passage and the person of the Altar-bread woman have a Mæterlinckian tinge. The Altar-bread woman seems to have no other name and no meaning aside from her Altar-bread function. She is tall, but stooping, and the straight-lined robe which she always wears, is black. Her cap is white and tri-cornered; beneath it her grayish hair is simply but strangely rolled. Her face is like the face of one who never speaks, and is the color of old parchment.

October 1. The Mother Superior has given the new teachers directions. We sat before her in fear and trembling when she

Louise Dudley, 1911.

told us that college graduates thought that they were well-prepared and able to teach, but very often they were not. And even if they know their subjects, they may not be able to impart them. None of us could write, but she wants us to teach writing and composition in every class. We ask for more books, but they are not what we need. Kemper Hall has enough books. We should make the most of what we have. The morals of the children are not in our keeping, and so on. Indeed, we are kept away from the children as if any informal communication between us would be corrupting. We teachers are necessary evils.

Miss Dudley had another interview with the Mother to-day. After many efforts, she secured permission to have a stenographer—a man—come to "The Pines" to typewrite her thesis. Like this house, that has no parlor; but that has not even a hallway, so the typewriting took place in the guest room. But the time for which she requested the guest room had expired before the thesis was finished. It would take a part of one more afternoon. Miss Dudley besought "Thumb" for the guest room, but in vain. She took the matter to the Mother. "Are you writing a book?" demanded the Mother, as if it were a wicked thing she contemplated. Then, "Where did you get this young man anyway?" On being assured that he is the only stenographer whose services were obtainable, and that he was well recommended, and coming upon a purely business matter, she said that nevertheless the guest room could not be used for such purposes any longer. Miss Dudley, in desperation over the thesis, suggested that her own room might do. The bureau and the washstand were hidden by a screen and the cot was covered with a robe and sofa pillows. "No, No, No, No!" cried the Mother, retreating before the thought. "We are exceedingly particular here! Whatever you do at college, we cannot allow it here!" But seeing that Miss Dudley would go to any lengths, she consented at last to the use of the guest room for one more afternoon.

Sunday evening reception was a stiff, unsatisfactory little function. Two by two, teachers as well as pupils, we marched into the drawing room to meet the Mother and meet the Priest. Then we talked for about two minutes, each to the other, a very much frightened girl sang, and a self-conscious spoiled child read a Riley poem. We sang two hymns and marched out. One of the girls had asked me to her room, so I went with Miss Williams to Sister Laura's floor, past the white angel, where everyone in a hurry slips upon the polished floor, and into "Saint Veronica." Every room is named for a saint or a quality—"Libertas" is one! Margery Thin, a stout little English girl in a red velvet gown for which she is presently to receive a lecture, was infatuated with a new book and play—"The Scarlet Pimpernel." She had all the autographs of the actors and actresses, for which she had written. The leading man had to have his palms crossed with one pound six. After she had shown us the book and we had drawn pictures in a sort of guest-birthday book, the bell rang for silence and we left.

Yesterday, I chaperoned four incipient shoppers on a tour in the "village." Candy is forbidden, and ice cream. The photographer may be visited only with especial permission. Nothing may be eaten on the street, or anything purchased as large parcels. Only half a dozen cakes may be secured at a time from "the cake woman." Chaperones are ever necessary. When the youngsters telephone, even, a Sister goes into the telephone box to overhear the conversation. And the telephone is always under lock and key, to be obtained only by much diligent searching. When the art or music teacher lectures or gives a lesson, a Sister always sits in the class room. O Men, Men, what fearful creatures you are!

October 2. Woes galore! "Thumb" entered my room brazenly to declare that my curtains must be secure from the fresh pea green paint which is lavished upon the house. They are "The Mother's curtains," and must be properly cared for. The teachers, she said, furnish their own and these are only lent to make the room look cheerful until my own are purchased. I wonder how much more of the furniture and fittings are supplied only temporarily.

Shirtwaists and white skirts and such things are not done by the laundry, it seems. Perhaps we should not wear them. At any rate, only unstarched things are washed without charge.

The Mother, too, "cannot" supply gas for the stove in the kitchen, which we use for an occasional cup of tea. The bills, says "Thumb" are enormous. As a matter of fact, the maid uses the stove for heating water and "Thumb" last year used it for baking apples. But a special meter is to be put in, and

179

we must pay for the gas. When asked the amount of the enormous bills, "Thumb" replied that such things were not to be discussed.

Letters and papers and books would make the atmosphere more genial to a newcomer, but not a newspaper is anywhere. We do not seem to be allowed to use the library, and mail is very, very scarce. Even catalogues seem to be strangely delayed—one that I wrote for a week ago to a town not ten miles away, has not arrived.

October 3. Another of those endless days is passing. I had recitations from eight-forty until one-ten. It made me think of the days at the Twin Creek school when there were twenty-five or thirty recitations in a day, but then we had an occasional recess.

A thunderstorm woke me early this morning from a very vivid dream. I saw my mother as she must have been when she was young. Her dark hair was simply combed up from her forehead in the old way, and her eyes shone dark from a pale face with pink-tinged cheeks. I could not look away somehow, she was so beautiful, and it seemed so strange to have her there, and yet it seemed strange that it should be strange. I remembered as I awoke, that she was dead.

October 4. Susan Thumb came into my room—to rescue my curtains from the green paint, as usual, I believe. I tried to be pleasant to her, and chatted about the arrangement of the room. Miss Livermore had the washstand in the closet, I told her. "Oh, I wouldn't do that," she said. "Miss Livermore sacrifices everything to beau-ty. I don't do that." It was all I could do to restrain myself. The idea of Susan Thumb sacrificing anything to "beau-ty" could not be borne with sobriety. "I like my bedroom convenient," she said, "but in the parlor I have things pretty." Oh the horrors which she has picked out for the adornment of the lower hall! The curule chair, made for anything but sitting in! The window seat! The mantel ornaments!

She told Miss Williams that the table manners of the children here were terrible. Last year, however, she taught them so that they would feel at home at the table of the king and queen. At the table, she says, you must "sit where you are sat," and "keep yourself to yourself."

The Altar-bread woman, it appears, has another name—Harris. She had formerly, perhaps has still, a great devotion to the Bishop, and used to write him wonderful letters, which he said might have been composed by a mediæval saint and mystic, full of religious ecstasy. For some reason, her own worthlessness perhaps, she did not join the Sisterhood. Now she makes altar bread, which the Sisters sell. The finest wheat flour she mixes with water, and pours this well-beaten paste on a kind of steel waffle iron, which contains moulds of different sizes. Strong pressure is put upon the moulds, which press the paste into thin wafers while it cooks. Afterwards, the sheets are put upon a damp sponge frame which makes them pliable. The Altar-bread woman, then, with scissors for this especial purpose, cuts out the wafers, small and large, stamped with I.H.S. and mottoes (the Aquus, three nails, the Host, etc.) She dries them and packs them away to be sent to Spaulding Bros., Chicago, to parishes in the state, and to some large jewelry firms which handle the wafers. Her thoughts must be far away even from this strange employment, judging from the look of her eyes. Her face is triangular—so No, not so.

I had suspected a renewal of calls upon me for the coming week and determined to be away from the hall every afternoon and evening. But Sister Lydia caught me through the mail and I cannot answer back. Her commands were politely in the form of a question—would I be so kind as to conduct the evening study hour next week, and every third week henceforth? And Miss Braislin asked me to "help along" pressure is put upon the moulds, which pass the paste into thin wafers while [crossed out] cooks Afterwards the Sheets are put upon a damp Sponge frame which makes them pliable. The altar bread woman then with scissors for this especial purpose, cuts out the wafers, small and large, stamped with I.H.S. and mottoes. She dries them and packs them away to be sent to Spaulding Bros. Chicago, to parishes in the state, and to some large jewelry firms which handle the wafers. Her thoughts must be far away even from this strange employment, judging from the look of her eyes. Her face is triangular — so — no, not so.

the Square, three nails, the Host etc.

I had suspected a renewal of calls upon me for the coming week and determined to be away from

A page from Ethel Waxham's diary.

outside of hours an exceptionally slow and almost defective child, who came into Latin late, and chose this course because she happened to have that hour free. Others are coming in late to Latin. I wonder whether I shall have to help each one along. The powers that be have a very surprising way of calling upon one for duties, or expecting them to be done without any word to the doer. One is never told anything except that everyone tries to make it pleasant for the new teachers. Truly, I wonder where we new teachers would be if we had not hurried about to discover things for ourselves.

We had a gay walk this afternoon down the sand dunes. Miss Dudley and I took off our shoes and stockings and paddled in the lake, and afterwards ran about upon the sun-warmed sand. Laura said that she would have given half her possessions to have the Mother see us. The Mother, by the way, is coming to visit my Latin classes, and Miss B. hopes to come often next week to see how I get along. O misery! On our return from our walk, we went through the graveyard to look in the funeral urns for spoils of sporelli or some such thing for Miss Williams. A large lot was assigned to "Sisters of St. Mary," as a stone step gave the carven message. Four unnamed crosses of plain wood marked the graves there.

BIG BEAR [FLORENCE RISLEY]
Winnetka, Ill.,
October 4, 1907

Belovedest Little Bear,

Lovely little bear-track just came and almost made my winter fur drop off with excitement. I live about two hours' ride from you on the Northwestern, just a few miles north of Evanston, about sixteen miles north of Chicago.

Now then, when is your first vacation, where will you spend it, and do let me be in the same cave.

No, Little Bear, we do not pray and sing before breakfast, in fact we do very little praying at any time. I think I am killed with twenty-six hours of work and what must poor

Little Bear do with twenty-four? But then you do not have to teach *Paradise Lost* to children who never heard of Mt. Sinai, and Burke's speech to the daughters of lawyers who know U.S. politics like A.B.C.

Outside of school time I take the children walking, keep them quiet during study hours, make myself useful and agreeable at meal time and go hungry to boot. "Ain't it awful?" Little Bear.

If you can run away for over Sunday, will you come down and make me happy? I dassn't go away except once in a long while on Saturday.

Big Bear has had a calamity that ruffles his feelings. During vacation all those possessions that were not completely in rags, he packed and left. When he came back every blessed thing was gone of two years' accumulation, clothes, silver, many presents, all but books for which *Deo gratias*.

Soon, Little Brother, make it very soon. B.B.

JOHN G. LOVE
Wolton, Wyo., Sept. 20th/07

[Postage Due: 2¢/postmark: Wolton, Wyoming, Oct. 11, 1907.]

Dear Miss Waxham,

I got home tonight about twelve o'clock after an absence of over three weeks. I suppose that I ought to be in bed now as I have a fifty-mile ride to make on Punch tomorrow, or to be correct, today, as it is now long after midnight. I would not go to sleep anyway, so I might just as well write a few lines to you even if I cannot mail them until after I hear from you. You may be thankful that I am in ignorance (but not blissful) as to your whereabouts. Had I known your destination when you left, I would have only been one day behind you, but as Burns says, "the best laid plans of baith mice and men gang aft agley."

The Fates were unkind. I got to Lander the day that you left on the train. I would have gotten there on Sunday if I had not lost my horses. Poor dumb brutes, they did not know the difference that one day was going to make to me or they would not have wandered off. If I had known, I would have hitched them up after dark on Sunday night and given them a chance to show their speed and endurance. So nobly would they have responded, that I guarantee that I would not have missed the train.

If I had it to do over again, I would go to the Mills' ranch and ask you to please give me your company for one whole day. After debating the matter pro and con, I decided it would not be good policy. I thank you for inviting me to come out there while you were there, for I was well repaid, not only by seeing you, but several things were made clear that before were in doubt. I never saw you look prettier or more fascinating than you did when I came into the sitting room to say goodbye to you. Did you note the change that passed over Mrs. Mills' countenence when I said that I would try and come again before you left? I did, for I was watching for it. When I arrived there that day Mrs. Mills never shook hands with me; but after having been there for over two whole days and never having shown any marked attention to you, did you notice how cordially I was invited back again? Unfortunately there was no possible chance for me to speak to you for even one minute alone, although I certainly tried.

I might have been forgiven for daring to aspire to win you without asking permission if Mrs. Mills had formed no other plans for you. That she in her own mind has other plans was also made clear to me. I was surprised to think that a woman of her intelligence and training should take the stand that she does. Mrs. Charlie Hall and some others including myself are wondering how Mrs. Mills got it into her head that a girl with your education and social qualifications was on the lookout for a boy—Sandford—to raise and support.

Mrs. Charlie Hall could not enlighten me as to just where you went from Lander. It seemed about an equal chance for you to be going to Colorado, Wisconsin or Illinois. I do hope that you are not away back in the East, but if you are, I will come back there to talk to you anyway, unless you absolutely forbid me to.

October 1st 12:30 AM

When I got back on the 23rd, my team had not yet returned from Wolton. I knew then that the man was drunk, so the next day I saddled up little Papoose and went to Wolton after the team and the mail. There was no letter from you. I know that wherever you are, you are busy. I know that you cannot possibly realize how slowly the time passes for me and how I have waited to hear from you.

As it is, I still in a measure contentedly build air castles for the future and hope that the time will yet come when you will say yes, and we can spend months at a time in the mountains and I will have no one else's pleasure or wishes to consider but yours. Of course, should you decide that it must be no, I will try to live a life so that you need not be ashamed to call me a friend.

> *"Let tomorrow take care of tomorrow*
> *Leave things of the future to fate*
> *What's the use to anticipate sorrow*
> *Life's troubles come never too late."*

Tomorrow, or to be correct, today is my birthday* and it will be a dreary one for me. I have gotten through with a good deal more work than I would have done had you written. It has been a case of

> *"Work, work, work till the brain begins to swim*
> *Work, work, work till the eye is heavy and dim."*

I am getting the full benefit of being boss. My men can get drunk and quit, but I have to stay sober and tend to business.

---

*John Love was thirty-seven.

I am tied here looking after a little bunch of 150 sheep. They cost me 16 dollars each and I do not want to lose them, but I have just about reached the limit of my endurance. If I do not hear from you before long, I will pen them up and locate you.

October 9.

I got the mail tonight, but no letter from you. When daylight comes, I will say "the cow is in the hammock," and before the sun sets, if Punch does not fall with me, I will know where you are.

I received the pamphlet that you sent me on Bradlaugh. Many thanks for it; I enjoyed reading it tonight. I have heard him and Annie Besant in Edinburgh more than once, and I have also heard him on the debating platform. He was certainly a fine orator, not even surpassed by Gladstone. If you had only written me a few lines, I would have been happy once more and asleep long ago. If I manage to get you located today, I will mail you this long, poorly-written letter. If I don't, I will keep the telegraph wires clicking until I do.

Hoping to hear from you soon I remain, with love &
kisses, ever yours,
John G. Love

In the same envelope:

Hailey, 7:00 PM

Dear Miss Waxham,

"Brownie" made a flying trip to Moneta, but the Western Union would not yet guarantee to deliver messages, so I saddled Punch and made record time coming up here.[3] I am indebted to Miss Edith Signor for your address. I was pretty sure that you had gone to Kemper Hall, but to save my life I could not think of Kenosha.

Since you showed an interest in fossils, I have located some

187

real ones—not little insignificant Belemnites, but huge anti-
deluvian monsters. I had some of the petrified bones in my
buggy when I got to Lander and found you gone.

We are having beautiful weather here now. I will start
back for home in the morning. Now, you dear little sinner,
be good and write to me or I will come back there and see my
native state.

> With love & kisses, ever yours,
> John G. Love

[Enclosed] "God's Country" by Louise Smith.

> *Sing me the song of the bit and spur—*
> *The song of the smiling plain;*
> *Blow me the breeze from the mountain top,*
> *And send me the Western rain!*
>
> *Mine be the light of the Western stars—*
> *My breath of the fir and pine,*
> *Where youth and joy and love come back,*
> *Like the taste of a rare old wine.*
>
> *So here's to the song of the mountain stream,*
> *To the shrill of the coyote's cry,*
> *And may I wake in that Western land*
> *'Stead o' Heaven—when I die.*

Evidently Kemper Hall kept its Latin department far too busy to
maintain both a journal and an extensive correspondence with friends.
This is Ethel Waxham's last entry for her year at Kemper Hall, but her
friends commented on her experiences there for years afterward in their
replies to her letters.

October 12. The new teachers waved me a hundred farewells
from the hack window as they all started on the way for home
or friends. Laura, bless her, wanted me to come with her, and
told me to be sure to use her poetry books. Miss Dudley's last
words were—"There's tea in the cupboard, and a *lemon* and
peanut butter and *saltines!*" as the carriage drove away.

We have been having consolation teas every afternoon in

Laura Hibbard's room, before one of us had to depart for study hour. Miss Dudley furnishes the tea, Laura a plate and a table, Miss Williams a few spoons, and for food we have an account at Scholer & Funks. Since none of us have cups, we use, respectively, a small mustard jar, a wine glass, a cup without a handle and a tooth mug. One afternoon, when we felt particularly rebellious, we patronized Laura's black bottle, and had whiskey in our tea. At these times, we share any knowledge which we may have gleaned with each other—for no one ever tells anything to those whom it concerns. My last contribution was that the Altar-bread woman has not only a name, but a hat, like other people—a black sort of dumpling which she wears as she moves listlessly about the streets. Yesterday she spoke—Miss Williams inadvertantly brushed against her in her desire for mail. After her apology, the Altar-bread woman spoke in unworldly tones: "I always stand with one foot at right angles to the other; it rests me to do so."

The Mother, we have discovered, considers any reference to money exceedingly indelicate. Our salaries, which must never be spoken of or asked for, are doled out to us when she sees fit, and in what proportion she pleases. A maid comes about, solemnly, with a silver tray, covered with a napkin. Upon this are little notes, sealed with the great seal. Within—money. But no one knows when these donations may come. Miss Hale was once greatly in need of money to repay a loan, and she was the only one of the teachers not to receive money before Christmas. She had to borrow the sum she needed at six percent—even though 'twas indelicate. When the teachers wish to leave over Sunday, they must speak to the Mother: "Not to ask permission," Miss Braislin explains strategically, "but to let her know." Still, if one does not "let her know," there is trouble. "You must not say 'May I go?'" instructed Miss Wells when the three new teachers asked how to confront the Mother. "Neither must you say 'I am going.' You must say tentatively, 'I should like to go home on Sunday.' And if she pleases, she will tell you to go."

Study hour is an invention of the evil one. "You may be a P.L. now, but you won't be after you have kept study hour for a while," warned Miss Wells, when I began. "P.L." is Miss Davis's shortening of "perfect lady." For one week out of three, from seven-thirty until eight-twenty, I sit at the desk in the study hall. I may not speak to reprimand the unwary. I may shake my head and glare merely at such as turn about and speak, pass notes, cross the floor unnecessarily, or make a noise. Every offense must be followed up, sleuth hound-like, to the death. All my days must be given over to picking out and punishing the offenders in ways that have no reference to the sin. And anything is a sin. "One of the girls," Miss Livermore told me in a rage—she is the dragon of the study hour—"had the audacity to laugh—to laugh!" She kept her sitting all recess time in her room—to come back worn out from the ordeal.

Tonight I had settled down in the most undignified and convenient attitude upon my couch under the light, to mark three stockings for the laundry when Sister Flora Thérèse hurried up the stair into my room. The Mother wished to see me instantly. I dropped my stockings and lost my needle in the flurry to follow Sister back. All my dissatisfied thoughts haunted my conscience, as well as the desire to see a bit of a checque. But the Mother only desired to ask whether I might not give Sister Flora Thérèse lessons in Greek two or three afternoons a week. I assented, with what grace I could, meanwhile reading upon the wall an illuminated motto "The sins of teachers are the teachers of sins." I thought, too, that I should try to make it one hour a week, if possible, for my hands are brimming full now of Latin prose papers and my brain is sick to death of the primer B's Galba and the farmers and the inhabitants of the island.

> MARCIA CHIPMAN
> Boulder, Colo.,
> Sunday, October 13th

Good Morning Stiddy!—
A fascinating "open and shut" day, when the canyon looks

gray and blue, and the air dances about your scolding locks between moments of scorching sun.

It seemed too good to be true when I really heard *directly* that you were going, or had gone to Kemper Hall. Rumor is a second-hand sort of a thing and one wishes personal news, where a "stiddy" is concerned.

My thought of Kemper Hall is such a loving happy thought; it is nearer to home than any spot on earth and I long to hear more enthusiastic reports from you. Still I am not blind to the fact that one hundred and twenty or thirty girls from everywhere might easily spoil even the dearest place I ever visit. My sojourn is always during the summer when the lawns are like emerald, the lake blue like sapphires, and the halls *quiet*. I associate the vesper hour with a handful of worshippers. The birds always call from treetops over shaded lawns into the cool dark aisles and feel in common with Sister and Mother and city dweller, the quietness of the time and place. How easily I can understand the difference, for I have twice visited Kemper Hall in term time. Perhaps you will not find it a "mill" always, Phoebe. Remember this about the Mother. She is loving down to her boots. A heart, oh as big as—you! But she is severe at times, and frequently misunderstood. I do love her dearly, and how she loves the girls.

No I did not lose my summer school credits nor yet my Tennyson hours, so my decline was not due to mental agitation—I simply could stand up no longer one day, and so, like a philosopher went to bed. My doctor will have me comfortable again within a few months, and will send me on my way with earnest entreaty not to take violent exercise, or physical plunges into "deep, dark rocky canyons." Never mind, the toiling up hills was good for my character, if not for "this mortal coil," and I am still a sylph, having kept below the one hundred forty pound limit "since we parted."

You are a darlin', although ornery. I wish you were here. *Please* write *soon*. My very best love to Sister Rachel and Sister

Ella and Sister Florence, and Sister Flora Thérèse, and the dear Mother. Tell her that Boulder is waiting for her visit.

> Ever Lovingly,
> Marcia

ETHEL P. WAXHAM
Kemper Hall, Kenosha, Wis.
20th October, 1907

Wolton, Wyo.

Dear Mr. Love,

Your long letter reached me last week. I was surprised that you had not received the note that I wrote you soon after reaching Kemper Hall. You remember that you asked me to send you my address? And I did. The Bradlaugh "Little Journey" I sent with unspoken contrition for being exceptionally sleepy on the evening that you told us about Bradlaugh's political efforts.

It did not please me to read about those "other plans" for me, which I shall not believe unless obliged to by unmistakable evidence. I came to Wyoming to visit at Mrs. Mills' invitation to fill a few vacant weeks and to see them all again. They were very good to me as they were before, and if they did want me to stay and if I was so tempted, there is nothing in that for all the gossip in Christendom!

Since coming here, I have heard from Mrs. Mills and from Sandford, and certainly was glad to get their letters. This is the first place that I have found where the days are long and largely unpleasant. So, you see, one appreciates fat letters. Then Kemper Hall is about as nearly opposite to the Twin Creek school on the ranch as can be imagined. Everything has to be done by the bell: eating, sleeping, studying, walking, dressing and most especially praying. The Sisters have chapel seven times a day; for us it is only twice a day. The children have to wear little veils while we teachers have small frilled oval caps. The pomp and ceremony of these occasions are often very tiresome and the sermons ridiculously childish.

My main duty is to be the entire Latin department. Every day from half-past eight until quarter after one, I am busy hearing recitations about Catiline and Cæsar and Æneas and second declension nouns and irregular verbs, until I feel as if I myself might "devastate Italy and urge on the troops" as Galba does in the sentences of the beginners.

My other duty is to serve meat and potatoes to twelve hungry girls, who keep the plates flying back and forth so fast that some day they will find me quite dead from exhaustion and starvation from not being able to get a bite. One of my Wellesley friends, Laura Hibbard, is here, and she certainly is a joy and a delight. No newspapers appear in Kemper Hall, but Laura gets them from her home in Chicago and tells us the news. Then sometimes we run away from chapel together and watch the moon rise over the lake. And, in the afternoons before time to take study hour, we have tea together with the other two "new" teachers. There is a distinction here between the old and the new. I always thought that tea drinking was a harmless but comparatively pleasant amusement for one afternoon out of ten, but now I find it intensely exciting every day of the week.

Last Monday I made a shopping expedition to Chicago, which seemed the most adventurous undertaking, from the convent point of view. I had luncheon with a friend at a German hotel and spent the afternoon at the Art Institute; then came back in the evening with the feeling I had been madly dissipating.

The music teacher is playing Scotch songs downstairs now—"The Land of the Leal" that Marcia sings, "Mary's Dream" and others. There are apples for refreshments, and I am invited. Must go before everything is over.

You will write to me soon, I know, and tell me the news. With birthday wishes, although they are late, I remain, as ever,

Sincerely Yours,

Ethel P. Waxham

Mary B. Mills
Red Bluff Ranch,
October 23, 1907

My dear, dear Girl,

I feel as though one of my own little girls was teaching way off in Kenosha, and I'm afraid she's a wee bit homesick among all those unsympathetic people.

But you know, dear, there are disadvantages everywhere, and it does seem to me you are far better off there, than in most schools, far better, I'm sure than in Rock Springs [Wyoming]. We had our opinion of that town very strongly confirmed the other day by a man who was here to dinner. He had lived in Rock Springs for a number of years. He added to what we said that the water they had to drink is enough to kill anyone. We are so glad you found some good friends.

The "paper doll" sister was a revelation to the children. They did not remember ever seeing one before. She is very good and looked very natural to me.

It's a pity we cannot send you that big six shooter and belt to hang up beside the snake skins for Susan Thumb's benefit.

The girls were rather worried when they came from the P.O. last. Edith had been telling them that Mr. Love had been there inquiring for your address. Could not understand why you had not written him and sat down and wrote a long letter which you probably have by this time. Don't you know, dear, it is far easier and much pleasanter to leave some things unsaid—if it was any other girl I should be tempted to, but you know how dearly we all love you and I confess it has given us a shock to hear sheep herders and everyone talking about Miss Waxham.

That Mr. Love should greatly admire you is not to be wondered, but that he should talk about you and your family to everyone until it has made you ridiculous to people has surprised me, as I really supposed Mr. Love knew the requirements of a gentleman.

He is a man, I believe, of good habits, as far as we know—

all but the habit of gossiping. As George Tweed says, "gossiping is bad enough in a woman, but in a man, oh, Lord." It is constantly getting him into trouble and one always wonders what he has done.

If this country is only peopled by a different class of people, perhaps it would be different, but they cannot understand a girl being civil to a man—and Mr. Love hardly seems to understand it either—at least, he allows people to put what construction they like on your friendship and does not deny it.

Forgive me, dear, if I have said too much. If you are interested enough in him to allow him the opportunity of talking, of course, I say no more, but I could not let it go on longer without saying at least this much to you. It should have been said last summer. The winter you were here, even.

We are waiting for the threshers to come, then the girls are going for a little visit down to Mrs. Charlie and Mrs. R. H. Hall's. They are occupied at present in making puffed rice brittle which they think is fine and so easy to make.

Have you seen "Big Bear" yet?

Write whenever you can — we enjoy your letters so much.

Ever most aff'y,
Mary B. Mills

NORA DUNN
Oakland, Calif., Nov. 20, 1907

Dearie Mine;

Your dear letter of so long ago is a reproach to me, as I see on it a date in September. I have *thought* many letters to the dearest little teacher in Kemper Hall, but somehow or other when it came to putting those thoughts on paper the flesh was weak. When I get home after a day with my fifty-odd incorrigibles, the thoughts fly fast but the fingers are weary.

And now I want to thank you for the gift which came on my birthday—dainty and pretty, and greatly appreciated. Sometimes, when the fire burns low, and all the family have gone to bed, firelight dreams begin, and among the pleasantest of those dreams is one of the old Hyde Park High School days, when we frowned over Greek verbs and smiled at Life together. I wish Kemper Hall were in California—or else the Swett [sic] School were in Kenosha, but perhaps we must put off still a little farther those blissful dream days that for nearly ten years we have been planning on. Sometimes I think maybe it is better as it is because then you don't see all my crankisms and my old maid habits, but with you, I believe those faults would fade, because of a *perfect* example.

How you must have enjoyed your trip back to Wyoming. After city life, it is such a treat to be with the hills, and the stars, and the vast silences of nature. In Texas I feel free and glad in spite of the potatoes and the dishes, and when one has mountains around there is nothing more to be desired.

Will you be back in Denver this summer? I had planned to go East—to New York—to see Mamma, as it will have been over two years since we parted in Los Angeles after the great earthquake, but if the present financial difficulties continue, I fear I shall have to stay here and try to get something to do during my seven weeks vacation. I am still hoping that someday you will come out to this sunshine land and teach with me, in a little school among the hills. But somehow those schools among the hills only want *one* teacher, and even the hills can't satisfy when one is entirely alone—which calls to my mind a line of a poem from the *Literary Digest*—"The heart that loves the lowlands is lonely on the hills." Isn't that true?

Oh, I must tell you of a "theme" I received from my prize "tough" of the class. It was on "Our Scoolroom," and this was it: "In our Schoolroom, they is six windows, three doors, five gass-pipes, and Miss Dun." I have a terrible suspicion that the joke is on me.

About that trip to Europe, Let's plan! We have had happiness in other plans even if no realization, so anyway—let's plan.

love from Nora

JOHN G. LOVE
Wolton, Wyo.,
November 27, 1907

Dear Miss Waxham,

Here I am once more burning the midnight oil. It is a month and seven days since you wrote, which, to me, seems ages. I sincerely hope that you are not sick.

Tomorrow will be Thanksgiving Day and I suppose I have a good deal to be thankful for. November 25th is the close of my business year and I have been figuring up profit and loss for the last few nights. The balance is on the right side of the ledger, but not by very much. My expenses have been very heavy and the storms last May cost me about seven hundred dollars a day for six days.

It snowed about two inches here on the 17th, but the snow is all gone now and the weather is nice and warm.

This will be the first year for many a long year that I will miss Christmas at the Mills' ranch. I will send the Mills children their yearly Christmas reminder as of yore. If you will not let me come back to where you are at Christmastime, I will stay here at home for the first time in twelve years.

When I started for Lander the other day, it was the first time that I had hitched up the buggy since you left Wyoming. I drove Blue and Essie, and I can assure you they made good time. The last eighteen miles on the way home was covered in less than two hours.

If you could have looked in at the window and watched how eagerly I looked over the mail, it would not have required any mental strain to know what I was looking for. I sometimes think that I would be better off if I was constructed as that party told you I was and got my head turned at every pretty face I saw. It certainly would have whirled around a good many times since I saw you. I have been wondering just what stage of lunacy I would be in at present if you had given me all the encouragement you could instead of none. I wonder.

With best wishes for your welfare and happiness I remain with love and kisses,

Ever yours,
John G. Love

ETHEL P. WAXHAM
Kemper Hall, Kenosha, Wis.,
Dec. 2, 1907

JOHN G. LOVE

Dear Mr. Love,

Your two letters arrived some time ago, but Kemper Hall has kept its Latin Department too busy to make the writing of letters easy—even for me! I'm sorry that my letter did not reach you, for I said in it what I would have said long ago, if I had written you at all since you began to sign your name as you do. You must have known that I would not like it and would not let it continue since we are only friends. I wrote you not to expect any more letters from me unless you stopped it.

Your plans for the winter seem ambitious enough to keep you busy—even without any work on the new dam. I have no plans yet, even for the Christmas vacation—may spend it with relatives near here, or in Chicago, or possibly in Denver. I will try to write you a letter then, but don't think of coming. Spend Christmas with the Mills people and make peace.

Mrs. Mills wrote me just about the time that your letter came, of gossip about me in Wyoming—the girls heard it at Signors—and she said that you were not unconnected with starting it, and at least would not deny it. Of all things I hate gossip, and try always to get back to the source of it. I hope that you are not responsible, for I have always thought that it was the part of a gentleman to keep idle talk of any kind away from any girl or woman, and never to spread it.

It is Sunday evening—Sunday evenings are trials here.

After supper, the children, dressed in their best clothes, file two by two and hand in hand into the drawing rooms. There stand a Sister and the Priest. The children bow and pass on. Then they scatter about the room, carefully with their backs to the wall, and talk politely to the teachers for some twenty minutes. Then someone sings in a high metallic voice and someone else plays the piano. We all sing three hymns, the Gloria, and the Priest gives a prayer. Then we disperse, two by two, hand in hand. It is called Sunday Evening Reception. When it is over, some youngster complains, "Aren't you coming to see me, ever?" or "Won't you come to my room?" You go after the fifth invitation, sit on the only chair, look at kodak pictures, or write your name in a guest book while a dozen children stand about politely admiring. The youngsters have all the polite externals; it is very nice but appalling. When you come into a room, everyone stands suddenly; when you come into a crowded hall, the girls make a wide passage for you. When you drop anything, they pick it up. When you rise after prayers, they carefully lift you to your feet. They help you up a step as if you were fifty and had rheumatism. In class yesterday, one girl asked if she might not go for my coat. I asked her if I were cold, and she said that she thought I shivered!

Over this Saturday and Sunday, Big Bear, or Florence Risley, a Wellesley friend of mine, has been staying with me. We went out to the lighthouse on the lake, and hammered copper and saw the alter bread being made, and had a delightful time. Now that she has gone, there is only Christmas to look forward to.

Marcia is working away at Boulder. Pater is in Denver again, and Little Sister Faith is keeping house for him.

It is far too late now to be writing letters and even my electric light is dim and sleepy, but I have still a little work to do. Spare time is very spare, you see.

Sincerely yours,
Ethel P. Waxham

JOHN G. LOVE
Wolton, Wyo., Dec. 6, 1907

Dear Miss Waxham,

Your letter reached me tonight. I was indeed glad to get it and learn that you were alive and well. I will write a few lines to you tonight, although I am very tired and sleepy from riding all day in the wind.

I will not go to the Mills' ranch as usual, as you suggest. Had you written me four months ago about Mrs. Mills' writing you about some gossip or about something that *I* was supposed to have said, I would have taken the trouble to look the matter up to find out the whys and wherefores, but *not* now.

I bought back all of Guinard's interest in the cattle and horses. I am breaking some more horses to work and nine new saddle horses. The snow is all gone and the weather continues fine but a little windy. The sheep are up next to the foothills in order to get snow. The wind is howling dismally tonight and it may blow up a storm. I hope not, as I have five days' riding after horses to do yet.

I will always sign all letters properly in the future. Please forgive my errors of the past. I suppose that I ought to be satisfied with your friendship, but I won't be. On the theory that half a loaf is better than no bread, I will try and be contented, and will always be proud to be even your friend.

Your letter came at a very opportune time. That day I had just gotten in my best saddlehorses to go after some that I wanted to break. I just needed a letter like that to give me back my old-time nerve and recklessness in the saddle. I have the grim satisfaction of knowing that not a single bunch of horses got away from me. My saddlehorses stand tonight with drooping heads from seven days' hard riding. I have no doubt but what they are comparing notes in horse fashion and wondering just what was the matter with their master. Even Punch, fast and willing as he is, for the first time since I owned him, felt the prick of steel in his steaming flanks. One

200

bunch had made good their escape from me twice this fall just because the world looked good, and I yearned to live forever and did not care to take any needless risk. I fooled them this time, however, and took ten times the risk I would have taken before. The day I got them, it was snowing and the [rabbit and gopher] holes were filled with snow. I had travelled for hours looking for the bunch. I led my horse across a good many gulches and rocky hills. I finally found them seventeen miles from where I had stayed all night. When I got off to cinch up my saddle for the run, I thought of what Mills has so often told me would be my finish. He has repeatedly told me that my horse would fall with me and I would either get my neck broken or be horribly smashed up. Then I said, "the cow is in the hammock," swung into the saddle and rode as I have not ridden for years. I finally got them in the corral at Delfelders' and got home (with all that three of us had gathered in seven days) tonight with no bones broken and only my left shoulder bruised a little. When my horses have rested a little, I am going back up in the Hailey country after some that I could not find this time.

I have thought and brooded over the contents of your letter, I suppose, a thousand times in the last seven days, and I am feeling rather sore over it. Mrs. Mills showed good generalship in her method of attack. Amongst all my villainy and cussedness, I confess that I was proud of the fact that right or wrong I would take the woman's side. I was proud of the fact that (no matter what depths of depravity I might sink to with men) there is not to my knowledge a single woman or child that ever heard a single word pass my lips that they could not with perfect propriety repeat to their mother.

In reading what I am going to fill out this sheet with, do not misunderstand me; don't think that I am trying to vindicate myself. The question, "little girl," is not my innocence or guilt in this specific case. Now, "little girl," you seem to think that I am wrong when I attribute the motive that I do to Mrs. Mills. I am absolutely positive that I am correct, but I would like it very much if you would give me your views on the subject.

To get back to the beginning: When you came to the Mills' ranch first, their boy Sandford was down here for a visit with me. You know that for long years I was welcome there at any hour of the day or night. The children were left for days at a time in my care. I was received if not as one of the family, at least on a basis of equality. Then you came. I was introduced to you as an equal. I was still a welcome guest. Not a word was said against my taking you to Lander or my going after you, but just as soon as they saw that I cared a little too much for you they changed fronts squarely and by the 15th of January, showed me clearly that I was not welcome.

Why did they not tell you if they knew me to be guilty of a single act unbecoming a gentleman? Why would they not answer my letters while you were there? Why was it that on the very day that you left Hailey, a letter was mailed from there saying "Come up the same as usual?" Why did they want me to believe that it was because I had not taken you to Halls that I was in disgrace? Why did they never say a word to you about it? Why would they never mention your name to me? Why was I to be made welcome only when you were not there? Why after all her sage advice to me on the subject of matrimony, did Mrs. Mills turn me down because I thought so much of you? Time and again for years she told me, "Mr. Love, I want to see you pick out a *good* girl and settle down and not make a fool of yourself like Mr. Bent." Bent's sole crime was that he married a girl that Mrs. Mills would not recognize as her social and mental equal. She could have no fault to find with you as you are certainly the peer of anyone that she ever saw. Why when I first came there this summer was I not made to feel welcome, but after having been there two days and not having interfered in the least with Sandford, was I so cordially invited to come back? Why, even if it was so that I had been talking about you, would Mrs. Mills go to the trouble of writing to you about it? I could propound queries indefinitely but if you can answer or explain those few on any ground other than the one that I have advanced, you can do far more than I can. Please try.

It may be for the best that you won't let me come back there for the holidays, but, of course, you can't expect me to see it in that light. I will either put in the day at home or in the saddle after horses. I have written this in a hurry and have written just what I thought. If you think it your duty not to answer it, all well and good; you have to be the judge and not I. If I am not crippled, I will write once more anyway on the last night of the year. With best wishes for your welfare and happiness and wishing you a Merry Christmas and a Happy New Year, I remain,

Yours Sincerely,
John G. Love

True to his word, John Love's next letter was dated December 31, 1907, but postmarked January 7, 1908. Ethel did not return to Denver for the holidays, but went to Rockford, Illinois instead.

Dear Miss Waxham,

It is the last night of the year and I suppose that I should be making good resolutions for the new year. Two years ago tonight, we came home to Mills' from Lander. Since then, I have spent a good many happy hours and a good many miserable ones. All in all, I cannot complain, for the world has generally looked very good. During those two years I have been guilty of nothing that I cannot look you squarely in the face and tell you.

There is only one thing that I would be ashamed of and that happened last fall when I got to Lander and found that you were gone. There was no use in my going to bed. I had to do something to help me forget and pass away the time that my horses had to rest. For the first (and last time) in my life, I went to the gaming tables for consolation. I played steadily all night and contentedly watched check after check pass over the green cloth. When the sun rose next morning, I was still playing. When I finally quit, I had won back all that I had lost and some more besides. I confess, "little girl," I am ashamed of that one thing. Fortunately very few know it and none know why. Not even Mrs. Mills living right here will ever hear of it.

The past week has been rather dull for me. I was not able to enjoy eating the luxuries of the season. I had everything that I could think of to eat, a good cook to cook it and felt able to do ample justice to it until the evening of the 23rd when I had to go to bed, unable to eat supper. I did not have much to say until yesterday, when I got out for the first time since the 23rd amongst the horses I am breaking. It was my own fault entirely catching such a cold. There was a raw wind blowing and I had off my coat, vest, and overshoes to ride. I got to sweating freely and did not get on my coat soon enough. I am about all right again but still very hoarse.

January 1st, 1908

Happy New Year to you, "little girl." The clock has just struck the hour of twelve and a new year has begun. I hope it will be a very happy one for you wherever you are. I had to in one way forget you this Christmas, as I did not even have a Christmas card to send. I sent the Mills girls five dollars each as I have always done for years. I am now curious to know if their mother will make them send it back.

I sold Jack back some of his horses again and I bought back *all* of the sheep, wagons, tools and machinery. Then I leased him the sheep on shares. I have added three geese to my list of livestock. I went out two miles east of the ranch after a load of coal yesterday. We drove one of the "broncs" and she worked first-rate, considering everything. I have one that certainly can make things lively with her heels. A very fast trotter, she surely can kick in grand style. I hope that she may get over it in time with kind treatment, for I would like to get behind her and her mate in the buggy.

I hope that you have had a fine time wherever you are—

and I hope that you will never want to go anywhere so badly as I wanted to come back there, never want to see anyone as badly as I wanted to see you.

This has so far been what I would call a cold winter, but stock of all kinds are still looking well.

What about that picture that I have been yearning for so long? Please be generous if I am expected to exist without seeing you until next June.

> Yours Sincerely,
> John G. Love

ETHEL P. WAXHAM
Winnetka, Ill., January 3, 1908

Wolton, Wyo.

[Forwarded to Moneta, Wyoming.]

Dear Mr. Love,

Stationery is short and poor and I have no time at all to write, but since I have not heard from you since that last letter of yours to Kenosha, I am a bit afraid that my answer to it went astray—which would be very unfortunate because I have practically forgotten what I said, except to scold you a bit for not being sensible and taking care of your bones as a grown-up should.

Vacation is almost over and my relatives and friends have been taking care of my bones and telling me first what I should and should not do. The only useful thing that I have accomplished is making paper dolls for youngster cousins. In gratitude, they named the dolls for me, Ethel (first name first), and Phoebe (second name first). Now I am visiting Big Bear, and making plans for amateurish arts and crafts work in the three days before time to return to Kenosha. Poor Big Bear burned her paws badly on a Christmas tree for the children before vacation began, and she has not been able to do much since.

Mademoiselle is waiting for me to go downtown with

her—Mademoiselle who paints pictures and teaches French and has great knowledge of Arts and Crafts and makes her best clothes and is a very, very wonderful person.

> Goodbye, and a Happy New
> Year to you
> from Ethel Waxham

MARY B. MILLS
Red Bluff Ranch,
January 28, 1908

My poor dear cheese-headed little Girl,

Sandford brought your letter to Kathryn this afternoon. I felt guilty that he should go to the post office without a letter for you, but when I tell you that Mrs. Hudson and the boys are here, you will know how almost impossible it is to do writing. How did you get ill, dear—such an unheard of thing for you. I see we will have to have you back in Wyoming again—hardships and pure air keep you well anyway. When it gets colder you'll feel better.

Your dear letters to Margaret and myself came a week ago. The Christmas letter did not get here before Christmas. It took quite a trip over the country, but it was just as welcome later. We laughed at your burst of poetry. No one else could write such a letter.

Your Christmas vacation must have been a decidedly pleasant change. I wonder why they don't make a special effort to have all the theatres filled with good things. You did enjoy the Italian Opera, did you not?

I must tell you of the delightful trip Mr. Mills and I took. We left for Atlantic [City, Wyoming] the 6th—not a bit of snow at the ranch; we struck it first about half way across the Flat. Then it grew deeper and deeper as we got nearer the mountains. The stage road through the Burnt Grove is the only one open. The two places I got out and walked, Mr. Mills stood on the buggy slip to keep it from going over. It was lovely going through the Grove for several miles—deep, deep snow everywhere, not a sound, some drifts fifteen or twenty feet deep, packed hard in the road. By the government bands on the trees and stumps, we could tell how high up we were getting. The highest mark reached 8,290 feet. We reached Atlantic about four o'clock and were the guests of Mr. and Mrs. Sypes for two nights. Mrs Sypes has a most beautiful voice. She had her training in Florence and speaks both French and Italian. She had expected to make great use of her voice when her health broke down, and she was banished to the mountains to regain it. She says that some days she feels that everything would be right again and others she is discouraged, but she was in excellent voice when we were there, and it was surely a rare treat for us. Mr. Sypes has charge of the mining property there, in fact all of Atlantic belongs to the mining company.

They live in a delightful house, an ideal living room about 20 × 30 ft.—the prettiest dining room I have seen in Wyoming. Six bedrooms, *two bath rooms,* great big windows, window seats, beautiful flowers, books, piano, everything to make them comfortable but friends, as Mrs. Sypes says. The next morning we took a big sleigh and all went up to the tunnel—1,800 ft. long in solid rock. The drive through the Rock Creek Canyon, all deep snow, cragged rocks and pine trees was fine—of course we flipped over. That's part of the sleigh ride. We thought how much you would have enjoyed it too. We must surely take the trip in the summer—the full length of the canyon and come out at Christina Lake.

While we were away "Smithy" came, all rigged out in new clothes and *shoes*—first he'd had in forty years. He was right sorry we were not at home. He thought that maybe Miss Waxham would be here, too. "But never mind, girls, I'll be up again soon. We'll have the phonograph open, a box of first-looks,* and have a great time."

I wish we were near you, dear. I believe you need petting, a good many big hugs, and some fried onions.

You will write just a line and let us know how you are getting along. Miss Thumb probably has you out of bed by this

*Stereoscope and pictures.

207

time. We will think of you all the time and it will be a great relief to know you are better.

It will soon be spring, dear, then summer will be here before you know.

Take care of yourself and write.

Ever most aff'y,
Mary B. Mills

Kemper Hall, Kenosha, Wis.
January 31, 1908

Wolton, Wyo.

Dear Mr. Love—

It is high time that your two letters were answered, and that I should thank you for the postal cards. The pictures looked familiar. I shall put them with my kodak pictures when I have them all made into a book.

I hope that things will continue to go well at the ranch— the hens to lay and the teams to move and the snow to come just at the right time. The Christmas letter from Kathryn spoke of your not arriving as usual for Christmas dinner.

"Poor you"—you are a little better off than I, if the world looks very good to you—I have just begun to wonder whether there is any good in Judah after all. For I've been sick abed for a week, and all the other nice teachers are just about sick abed, and examinations are here, and we have to mimeograph our own examination papers, besides making them out and correcting them. Moreover, the thermometer is twelve below, and we have a Feast day on Monday. I hate Feast days, because they starve us for a week before, and we have to go to a long church service. Besides, it takes away our holiday. Big Bear has sprained her ankle now, and Marcia, who came for a while to visit, has gone away too far to come back. So Little Bear goes about saying, "Brrr," which is half way between a shiver and a growl, and means, "Don't come near me, or tell any bad news, or I'll swallow you up quick!"

The only amusement for the whole week that I was under the weather, was Miss Thumb. She brought me my meals and scolded me all the time that I ate, broke two whiskey bottles in a day and salted the grapefruit instead of sugaring it. She told the doctor about me, "She's got to get sick or well. We can't waste any time at Kemper Hall." And she thinks that I am trying to commit suicide by not eating meat, and that I show how useless a thing a college education is if it turns out a person who takes so little thought about food. But she really enjoyed looking out for me, and I was afraid that she would not let me recover. The Seniors sent me some lovely red roses which made the days easier—and the Mother even came over to say, "Don't let Miss Thumb be too bossy!" Think!

Brrr! I wish I were a tall green tree, because they don't ever have Latin grammars and examination papers and Miss Thumbs. Perhaps if I am very good and correct the papers neatly, and go to chapel twice a day and three times on Sunday, and always get up when a Sister goes by, and never stay away from breakfast, and never say that study hours are not delightful—maybe I'll be a tree in the next life!

Listen—I hope that you will be soundly berated again for not going to the Mills people for Christmas. You deserve it! Don't gossip with anyone—and if you do not, I cannot condemn you, heard or unheard. And wouldn't it be better to write to me than to go to gaming tables?

> Goodnight, and write to me soon
> Ethel Waxham

> BIG BEAR [FLORENCE RISLEY]
> Winnetka, Ill.,
> February 10, 1908

This is for to cheer up Little Brother Bear what is all mis'ble with a misery. Why you go and get sick when B.B. is far away and can't say cheering things to you. I pity you, L.B.

Examinations are all over and only four of the dear children failed, which is interesting because they have to have a second dose in six weeks. And now all kinds of extra things have to be done because Susie never had this in the Saxypuddle High School, and, who ever heard of reading *that* before senior year? They never do where Janine came from. So poor B.B. is all took up teaching what he never had to learn in his days.

The opera was here and both Nordica and Alice Neilson sang; more yet, Nordica acted. B.B. sat with his row of children and stretched his eyes and ears and listened with all his might; it was such a long time since he has heard anything very nice. B.B. has not said it was "Les Hugenots" with the murdering last act omitted.

Mademoiselle is very sorry L.B. is all sick abed, which she hopes he ain't by this time.

Is L.B. thinking about rustling a new job for next year or of perhaps taking the veil at K.H.? If he takes the veil, B.B. will come too, only he would prefer it in a really truly Roman convent where you say prayers in Latin and know even less about why you do things. Besides, think of the hair shirt B.B. would be always wearing and thereby saving laundry bills.

B.B. has Lincoln's birthday for to suck his thumb all day if he likes and if Lincoln would only be home on a respectable day like Friday, B.B. would p'raps go visit his little brother. Anyway, it will be sometime soon when L.B. most would like it. Are any plans made yet for Spring Vacation?

A Big Bear Hug from B.B.

JOHN G. LOVE
Wolton, Wyo.,
February 7, 1908

Dear Miss Waxham,

I got home to the ranch tonight with two four-horse loads of building material and found two batches of mail awaiting me, including your letter. I am indeed sorry to hear of your being sick and I trust that long before this you are well and enjoying life once more. Poor Big Bear is indeed unlucky. I do hope that she is all right once more and that her misfortunes have come to an end. Did Miss Chipman go back to Boulder?

I am afraid, "little girl," that you would make a dismal failure trying to look fierce and saying "Brrr," for that would be out of your line entirely. Yes, I would be a good deal better employed in writing to you than gambling. It was my first time and it will be my last. At that time, I did not know where you had gone, so I could not very well write. Had I known, I would not have written anyway, but I would have been in Denver the next day.

There was a fire in Lander and Collins the tailor and his wife were burned out of house and home. A lady was taking up a subscription to help them get a start again and I donated my winnings. They got together about six hundred dollars and gave it to Mrs. Collins. That night she eloped with a gambler, one who follows that for a living. I hope that the money will do her more good than it would me.

Now, "little girl," you say, "Don't gossip with anyone. What constitutes gossip? When asked a direct question, I cannot very well remain mute. I do not think that you want me to tell deliberate lies. If I do not write and explain some of the queries that are propounded, I will tell you one or two of them when I see you and tell you just how I answered them to see if you think that I erred.

The weather here has been warm and pleasant and there is not very much snow left at present.

I am adding another room to this house. It is $16\frac{1}{2} \times 17\frac{1}{2}$ feet with one double window, one single window, a fireplace and a porch. After I get it fixed up to suit me, it will be nothing grand, but it will be comfortable. Then if Fate decrees that you must say no, I will say goodbye to it and travel, for there will no longer be any incentive to get money ahead. I have plenty for all my wants as long as I live.

I did think of selling the sheep, just keeping the ranch,

George Rushton, John Love's friend and employee, handling a horse-drawn scraper during the construction of the dam at the Love ranch.

the cattle and the horses, but I finally decided to keep the wooly fellows for a while longer. I could have gotten over four thousand dollars for them. If they die off, I will wish that I had sold them, for all the money that I have is tied up here in this ranch and livestock. I have to be in Lander on the 10th to see about getting more land. I have used all of my rights except the right under the Stone & Timber Act and I am going to use that. Then there are still another 320 acres that I want. One quarter section is a meadow with a little spring on it that I have under fence; the other quarter is farming land below my big dam.

I am having a new sheep wagon built for my own special use so that if I want to go to the mountains or the "Park," I can go in comfort. (In place of *I*, it really ought to be *we*, because, "little girl," I always think of it as *we* when I am contentedly building air castles. I have a good deal of satisfaction in building them and get a good deal more work done than I otherwise would do.)

I wish that it was June, that your school was out and that you were once more in the West again. It certainly will be a great relief to me to know that you are once more safely back in Denver away from that miserable damp, cold place.

So you think that I deserve to be soundly berated for not going to the Mills' ranch for Christmas. Perhaps I do. However, I was being ill. I was not out of bed until three o'clock on Christmas day.

With best wishes for your welfare and happiness I remain
Yours Sincerely,
John G. Love

John Love dreamed of making his part of the Wyoming prairie bloom with hay meadows, grain fields, fruit orchards, and shade trees, with water from the dams and irrigation system he planned to build. He applied for his homestead on December 7, 1897, and it was granted on August 5, 1905, signed with a flourish by President Theodore Roosevelt. The smaller of his two planned dams across Muskrat Creek was completed sometime in 1907. It was about 700 feet long with a maximum height of 15 feet. Unfortunately, it proved inadequate, so he filed a reservoir application on May 28, 1908 to be completed two years thence, September 1, 1910 (later extended to December 31, 1911). Its dimensions were to be: top length, 767 feet; bottom length, 710 feet; top width, 10 feet; bottom width, 110 feet; height, 20 feet. The final version, however, was much larger. The cost was estimated at $3,500.

The dams were to consist of steel headgates, clay cores, with rip rapped earth and rocks on the sides. A rough estimate of the volume of the earth and rock is about a million cubic feet (37,000 cubic yards). No record was kept of how many men and horses were used, or how much equipment, such as fresnos and scrapers. No motorized earth-moving equipment was known at that time. An idea of the effort involved in the construction of these dams may be reached if one considers that a fresno load was about one cubic yard, a scraper held less than half a cubic yard, and that the clay core of the dam had to be carefully selected, then hauled many hundred yards by fresno or wagon before it was tamped down.[4]

John Love's letters for the next thirteen months are missing.

ETHEL P. WAXHAM
Kemper Hall, Kenosha, Wis.
March 1, 1908

Wolton, Wyo.

Dear Mr. Love,

The only time that I seem to have for writing letters is study hour—now—and it puts me in such a villainous frame of mind that it would be better, I am afraid, if I didn't write at all.

It is foolish, isn't it, to bother, because these little imps never want to study, and it is foolish to care whether they ever learn anything or not. I am quite out of love with the profession at present, and make faces at Kemper Hall behind its back. Nothing has happened for ever so long—we haven't even had a Saint Day. I go to chapel once on Sunday, and once or twice every other day. Sister Mary Elise plays the organ instead of Miss Lentz, and oh, how she mangles the hymns! We had a truly pitiful performance this evening—the organ going or stopping at its own free will, and we, faltering after, or gaining courage and going along before.

There were three different snows on the ground and another is prophesied for tomorrow—which is, I suppose, a sure sign that spring will come in due season.

Big Bear is better—I have written her to come and spend next Sunday with me, and only hope that she will accept. Things aren't "stale, flat and unprofitable" when she is about.

The tale of your winter doings sounds energetic and interesting—and the new sheep wagon ought to be attractive. Have you given the Mills people their chance to explain things to you yet? Friends are too valuable to let go their way for uncertainty.

Sunday

Study hour was not quite long enough to let me finish this letter to you, and now things are quite different. We had a heavy cold rain last night that froze the trees, leaving them encrusted with silver, and the ground like a frozen lake. The barberries are a lovely red through their coating of ice. Kenosha was never so lovely before. For that reason, I was glad to have had two visits today—one from Big Bear and one from my father. He appeared this morning, we had dinner together, and he disappeared this afternoon—leaves Chicago early tomorrow morning. His latest hobby is ever so interesting; it is carbon dioxide snow for removing birth-marks, and he has been wonderfully successful with the cases that he has had, and more are waiting for him.[5]

My own hobbies are not nearly as interesting. I wish a splendid hobby might come my way. I am merely pounding copper for an electric light shade, and making a new rug of lovely greens and yellows that make you think of a fresh bed of lettuce in spring.

School is over the first week in June—would that it were that time now! I want to go west—

Sincerely yours,
Ethel P. Waxham

NORA DUNN
Oakland, Calif.,
March 27, 1908

My dear Ethel,

Your letter brought smiles of joy to my frowning brow, and I decided to send you a line in answer even though I have nothing of interest to say.

My dream of spending a summer in Denver is fast fading, as sister has decided to spend her vacation in Texas on the ranch, to be fresh for next season, in preference to playing her engagement with the Baker Co. in Denver.[6] For her sake I am glad, as she needs a rest, and enjoys horseback riding and fresh air of the prairie life.

You say "stale, flat, and unprofitable, seems the teaching profession"—yes, I fear I too find it so. Perhaps I have not resources enough within myself to make this word-of-one-syllable-existence joyous. I am growing rusty; I do not read, or even think. I just eat supper, then drop into bed, read a while—and sleep.

I was very happy the last weekend in paying a visit to college, and even though things are in a very "up-roarious" state just now, I felt as though I had gone back to my own college days again, with the blue hills calling to me 'mid the starshine, and the pines whispering of old, fond memories, buried now beneath two years of sordid chalk dust and addition. The meadow larks sang so gaily I laughed aloud and skipped as of old. I laid aside my professional (in)-dignity and poured out all my absurd enthusiasms into the waiting gold of hosts of daffodils—the roses, my one-time playmates, had not bloomed.

Did I ever tell you, dear, that once in my Springtime, I gave a man—no just a pure hearted little boy—a rose? I was rehearsing "Sylvia," and I flung him a "Gold of Ophir" blossom as he passed me. I forgot all about the incident. Then came earthquake and fire, and a year afterward I heard that in the terror of the trembling earth and the mighty blaze, the boy thought of and saved but one thing—a with-ered rose—a "Gold of Ophir." I was truly happy, I who so love the roses. I have told you this because I thought it rather a pretty incident—but there is no end to the story. The boy grew older, and doubtless the blossom, faded and fallen, was thrown away. But ever in my soul there will be the fragrance of golden roses.

Why isn't it always Springtime? With daffodils bloom-ing, one doesn't miss the roses.

Where will you be in June? I expect now to go to New York to see Mama, whom I have not seen since the earth-quake. I thought if you should be near Chicago some time after June 19—when my school closes—we might have a visit.

The thought of you makes the world bright,

for,

Nora

ETHEL P. WAXHAM
Kemper Hall, Kenosha, Wis.
April 3, 1908

Wolton, Wyo.

Dear Mr. Love,

It is already the third of April here in Kenosha—*"tertio di ante monas Aprilis,"* as I make my children say in Latin. These are for you busy days, I suppose, from now until June. I hope that the weather will be more favorable than it was last year at this time—and that the dam and the currant bushes and the ducks will all grow marvellously.

We are counting the days until spring vacation now. Louise Dudley's sister Ann has invited all of our "happy family" to visit her in Kentucky, and I am going. There are an orchard, and a baby, and an old horse, among other attractions. The horse I am going to ride, unless he is too stout, and if he is too stout, we will drive him until he is thin. Ann lives in the country, and Kentucky country in April is very alluring.

Kenosha is barely beginning to show signs of spring—the last sign was the taking up of the boardwalk, and uncovering the vines. The other signs have been here for several weeks, without any change—pussy willows, robins, grackles, and the faintest green in the grass. I have looked vainly so far for blue birds or red-winged black birds. Gardening I recommenced today. Several weeks ago, I planted some flowers in a little pot for the Latin room, but someone ran away with the pot before anything came up. So today, having given up all hope of its return, I planted more flowers, but kept them here in my room. They are to be tiny little blue flowers— Ageratum. Three large yellow tulips I have too, in a green vase, and the room is sweet with their fragrance.

Did I tell you why I am pounding copper just now? For a wedding present that must be ready by June. Present is to be a sconce to hold two candles, and it is very elaborate. The

Ethel Waxham. April 18, 1908.

vacation will be a grand time for pounding, and I have more things planned than I can ever accomplish.

Kenosha has gone wild about roller skates. It is worth one's life to cross the sidewalk when the youngsters are flying about. It will be a wonder if we are not all driven to it in self-defense. Even now at ten o'clock, the boys are scraping over the sidewalks under my window.

I'll find out the Kentucky address from Louise tomorrow, and send it to you, for Kemper Hall usually fails to forward mail, and I should be glad to hear from you during the vacation. Holidays begin the sixteenth, and last for ten days or two weeks, no one knows which.

Goodnight to you from
Ethel Waxham

MARCIA CHIPMAN
Jamaica Plain, Mass.,
April 25, 1908

Kemper Hall, Kenosha, Wisc.

Dear little Stiddy—

Your most welcome letter brought unwelcome news. I had counted on having you at my wedding—on June fourth, sixth, or eighth—I shall decide today. Phoebe, is there no hope that you will repent? How can I take the plunge without your parting words, "Be always kind and true."

Have I told you about my four little cousins, who live in Newton (with incidentally) their father and mother? They are pretty; they are loveable; they are blond; they are to lead me down the (aisle) living room carpet to Mr. George,[7] waiting in a bay window. First, a fat cherub of eleven in white, carrying a basket of sweet peas; following her, two older sisters of thirteen and fifteen, both the same height but varying widths; then the oldest, nearly seventeen. The bride is to wear a veil, with a booful non-destructable wreath of orange blossoms, guaranteed to make anyone presentable. Gown simple white batiste—but pretty lace—Mudder's choice (and Marcia's) three inches wide train only twenty inches from its first introduction to the living room carpet. Cunnin is to give me away, and only a few choice spirits are to be present. Are you penitent? One more item. The bride is *happy, happy,* she can't 'spress it. She must try.

Boulder was so surprised, Phoebe!

I am going to board for six months. Mr. George has bought land next to Mr. Pease's house. We may not build till next year. I want to see my stiddy.

Ever Leisurely,
Marcia

ETHEL P. WAXHAM
K.H., Kenosha, Wis.,
11 May, 1908

Wolton, Wyo.

Dear Mr. Love,

I am sorry that my not writing to you has troubled you—
but I have had no letter to answer until the one today.
Perhaps you wrote to me in Kentucky, although Louise says
that no letters came to me there. The vacation turned out
quite otherwise than it was planned, for just at the last
moment when I was about to start with Louise, a telegram
came from my father saying that my brother-in-law, Will
Shattuc, was dead. So I went home instead, and I was very
glad to be there to take some share of the responsibility and
work of the time that was so hard for Vera. She is only a year
and a half older than I, and is left with a little family.*
For the present she is living close beside Will's father and
mother, for Will was an only child and they feel his loss very
deeply.

The days seem to go still more slowly now that I am back
again at Latin, although by this time we have almost reached
Idus Marias.† If Pater comes to the American Medical Association in Chicago on the first of June, I shall stay over a week
or so and visit some of our old friends near Chicago, and not
reach Denver until the fifteenth of June or a little later. It is
miserable weather for a person who is used to sunshine. For
two weeks now there have been only two days with sunshine,
and no rain. The leaves are only just putting in an appearance
on the trees, and we see flowers still only in our mind's eye.

I hope that Punch and Papoose were not among the four
horses that died. It is a great pity about the sheep—they
have a precarious sort of existence at best, haven't they? I

---

*Vera Waxham Shattuc was left with one small child, Robert, and was expecting a
   second.
†The Ides of May.

read in the Denver papers while I was at home about the poor wool market this year. Will you sell the wool just the same as usual? Best wishes for the lambing—you must be in the middle of it now—and for you.

Her next letter was dated June 1.

There are two letters of yours before me—both unanswered—but I was looking for time to write before the first one came. Now will you believe in the doctrine of free grace? And the time that has come is little better than nothing— the tail end of a Sunday evening after a week of examination days and as a grand climax, high tea. Whenever I tried to write the girls would come in to see me because it is the last Sunday.

Pater will reach Chicago tomorrow probably—It depends largely upon his plans what time I get to Denver—though Louise Dudley and I have concocted a wild goose scheme for going abroad that will probably come to nothing. Truth is, we are quite tired out.

Tomorrow is Field Day, awarding of prizes and so on; then come the Greek play, and little and big commencement. After that, I leave to visit Mrs. Wood at Winnetka for the few remaining days of the Medical Association. Denver address is 1425 Washington Street. If I do not come back to Denver soon, I will let you know. Pater has some idea of visiting for a while in Rockford, Illinois. But his work keeps him very busy just now and he may not be able to spare the time. This is just a note to say "how do you do."

Hastily yours,
Ethel P. Waxham

7

DENVER: 1908

The Kemper Hall experience was at an end and Ethel again returned to
Denver, to a new address this time, where a more complex set of
household responsibilities awaited her—the care of her newly widowed
sister Vera, young nephew Robert, and her two-and-a-half-year-old half
sister Ruth, whose rather sudden arrival and previous whereabouts are
never explained. Ethel Waxham's poem "Night Within Doors" reflects
some of the pressures of this period.

Some of her friends were abandoning their careers as teachers to
become housewives, some were continuing to pursue their academic
goals, some were going abroad to become well-rounded, and some were
merely trying to earn a living in their chosen fields. As Mr. Hyde had
predicted, Ethel seemed to bear on her own back her share of the "world-
burden" and feel in her own heart her part in the "world-sorrow" in
normal experience within the home, the shop, and the market.

ETHEL P. WAXHAM
1425 Washington St.,
Denver, Colo.
June 12, 1908

Wolton, Wyo.

Dear Mr. Love,

It is not my turn to write! But I am answering one of the
letters of yours that have not been answered, perhaps.

My father came [to Chicago] for the American Medical
Convention, and he and I came home together—I had to

miss most of the Convention, much to my sorrow, for the doctors did everything to give their wives or daughters or sisters a good time. I could only go to a reception at the Art Institute. Pater wanted to stay to see an operation by the celebrated German, Dr. Jansen, so we left on Friday. Big Bear and Louise Dudley came to see me off, and Pater took us to dinner at a place called the Tip-top Inn on the twelfth story, perhaps, of a tall building on Michigan Avenue. We felt as if we were taking dinner on the stage, the setting was so theatrical, with the view of the lake through the latticed windows, and the ivy winding about the pillars—artificial ivy, I am afraid. Sunday morning we reached home, and nothing has happened of particular interest since.

Before leaving Kenosha, Louise and I went to Chicago to visit a girl who is to be married in August. Her mother must have been preparing for the event ever since she was born, judging from the quantities of linen and silver and china that are to be hers, without speaking of the clothes for the trousseau. Her mother is an inveterate collector of porcelain vases, tea pots, odd plates, tea sets, and so on, and delighted in showing some of the things to us, and telling where they all came from. She said that she had so much of it that she could serve six dozen people without changing a dish. We saw enough to stock a good sized shop, and some pieces that were worth several hundred dollars. Never saw a woman with that hobby before—or at least to such an extent.

Marcia was married during the first week of June, near Boston, to one of the professors in the University [of Colorado]. I was sorry not to be able to go there, but expect to see her before long because she is going to be in Boulder, where Mr. George has a lot, and is going to build.

My sister Faith is going to Colorado Springs to visit, probably in a week or so, and to the mountains for a rest. "Domestic duties" are coming my way!

Goodbye and good wishes
from Ethel Waxham

HELEN WATSON[1]
East Braintree, Mass.,
June 15, 1908

[Forwarded to 1425 Washington St., Denver, Colorado.]

Dear Ethel,

I am glad that you are still the writer of official communications for that College Settlement Association and that I did forget to pay my dues, for you had to write me. Now I dare write you and tell you how ashamed of myself I am for not answering your other two dandy long letters.

I suppose you know that I am studying at Johns Hopkins Medical School. It is just splendid, the work is and the school. The other students and the Teachers and the hospital and everything. I never was so supremely happy in my life so continuously I mean, as I am just studying medicine as hard as I can.

One of the medical school girls says she is going to write up her entire correspondence after she has her office and is waiting for patients, and I kind of had a similar vague hope concerning this same letter, but I am glad now that I have started three years sooner.

There are only four girls in my class, but one of them is a Holyoke girl just about my size and age and just enough brighter to keep me always trying to keep up but never quite doing it.

Our classmate Rachel, as I suppose you know, *is* as happy as larks. She has her own little house just exactly as she wants it and she is what she has always longed to be—a most respected and loved lady of leisure. Washing dishes is leisure if you can do it when and how you please.

Do you know, Ethel, I just can't imagine you as enjoying teaching in such an eminently respectable school as I hear yours is. I know you must have loved the wilds better and I hope you can get to them on your vacation. Pearl [sic] Strohm has gone abroad with 3 other school teachers and Florence

Woodruff is fluttering up and down the country to her heart's content—doing what pleases her most—the social act.

I just can't tell you how much I like what I am doing or I would. I am enclosing two dollars for I have a faint suspicion I didn't pay my dues last year either—anyway, it won't do any harm to the cause.

Wish I could see you again, Ethel—If you ever come East, do let me know and if I ever come West, I'll write to you when—

Lovingly yours—
Helen Watson

ETHEL P. WAXHAM
Denver, Colo., 24 June, 1908

Wolton, Wyo.

Dear Mr. Love—

Your letter telling of your trials and tribulations of late has just come. And the moral of that is—"what! Don't trust fickle fortune." Wish myself, that the good lady would smile oftener.

This note is to say "glad to see you, when you come." and that we are on the verge of moving. It happens from the twenty-ninth to the thirty-first or thereabouts, and we go to 1364 Marion St. My small half-sister, Ruth is now with us, and she needs a back yard and other accessories. Presto! We move!

Sincerely yours,
Ethel P. Waxham

DONALD MCLEAN[2]
Hay Creek, Oregon,
June 25, 1908

Dear Ethel—

I was surprised to know that you knew about lambing. No one else at home seemed to have ever conceived of such a thing on earth. I wish you might be in it for a month. It would be judged highly improper here for a lady even to go near a lambing camp. There are a lot of white washy conventions here which are the more futile because they haven't the intelligent understanding of conditions to back them up. And all the sticklers who wear these undergarments don't seem to consider that there are even seasons when they should be shed or lighter ones worn.

I read Harper Scott in *Colliers*. I wish there were more of that kind of story. It's the kind I need all the time and can never get enough of. I was going to send it to you, but before I did I got a letter from Mother that showed she was unsettled and I sent it to her. She's never mentioned it. But I know it did her good.

I just got a lot of pleasure out of "From Generation to Generation"—a short article in the July *American*. It gave me scientific facts, too, for several more points in my "Equalization Theory." (I wonder if you remember my theory. You didn't seem to care for it as you did for "The Conservation of Souls" one.) I think you'd like the article.

Don't you want to take a walk with me? I'm enclosing a map of my route and if you feel that you'd like to, I think it would be great. You could meet me at Wamsutter, Rawlins or Baggs, Wyoming, or any place along the Moffat Road and we could walk into Denver. It would take a week or two. I shall leave here October the 5th and go to Wamsutter, and from there along the line of my pen on the map to Denver. I have to be home the last week in October as I begin the Short Course Nov. 1 at Ft. Collins [Colorado]. It will be the glorious time of year then, when living is too good and walking through the fall-tinted mountains in the crisp air is heavenly. You better come. I mean it.

I must get busy now. I hope that Vera is better and that Ruth won't chafe too much.

Donald McLean

Enclosed is a map showing the "Little Snake River Canal System and Land to be Irrigated in Routt County, Colorado" and the route Donald intended to walk—at least 250 miles!

MAUD THOMPSON[3]
Norfolk, Conn., June 30, 1908

Dear Baby,

Tell me about the Greek Play. You got it up, of course. I did not know you had enough Greek pupils. I am so glad you have left Kenosha. By the way, did you know that the Socialists were strong in Kenosha? Did you know Harvey Brown? Why don't you look up the local in Denver. The address of the Secretary is A. H. Floaten, 1026 Broadway, Denver.

The "unpleasant" thing is that I have no money and no job. I don't mind not having a job for a few months, but I do mind not having any money nor any job for next year. It is not merely the anxiety about living, but also, or chiefly, the sense of failure, the fact that with all my preparation, I am not in demand. I suspect that you are not unlike me in this. In every profession, but especially in teaching, the demand is for the conventional. I guess we are in the wrong business. I am sure you are, because you don't like to teach and it weighs on you. I like it, always have, so that I think I would be a success under The Cooperative Commonwealth. I am as well equipped as the average teacher—better? perhaps, and I can teach, but I shall never be "successful" in the sense of getting well-paid and responsible positions. Perhaps I can't even make a living. I am still convinced that you should write and not teach, but with you as with me, it is not a question of "should" but of "can." Oh, the curse of struggling for a living! You and I are both ready and anxious to *work* for our living, but we are not ready to *fight* for it—and no one should be. I wish we could be together next year. If you hear of a job in Denver—not just Greek, but anything—let me know.

Did you get the paper with an account of May Day and what did you think of yours truly? I have an article coming out in the *Union Advocate* this week and am working on another. But I have no real working blood just now.

Why is the baby* with *you?* Does the baby's mother give

*Ethel's half sister Ruth.

her up willingly? Or was she awarded to her father? You know I feel pretty strongly on the rights of motherhood. Besides, I don't think *you* ought to have the burden. It is too much for you with the housework. You are not big enough nor strong enough and I am afraid you will break down. I wish I were there to help you with the housework. I would decline the baby, if she is spoiled.

If you were here we might go off to the woods, by the purling brook, and be quiet or talk as we chose. The country is as lovely as tho' no one had ever noticed it before and I have books and nothing to do but read and look.

I am going to write to the mother of the "ideal man." She is a rare and wonderful woman—no wonder she has an attractive son. Though, as he himself says, he is not worth one year of her—he thought it a waste that she should have borne him when she might have been writing books! She doesn't.

Good bye, Fairy-mine

M.T.

P.S. I prefer Bryan to Taft—don't you?

Maud continues in a letter dated July 6:

I hate to think what you are probably doing this warm morning. Cooking—which I know you detest—and bathing the baby, which is at least fatiguing. For no reason at all I am exhausted. Yesterday, on the glorious Fourth, we did nothing at all exciting. Fired off a few crackers in the morning, tried to do a bit of work, and in the afternoon went to a local ball-game which proved rather a bore. Followed a band concert on the Village green which might have been interesting but wasn't. What a Socialist celebration one could have! By the way, Kid, will you have a vote in Nov. if you stay in Denver? or shall you have lost it by non-residence? You will vote for Gene* of course? How it makes me rage that I can't!

*Eugene Victor Debs was nominated for the Presidency in 1904 and 1908 by the Socialist Party.

What fun you will have this week! I hope John Mitchell won't take the V.P. nomination. I admire him and don't want him in that crowd. Debs more and more gains my admiration. In the *Daily* for July 3, he has two fine articles— one about women in Socialism. It is his delicate and loving spirit that I delight in. He reminds me very much of Jesus.

You don't attempt the washing and sweeping? Be careful, Dear.

Is Vera to come to you when you move? How is she mentally? When is her baby expected? What a burden you all have just now! Three babies! How do you get on with your housework? Make it as easy as you can. Don't be too ambitious. Isn't it likely you will stay with your father next year? I suppose he needs you, and perhaps you would like it better than teaching. Tell me what the oculist says. The muscular trouble is serious, but can be cured, as I know.

I have been rereading Stringer and like it even more. Also am working on the book—law in regard to Mohammedan women just now. I have lots to say to you—yet—but back aches (for reasons) so I will quit and write again—after I hear from you!

Maud

BIG BEAR [FLORENCE RISLEY]
Boston, July 15, 1908

Belovedest Little Bear,

Once there was a big brown bear what decided he would surely have time to find a new hollow tree cause all the honey bags were sucked dry in the old woods and besides he wanted a new kind of honey. So he hunted and hunted. . . . Bymeby when he had just made up his mind to be an anarchist bear and burn up all the trees so there wouldn't be any houses for anybody, he found instead possible little deserted cave what is called 29 Cottage Street and is most deliciously commodious and what appeals still more to B.B.'s instincts— clean. Nice Brer Man what owns it has put new thatch and new grey coat on outside to say nothing of nice new clean trimmings all over inside and spring new bathroom with a tub exactly the size of B.B.'s hind foot—fits him as if it had been made to measure.

Meanwhile, Brer Bear is in lodgings polishing his toenails and combing his ears and otherwise passing the time until Brer Man says can move into new cave. . . .

Win [Hawkridge] came sauntering by to find us one day in most becoming new clothes which it pleased her to have us notice. Win is taking vocal lessons—study of law did not touch her appetite, and she is going to Europe in November with 2 other girls.

Bad, most Baddest Littlest Bear to go spoil "booful" eyes. That comes of wasting those killing glances on the vulgar heads of K.H. children.

Who is Baby Ruth? and how did little sister like kimono? and do shoes fit the baby boy?

I 'spose you have heard all about commencement from a dozen sides?

Want to hear any more?

Friday night, the seniors gave *Cyrano de Bergerac*—it was rather heavy, but extremely well done—of course, that meant Cyrano was good enough to carry it off. D. Hazard was the player within the play—a comfortable mountain with a thunderous voice.

Saturday morning a ragged remnant of 1905 gathered at Agora to practice songs and have picnic brunch.

Saturday afternoon Garden party and dancing. The senior dancing was the myth of Demeter. The faculty recommended them not to do it, but they went ahead.

Sunday, Goldy L. and Win and I blew ourselves to a Sunday dinner at the Inn and Win's father came out in his auto and took us for a drive in the afternoon. Evening, vespers with lufly music such as I have not heard these many moons.

After supper 1905 shook off its fine fur and adorned in petticoats and sweaters it sallied forth to serenade. Again

B.B. avoided Alumnae luncheon—when he comes back for 10th 1905 will have place of sufficient honor to warrant his parting with all of $1.50.

L. B. Hurry up and make eyes all well and let the Pater feed you on beefsteaks so when you come visit B.B. you can dig garden in his back yard and make beautiful copper improvements on the interior furnishings of 29 Cottage Street.

B.B. is daily holding herself in readiness for the summons that cottage is ready. In the meantime has read nice fat biography of Aubrey de Vere what B.B. always has been liking for some time and Coventry Patmore's nice poems. If house isn't in a hurry B.B. will take to reading philosophy and no mistake.

The real reason, dear Little Bear, for this painfully long letter is that Mlle makes me write to her in French and naturally my powers of expression having no exit to her, I have to explode on you. If you will hurry up and write, I'll promise to tell you all about the apple tree in our new back yard and other things maybe.

Bye—a 20 mule team hug from B.B.

Enclosed with the following letter was a newspaper clipping of an editorial entitled "The Socialist Program," from the *Detroit News*.

MAUD THOMPSON
Norfolk, Conn., Jul. 17, 1908

My very dear Baby,

That adorable letter must be answered at once, tho my editor is expecting an article which I have not yet begun. It is on women's wages. The wages we get from teaching are certainly not commensurate with the exertion, but is there any trade we can enter which will treat us better? I don't know. I am rather inclined to think that for the same amount of effort, we get more than the business woman. What do you think? But the real trouble is not wages but the difficulty of getting a job, the necessity of begging for one. The stupidity of a society which does not care to use well-trained workers! For we *are* well trained, willing to work hard, and competent to do our work. Yet instead of society organizing to utilize such workers, and assigning them a field where they could live and serve others, it is left to chance and one's living is dependent on whether one is a member of an "evangelical church"! Yes, the Chicago agency told me that there was very little hope of getting me anything to do, because I was not a church member! That is economic justice! And the public schools shut me out because I am a socialist. I enclose a clipping thereon by my good friend, the *Detroit News.* Please return as I have no other copy. But how can you help working for money if you are going to live? As you are now, you are doing very hard work for board and lodging aren't you? I would not want to have you be your father's housekeeper only, for life. I want you to write and I would to heaven I could give you leisure to do it. Don't try now, for you are working too hard and are not in physical condition. But sometime you must. That you are not sure of yourself is due wholly to the mauling, physical and mental, that you got at Kenosha. You will recover from it. As you get more used to housework and learn to systematize it, it will be easier.

The "Ideal man's" mother is Eliza Burt Gamble, author of *Evolution of Woman.* You read that, did you not? She is perhaps 60, and a sufferer from rheumatism. She cannot walk at all or stand and suffers agonies much of the time. Yet she never talks of herself and is always enthusiastic and cheerful, one of the most optimistic of persons. I suppose it would not be possible for her to endure it this way, if it were not for the devotion of her son and husband and the care and comfort with which they are able to surround her. They are all theosophists and socialists. She is very fine looking, with white hair, brown eyes and a strong face. She is wonderfully refined and courteous, sensitive to every impression. She is indeed one of deep impartial thought. She is self-educated, not a college woman, and that has been a handicap to her in her work. She can do very little now, of course, but live and endure. She writes for the papers now and then.

If you fear that your people would oppose your interest in the socialists, it need not be known. If you go to the Denver Local and tell them that you can't come out openly, but want to do what you can, they will welcome you and keep it quiet. That is a part of socialist honor, and has to be done often to keep people from losing their employment. I want you to *join* anyway. It is only 25 cents a month and I want you with us. The names are not published. Have you seen about those heroic women who were imprisoned in Los Angeles for speaking on the street? They were put with prostitutes, *diseased,* and refused disinfectants. They refused to give bail, as did the men, so as to draw attention to the infamous wrong. It makes me feel so small and selfish.

I was amused at your asking if I read the Republican platform. What kind of a heathen do you think I am? Wasn't it "buncum?" The Democratic platform was at least better. I hope that Taft will win, however, because it will hasten on Socialism. I am anxious lest Bryan draw the Labor vote from Socialism. Have you seen Roosevelt on Socialism? I have lost all admiration for R. but it is not safe to say it here, for this family positively worship him! How did you like Thomas Hall in the last *Review?* Have you read Nietzsche?

My friend George came when I was packing and worn out and sad, and he was not well, and so there was material for a scrap. He is fairly liberal, but we struck all the things we most disagreed on. Chiefly he tried to argue that I should not do Socialist speaking but should live for the sake of getting a better "place." Also he abused Socialists. So we quarrelled— silly! It was a shame of me to allow it, for he had come so far to see me and it was really my fault that we quarrelled. However, of course, he took all the blame. I am not fond of him and never can be—have had some 25 years to try! But I do respect and often like him and I appreciate his constancy to me, but his conservatism wearies and irritates me and he doesn't understand me.

Your characterisation of Noyes was good. Music but neither thought nor feeling. By the way, do you like Kipling's verse? And William Morris? I forget. I brought only two poets with me, Walt Whitman and Arthur Stringer. Is there any definite reason why you demand feeling in poetry now?

I am anxious about your eyes, Dear. Do let me know what the doctor says. Is it muscular weakness?[4] What does Vera have to live on? I am rather in the depths myself lately, chiefly over the bread and butter question. If I can't get a teaching position, I shall have to get what I can, a shop position? I won't be dependent. No, death first.

But meantime life is pleasant except for that cloud. I am riding, playing tennis, writing, reading. And rereading Thucydides. I wish we could read together. And most of all, I wish we could go down by the brook in the birch woods, and lie on the moss and read poetry and talk. Oh, I do miss you, my precious child!

> Yours for the revolution,
> Maud Thompson

John Love made a trip to Denver.

> ETHEL P. WAXHAM
> 1364 Marion St., Denver, Colo.
> July 21, 1908

Wolton, Wyo.

Dear Mr. Love—

Your letters from Cheyenne and from Moneta reached me last week. And I suppose that your deserted gloves have rejoined you by this time.

Faith is away; Robert has the measles; "Boots"* is an imp, cookery fails and it is a weary world. (For authority see line 1, verse four, hymn 7, Episcopal prayer book, used by the Sisters of Kemper Hall and the rest of the church.)

Marcia's good example has stimulated us into drawing plans for a bungalow-in-the-air, and Pater has even gone so far

*Ruth.

as to talk them over with a flesh-and-blood architect. But while the lots exist near Montclair, the boulevard is still a day-dream; while *we* might live on a daydream, an automobile couldn't, so I suppose the scheme is not practicable yet.

There was a wind here yesterday which would have been a credit to Boulder; a slam-bang wind that broke one of our glass doors to shivereens—nice word? All the autos were spinning by and people running for shelter and horses making for home, black clouds, tons of dust flying about—and no rain after all. A sort of dry cleaning process that cleared the air quite as effectively as rain. Ruth howled throughout. I sometimes fear that she has "inner troublins" like a poor lady of the New York settlement.

> Dearth of news, so farewell—
> Ethel P. Waxham

ETHEL P. WAXHAM
Denver, Colo.,
15 August, 1908

Moneta, Wyo.

[Forwarded to Shoshoni, Wyoming.]

Dear Mr. Love—

Your letters arrived some time ago, and I was truly sorry to hear the bad news about the berry bushes and flowers and the garden. I hope, however, that the sheep are doing well, and that you found your bride and groom* at the ranch, waiting, when you came back.

Faith has been away a good deal of this last month, so I have kept busy. Life isn't worth living unless things are neat and sweet and clean round about, but somehow it takes most of the living time to keep them so. I am faintly hoping that it is because I don't systematize enough.

*Mr. and Mrs. Jack Guinard.

Cooking has gone better. Tonight you should have had some of our luscious mushrooms "à la Poulette." And Monday night I made a pink dinner, with both hands, for Faith's chum and her fiancé. The cherry sherbet was a dream! And tomorrow—it's a secret, but you won't tell—there is to be "Angel Parfait" for dessert. Food isn't all names, either.

Faith's chum was married on Wednesday, so of course we had to meet the groom. He's about two inches shorter than she, Scotch, and possessed no doubt of all the virtues. But he puts his head on one side when he laughs, and curls up his fingers and toes. At least he gives one that impression. Did you ever notice how a laugh tells tales? Man is nice anyway; has house all ready waiting for Hester in Toronto with a reformed missionary for a cook, and jars of raspberry jam already on the shelves, and half a dozen Persian rugs already on the floors besides other furniture. The wedding was very pretty. Hester bought a book on "Modern Weddings," so as to have everything prim, precise and proper. So 'twas. Faith had the time of her life—served punch, and caught the bride's bouquet—which means you know that she is to be next of the company married.[5] We have been sleeping on wedding cake ever since, but to no avail. I dream of sewing, and teaching youngsters, but of nothing more romantic.

A countryman of yours from Rock Springs called not long ago to ask me to teach English in his high school—"it's not education they need so much as inspiration," he said. Is that complimentary or not?

And today a letter came from a lady in Washington, who has a fashionable boarding school like Kemper Hall, I suppose. Oh deary me, why doesn't somebody in Japan or Honolulu or my flamingo-on-a-coral-island write and ask for a course in world-drama or metrics? It would even be less dreary to starve in a garret a-writing verses to the moon. Cheer up—that may happen yet!

> Meanwhile goodbye and good
> wishes from
> Ethel P. Waxham

NIGHT WITHIN DOORS

Night within doors, and murmur of the rain
  Falling without, yet neither sleep nor rest
For tortured nerves aquiver from the strain
  To meet the day-long, life-long, endless quest;
Knowing for dust and ashes love is spent,
  And feverish from urging on and on
The lagging limbs and wandering thoughts intent
  On beauty dreamed of or on splendor gone.
But in the dusks of self, the captive soul
  Shrinks cowering, sick at the thought of day,
Pining for freedom from the weary stress
  Of sordid toil toward an unhoped for goal;
Or vainly beats with tired wings the gray
  Hard, adamantine bars of Consciousness.

Ethel Waxham   1908

Florence Risley was beginning a year as a graduate assistant in English at Wellesley.

> BIG BEAR [Florence Risley]
> Wellesley, Mass.,
> September 5, 1908

Belovedest Little Bear,

My hand is so horny and callous from manual labor that a pen feels like something much too delicate for my handling. Nevertheless, I take my pen in hand.

Since B.B. and family moved to Wellesley great commotion has gone on every morning in the cellar where there is a galorious work bench and indefinite supply of old boards, hard wood, soft wood, warped and knotted, all of which are being gradually turned into most wonderful things* excelling for their beauty and utility. They must be done before the first of October when the sun goes down and bears can't make any more hay.

Little Bear did not say anything about eyes in last letter.

*Household accessories.

Are they all better or must she not use them and not read any old scratchings from such as B.B? I hope she will be marvellous good and not read her prayer book too steadily for a while. Surely you must know enough by heart to tide you over until you go back to K.H.

The first week we were here I dug a patch of garden as big as a bed and for two weeks we have been eating lettuce from our own garden. Mother goes out now and then and gives the apple tree a bath and scratches its back so next year when L.B. comes to see us we'll have apples as big as your head.

Little Bear, write a nice fat letter soon to B.B., but do it with her eyes shut 'cause I would rather not have a letter in a year than help to spoil your eyes.

Bye and think up a scheme for coming to visit. B.B.

Enclosed with the following letter is a long clipping from the [torn] . . . *Socialist* (National Edition, Sept. 15, 1908) with "Hurrah!" scrawled in large letters across the top. The headline reads: "10,000 Listen to Debs Speak—Enormous Skating Rink at Portland, Ore., is crowded to the Doors—LARGE PARADE IS HELD—Ten Stops Made and Much Enthusiasm Is Shown at Every Place—(WORKERS PRESS ASSOCIATION) Portland, Ore."

MAUD THOMPSON
Norfolk, Conn.,
September 19, 1908

[Scrawled in large letters in left margin: I hate other people's clothes!!]

Dear Baby,

I am going to Detroit and I am tickled to death. Really, ever since I heard, I have been happier than all summer. It seems like home—and how I do hate change! Mrs. D. will pay me $75 a month (8 months) and I can live on that; tho, of course, I can't pay Dad what I owe him, nor save for the summer. But Dad is not in a hurry for the cash, and I am willing to trust to finding work next summer. I would rather go there than to a new place, unless it was a college position and just what I want. I am really delighted that I did not get a high school position at twice the salary! Like you, I fear I have no worldly ambition. I want to be with the people I like and do the work I like and have time for study. I won't like the teaching—have to teach some English! but it is not hard work and I shall have time for suffrage and socialism.

I have not bought any clothes for two years, but have just had three dresses given me. They belonged to a relative who died and I hate to wear them, but they are good clothes and beggars can't be choosers. My crying need is a coat. I haven't a thing, but doubtless it will be found somehow. I have two good black silk dresses (besides the one given to me) and a good crêpe de chine for the house and a grey silk that is not worn out, besides plenty of thin clothes.

I can get the rooms I had last year or those I had year before. I think I can't afford the last year rooms—$20—and shall probably take the Third Ave. ones, which I can get for $15 and *my own gas!* d[amn]! The two objections are the distance and the lack of a telephone. As I can't walk to school anyway (since my feet are crippled) it does not matter much anyway to be a bit farther but I shall miss the telephone in my work.

I am awaiting with some amusement the outcome of my affair with the editor. It is growing mightily and what will propinquity do to us? I have not thought about the "ideal man" all summer—*sic semper!* Do you remember my "sailor lad"? He is in Buffalo and has written me to visit him there.

Will probably spend Friday at Niagara with him. He is a case.

Are you interested in all this detail? Must end and go to town.

Yours as every day—Maud

ETHEL P. WAXHAM
Denver, Colo.,
15 September 1908

Moneta, Wyo.

Dear Mr. Love—

Your letter reached me today, and makes me your debtor

by still another. The days have been so full and the evenings so strangely short that I have written practically no letters during the last month. Vera is in the hospital* and little Robert has been with us. Faith has been teaching in Kindergarten again. A little Black girl has been here helping with Robert and in the kitchen, which made things somewhat easier. But she was powerless in respect to Ruth, and could not so much as boil an egg. We hope to have Vera back by the twenty-fourth.

The State Medical Association has held its meeting in Denver during the last week. I went to the President's reception, dance, and supper with Pater. The festivities were at Lakeside Amusement Park, and best of the entertainment consisted of free tickets to most of the attractions. I am afraid that Pater wanted to do more in that line than I. We compromised on a launch ride and sight of a celebrated picture. Supper was supremely Dutch—a bottle of beer apiece along with the wienerwursts and rolls and cheese served in regular banquet style. Pater and I were ashamed of the Doctors, for they usually have fine banquets.

It is late for me, though not "long past midnight," so this must be merely a short note to say "why be lonely?" Analyze the sentiment, until pouf! It is gone!

I have no position yet for next year, though if a very enticing offer came from Japan or Honolulu or Greece I fear that I should not refuse.

In haste, I am

Sincerely yours,
Ethel P. Waxham

In a letter dated September 30, she continues:

This letter must be only a note to tell you not to hope for the impossible when you come down to Denver for your dentistry work.

It has been a busy week, with a dressmaker for Faith here, and Vera. Besides it is preserving season. I like preserves. But

*William Hugh Shattuc was born September 3, 1908.

the thought of putting them up makes me quail. When old housekeepers talk them over in such a learned fashion, my inexperience grows and grows in my mind's eye until it darkens the landscape. Well,—there are pears on the top pantry shelf, and watermelon pickles and preserves, and tomato preserves, and crabapple jelly, and Waldorf Astoria relish—due to the exertion of my two hands.

We had ducks today, ourselves, that a friend of Pater's sent him. On the strength of five ducks, Vera came over and we celebrated with a big dinner.

The storm that you had must have been the one that started the furnaces in Denver, and made people get out their winter clothes. It lasted several days and nights, and the frost killed the flowers, and vegetables too, I suppose.

Taft speaks in Denver tomorrow night. Pater has just asked me to go to hear him. Wish we could hear Bryan and Debs, too, all at once, so as to compare the men.

It is not late, but I am tired. Tomorrow will be another crabapple jelly-day, too. So good-night.

Ethel P. Waxham

LOUISE DUDLEY[6]
Georgetown, October 14, 1908

Ethel,

Sick? dead? wounded? teaching at Boulder? tired? dreaming? You see I won't believe but that there is some good excuse for your not having written to me for so long.

Don't know yet when we sail. Jean, my traveling companion, spends five months in Berlin and I suppose that means that I will put in the greater part of my winter there. My! but I wish you were going with me!!

I ought to be terribly busy getting ready to go, but have not worked myself up to the point of doing anything yet. Guess it will be one grand rush at the end.

Did I write you that I am teaching a Sunday School class now? I shall be real sorry to leave it. We are studying the Psalms, and I am learning in strides almost as great as when I tutored Virgil and Cæsar. By the way, your friend Mr. Moulton's Bible has been published in one volume so it is more accessible than before. I should like to have your opinion of it when you see it. A lot of it is bosh, and a lot may be bosh that only a person better acquainted with Hebrew would recognize as such, but he does put in bit letters the things you want to know, the things the authorized versions usually hide in notes, which is a great deal.

Some of the leaves are quite brilliant, I am surprised at that for it has been so dry here, I was afraid we would have no coloring at all. Why do you suppose it is that we find nature beautiful, and why is it more satisfying than anything artificial even its dullest yellowbrowns? Is it because there *is* an absolute standard after all, or is it due to the fact that we ourselves are a part of it? Give one of the lower animals ability to appreciate beauty, would it find Nature beautiful—and how about that much discussed visitor from another world?

I am going out to Bryn Mawr tomorrow to see Dr. Brown and the few friends I have left there. I am so glad I am sailing from Phila. on that account.

The words to that Old English song I promised to write you are:

> *Here's a health to the King*
> *And a lasting peace*
> *To faction {sic} and end*
> *To wealth increase*
> *Come let's drink it while we have breath,*
> *For there's no drinking after death.*
> *And he that will this health deny—*
> *Down, Down, Down! (fortissimo)*
> *Among the dead men let him lie.*

The third stanza begins nicely, too:

> *I'm sinking {sic} Bacchus's joys I'll roll,*
> *Deny no pleasure to my soul—etc.*

243

Maybe this last is my motto, at any rate, *"carpe diem."**

Goodbye, Ethel, keep well and in good spirits this winter, and if you just can't seem to anyhow, come over to me and I will help you hunt Sethe (lethe).

Best love from Louise Dudley

ETHEL P. WAXHAM
Denver, Colo., Sunday

Moneta, Wyo.

Dear Mr. Love—

Sunday is my busy day, and I have only a few minutes tonight for letters—but I seem to owe you several!

The new dam, and the sheep, the cattle, and the horses, and the men must fill your days pretty well, with plans and work.

Did you know that Marcia's husband was State Geologist of Colorado? He has a business trip to make at Christmas time, so I expect Marcia to spend Christmas here with me, and I may go to Boulder with her afterward, for a while. Her house is going up rapidly; it has walls and flooring already. They expect to have their house warming by February. I know so much about Marcia because she was in Denver last week, and we spent about an hour together.

Arabella Draininta, the latest in the kitchen, has left. She could not wash or iron or scrub on account of her back; and she could not cook, although she thought she could. But she did admire my German! She had store curls that drooped over her ears and pinky cheeks—store pink—and she was tall and mostly bones. But she hungered for things of beauty, like the rest of us, and she did want to be strong. We almost came to tears when I told her not to come back. She liked us; she did not know what she would do if "her peoples was tough." And she has telephoned—five cents!—to know whether we will take her back. The poor girl has not even the

*Seize the day!

consciousness of some of us that we have been denied by nature, or the wistfulness that comes of knowing that we are wishing for something beyond us.

So now I am cook again. Uncle Ernest was here again today. He will be here again tomorrow for a duck dinner. Poor Vera will have to be putting the babies to bed, so she can't be here. The babies take up almost every moment of every day. I am afraid that by the time that they are grown and need what she alone can give them, she will be worn out with this work that anyone might do. And yet some people say that a child's disposition is formed during the first six months. A little training is necessary beyond that point, however I dare assert, with only one specimen from which to draw examples.

When I reached this point last night a caller interrupted me—one Donald McLean, just back from a sheep ranch in Oregon. He is anxious to start in the business himself, this fall, or take a course in some agricultural college as preliminary training.

I hope that this letter will find fine weather in Wyoming, sheep in good condition, and Mr. Love without any blues at all. Whenever you come down I shall be glad to see you. Forgot to ask Pater about the best dentist, but will let you know.

Sincerely yours,

Ethel P. Waxham

P.S. Don't read my letters until after supper. That "impossible" was entirely psychic.

ASPEN LEAVES[7]

> *O Little leaves in the uneasy wind,*
>   *Do you know sorrow, have you heard of pain,*
> *That lingering here, I dream that I may find*
>   *The meaning of your chant to wind and rain?*
> *Do I regret far, long forgotten hours*
>   *Of life like yours, where only winds astray*

Touched the tempestuous leaves and quiet flowers
Until death wandered slow along the way?

Or 'neath the trees in some life long ago
Did sorrow gently come and gently pass,
Like summer wind over the bending grass,
Did sorrow come, but leave no memory,
Only a shadow on the heart to see
The waving of green branches to and fro?

Ethel Waxham   1908

MARY B. MILLS
Red Bluff Ranch,
October 1, 1908

My dear little Girl,

Do you think we are all bad and have forgotten you? Indeed no, dear, but it has been a busy, busy household this summer. Lots of time to think and talk, but when it came to letter writing, ah me!

You have had a busy time, too, poor child. Your little letter of September 13th was welcome indeed, for I had been thinking a great deal of Big Sister. The birth of her little one was sad with no father to welcome it, but people live through such griefs. How, I don't know. They are probably at home again and little Robert with them. Was little Ruth with you, too? You must have had your hands overflowing.

Ever since the opening of the sage chicken season we have hardly been alone a single day. We would plan to have everything done so as to have the morning for letters, but it was hopeless; someone would come.

The new neighbors that are to be on the Schlichting place came last week. It will be good to get some real neighbors.

Have not seen the Schlichtings this summer. Otto and Emmons have both the scarlet fever. Haven't an idea where they could have contracted it; don't know where they intend to go.

Our other neighbors, the Ehlers, are settled at last, I

think. He committed suicide in prison and the family have gone to Greeley, Colorado to live so you see we are well rid of them at last.

You seem to have become very domestic this summer. Such an accomplished little cook. You have not forgotten how to prepare fried onions and bean soup? The former are probably taboo in the city. They used to be. You said nothing of your eyes in your last letter. We hope it is only a temporary trouble. Was it too much study or too much Latin or too much pounding on copper?

Oh yes, we heard of Mr. Love's visit. He was up to spread the news around the country.

How near we are to the election. Are you interested at all? You know we have another voter—Kathryn was twenty-one the twenty-eighth. She feels very important.

Do you know, dear, we looked longingly all summer for a letter saying you would be up. Of course, I know you were needed at home, but we did want you so much.

How about a trip abroad. Entirely given up or living in hopes?

Take good care of yourself dear, and just let the cook think she can cook, and she will surprise you. The pears haven't started to ferment, have they?

Write when you can. You are always in our hearts and minds—if we cannot write.

Ever most lovingly
Mary B. Mills

LAURA HIBBARD*
Mt. Holyoke College
South Hadley, Mass.
October 18, 1908

Dear Ethel;

It seems a very long way to "housemates" today, with you and Billy† at your respective lands' ends, and Louise on the

*Laura was now at Mount Holyoke earning her master's degree.
†Elizabeth "Billy" Williams—now Mrs. Chandler—the "Science Department" at Kemper Hall.

briney deep. It isn't quite credible yet to me that she is really gone, but once in a while the sense of adventure has come winging in and I realize it because I, too, am trying in some dim and clouded way, to go down to the sea. Off in Denver, are you feeling the need of wings today? Perhaps our wings are signaling each other and that is why I miss you so especially today. What wouldn't I give for even a "retreat" walk. We fared so well that day—do you remember? and we waxed so intelligent?

Do you want me to confess to an act frankly sentimental? For two weeks I didn't wash one of the two white and gold tea cups which still survive—solely because it was yet unwashed from one of our last tea parties. Perhaps I ought to tell you more logical things, but not to is such a comfort! All day one has to be pretending one is wise and very, very old, and one never dreams of having "sentiments." One has to live, humbly or rebelliously, in the vast impersonality of the "Ladies Collegiate."

I don't know why my pen sheds such grumbly words today, for the world is very beautiful and wee birds are singing as if it were June and presently I am going out to lie under a pine tree in the drifted red and golden leaves beneath it. The richness of this autumn beauty is a continual recompense; one oughtn't to be lonely in it, even though one would be happier were there the possibility of sharing it with someone who would care.

Things have settled into a wonderful work routine, in which one jogs more placidly. I now know my way and am not quite so much in awe of giving lectures and such! It saves time when that first vast respect for the students is over— though as a matter of fact, I still seem to be working most of the time! But sometimes it is work on the secret—do you want to know about it? I think Mr. Mutt of the London firm is going to publish Guy [of Warwick] and three other translations: Bevis [of Hampton], Havelok [the Dane], and Horn [Childe]* for me. I work on them in what would have been last year—in tea party times.

*All 14th century romance verses.

There, that's the end of me for this epistle for I have news of Kemper Hall and of Billy. Do you remember a red-headed young Shakespearean, 1907, Margaret Ervin? She has gone to Tucson and has seen Billie and met Mr. Chandler. Margaret wrote enthusiastically of them both, says they are adorable together, that they live in a "dear little flat and make everything themselves" and altogether produce in the young a desire for the same state of conjugal bliss. When do you suppose Billie will come out of her bridal seclusion and tell us a few details of herself? Perhaps you have heard already? I haven't heard a syllable since she wrote asking me to the wedding.

I want to send you an extract from Rowena Osbourne's letter. Does it not make vivid again the Mother Superior's office, and the "sins of teachers," and the little awesome figure of the Mother herself? She wrote:

"Our psychology class is another source of woe—The Mother looks over her mail while we recite and we are left to talk to thin air. There is nothing that insenses her so much as to have us say 'recite' or 'study' or 'it said in the book.' We are supposed to discuss the subject in a scientific manner, taking particular pains with our English. The result is that we are so divided between fear of using the wrong word, fear of having the wrong idea, and fear of the Mother in general, that we are reduced to a state of helpless imbecility." I think that is a really choice description.

Little Bear, it is time to say goodnight, though I don't want to. I want to find something beautiful up in the sky or down in the earth and send it to you and make you very happy. But I am glad you are not teaching—I wish you would see it that way, too!

Always faithfully yours,
Laura

ETHEL P. WAXHAM
1364 Marion Street,
Denver, Colo.
November 10, 1908

Moneta, Wyo.

Dear Mr. Love—

Paddling butter all morning and preserving apples all afternoon, and writing letters all evening, and running after my baby sister Ruth and prodding Bentra, the cook, in the "Betweenties" makes a full day, doesn't it? When I came home I found two piles of letters that needed immediate attention—not answers like, "yours of the 1st inst. received. Forward goods at once—yours truly etc.," but answers to make other people as glad as I am to get their letters. Have written to five girls and two men, and then you come. Aren't you glad, instead of waiting for eight more?

My younger sister Faith came home [from a trip East] last week, by way of a hotel in Suddington from which she sent us a postal card. The name of the hotel was "Bugg's Resort." Wouldn't you have kept your name secret if you had been Mr. Bugg, instead of naming a hotel for yourself?

There is a crisis at hand in the kitchen. Evolution is too slow. Either Bentra will reform within the next week, or, I fear, go back to Kansas with the railroad porter. Not only does she lack godliness, but also the virtue usually placed next to it. And Oh dreary me, I caaaaaaiiiinn't stand that! Hope the porter can say, "The cow is in the hammock" as often as she.

Speaking of good—I've been working eyes very hard, and read four cookbooks in four days, not to speak of other books and magazines. One book was on "The Chemistry of Cooking and Cleaning," as if one did not know beforehand which foods were carbohydrates and which nitrogenous, and why bread rises, and why after using muriatic or oxalic acid there should be an alkaline rinsing. But I did learn a few new things about washing clothes!

Mrs. Kingsland [the landlady] has found me out, in spite of locked doors and closed windows. In company a few evenings ago, she accused me of playing the piano and singing! She said that it was not the fat little soprano next door and the music was "beautiful"—I still think that she was dreaming. But I'll have to watch for her to go out before daring to touch the piano. Such is life in a tenement house.*

Our garden, even, is more of a public garden than ever. But cheer up, a toad has moved in. It may yet be a success in years to come.

Now I've told you about all the news except that Vera's babies are at home, taking naps and missing them just about as they did here; Hugh is growing fatter every day, and Robert is growing jollier, and Vera is growing thinner and more nervous. Mrs. Kingsland told me a moral tale (hoping, I suspect, that I will tell it to Vera but I didn't dare) about a woman who wore herself away over four children. I told it to Faith, but it has not gone any farther yet.

When you write, tell me how are the teeth, and the sheep wagon, and the fat girl and Rosey and the horses and sheep and the weather.

Sincerely yours,
Ethel P. Waxham

P.S. Your letter came before this is mailed—in fact I was wasting time on an article when I read about a family's phonograph. "Dispatches from London inform us that there is discussion concerning the peptic value of music. The verdict of alimentarians seems to be that it mainly depends upon the quality and loudness of the music etc." EPW

*The Waxhams lived in a two-story building of four apartments.

251

"BILLY" WILLIAMS CHANDLER
Tucson, Ariz.,
Friday, Nov. 13, 1908

Ethel dear—

Well, now I'm in Tucson, and Ethel, it's great. As Louise
Dudley says "Gee! but it's great to be crazy!" We live in a
cunning adobe, four rooms and two great porches, and I'm
horribly domestic. Your letter caught me Wednesday making my first bread. It took me all day and came out fine, and I
had to take off yesterday to recover! Wednesday evening, the
first meeting of a Spanish Club, which husband Harry has
scared up, was held here, so that day was a wildly hilarious
one for me. Harry has dubbed this club, though only on the
side, the Romance Club, mainly for the reason of several
young cases which he sees developing!

Ethel, *when* do you get time to do anything art-y or craft-
y? You from all accounts are every bit as domestic as I and I
have very little time for extras. I am determined to learn to
speak Spanish in this Mexican country, and as a last resort, I
study my Spanish as I wipe dishes and sweep. There is a plan,
an extravagant plan on foot to make me husky, a true Ama-
zon, and so it is required that I lie down one hour each
morning and at least one in the afternoon, so that is where a
lot of time goes.

What do you think of Louise [Dudley] on her wild goose
chase? I'm glad she up and did it. She'll have a lark and I believe when a person wants a thing as badly as she wanted to go
to Europe and it is at all possible, he or she ought to have it, so
there! I wish we had you and Laura [Hibbard] in this place.
You'd think it was a lovely springtime and not close to Thanksgiving. It is hard to believe that they are shivering in Chicago
and I'm sleeping outdoors. Do you remember our first cold
days at K.H.? *Could* you ever forget them! Thank goodness
those days are gone! I wouldn't give anything for the experience, for I certainly learned a heap there, and if it hadn't been
for K.H. in all probabilities, the "family" would not have

come into being, but I'm mighty glad that no one of family is there now. Fancy one being stranded without the others!

Ethel, *can* you make out Louise's address in Germany? If you have it clear and plain, do send it to me. Wish you could come and see me. If I could have our "family" around our grate, and turn off the 'lectric and have a grand old pow-wow punctuated with tea and sandwiches, oh!—

Remember me to Pater, who I have never seen, but have heard so much of, and give my love to little sister Faith and the little sister who has come to live with you.

> Devotedly as always
> Your twin mosquito bite
> Elizabeth W. Chandler
> Which is the same
> Billy

Louise Dudley
Paris, November 23, 1908

Ethel dear—

You have yet to learn how much pleasure that little blue picture of Abe Lincoln* can bring with it; when I see a certain yellow envelope and a certain funny twisted "L," my heart jumps within me.

Don't talk to me about an absolute standard of beauty, though. I have not thought a real *think* since I landed. I have been places and seen things aplenty—read little—but thought never! You can do that when there is nothing else to do. In fact the infantile preparation for my French lesson every day—transcribing into phonetics, writing a "petite histoire" etc.—is almost too great for my mental ability at times. One is always tired—it is partly the climate, warm and damp—and there are always so many things to do, just as yesterday afternoon when I had made up my mind to be very sensible and stay in and rest, off I went to see an exhibition of pictures, and ended by standing out in the cold

*Five-cent stamp.

and damp an hour and a half to catch one fleeting glimpse of the King and Queen of Sweden. It was worth it, of course, the long lines of soldiers on each side of the street so far as you could see, and then the lovely, lovely *cuirassiers* with their steel breastplates and long horsehair hanging from their helmets riding fore and aft—port and starboard of every carriage. All I could see of the king was cocked hat and gilt lace, and all of the queen violet hat and dress, and a bow very formal, unsmiling, and rather bored, it seemed to me.

So you are being worried by domestics? Presto, I *think* you a French maid, and here she is already! Small, dressed in black with a tiny button of tightly plaited hair on her neck, and you call her "ma petite." I give you the little maid we have here. Those at the Club were too dressed up and American looking, pompadours, frills, etc. For I have moved to a French family, and am kicking myself for not having come before. However as this is my first afternoon here and I have not had a single meal, I really do not know so much about it—but they are awfully nice so far. M. and Mme Meunier are an old couple, exceedingly friendly and kind without losing in dignity, and everything is so deliciously Frenchy and foreign. There at the Club it was exceedingly nice and I would advise anyone to go there to get her bearings—but it was about as French as Kemper Hall and something like it, one round French table with one person there who could speak well, and all the others stuttering and saying, "je . . . j'ai," etc., talking English when Mme was not there, etc.

I forgot to tell you that I am to have practically a small apartment to myself here—that is, I will have a tiny bedroom and salon with perhaps the microscopic kitchen for a "wash" room. There is another bedroom there which is to be occupied by an American girl after the first of December. I am particularly pleased because I am going to exchange English for French with a young Frenchman. It seems I would have to take him in my bedroom, and I have not gotten to the point where the feasibility of being in an apartment alone with a young man is so terrible as having him in a bedroom. *He* is a man I met at Mlle Puthod's and she assures me that "he" and "it" are all right. Of course I could not say anything to him at all—he does not know any English, I believe, and so far all I know is that Mlle P. says he is very anxious to exchange. Of course, "Barkis is willing" so I hope it will be a go. His name is Étienne Drugeau—don't you fall down and worship? I do. Don't you think it will be much more interesting to exchange with a man than a woman, to get the other point of view? Then too, I like to be exchanging with someone of the same social status as myself while the little woman with whom I have been exchanging does not seem to be so—that is as nearly as I can make out about French people. They are absolutely incomprehensible to me. You find the nicest people often living in houses which would contain only the bummiest flats with us, and after you get there, it is a nice apartment. When I went to Mlle P.'s for the first time, I thought I surely had gotten in the wrong house, for the stairway there at bottom was rather dusty and not even polished. It got better as we got up, however—and yet the Italian ambassador lives in that house.

Mlle Puthod has been awfully nice to me; just the other afternoon she had me to her house to tea. Then we went out and bummed around the shops, went in one store and looked at the beautiful artistic jewelry, very fine and of course, very expensive. She shows me so many things and tells me so much about the different places, stores, customs, habits of people, etc. that one never knows except by living here.

You are not wondering at my not being able to talk French, are you? I am able to talk a little, but when I get out in a crowd, I lose my nerve entirely, and I am afraid to say a word. Then the understanding is so difficult. I am beginning to catch on somewhat now, but I don't keep up with a conversation even now, well enough to answer or enter into it. I hope I will improve now that I am here, and they speak it all the time.

What are you doing this Thanksgiving Day, having a big family party with the children, etc.? Heard some Kemper

Hall news—Miss G. brought Sister Laura over here for the summer; wasn't that nice of her? "Sister, however, didn't enjoy it much because of the way the Sisters have been treated in France, and there is so much dirt in the churches. I really think her feeling that way took away from my pleasure in being here, a great deal." Miss G. also felt that the girls at K.H. are much nicer socially this year than last year.

What I shall amount to is really quite a vital question now as my future for the next year or so is "on the carpet." When I stopped at Bryn Mawr on my way here, I had a long talk with Dr. Brown about my work, etc., and told him I would like to work in the libraries here. I had a letter from him last night offering me a special research scholarship of $200 to work in the English *librairie*. It is understood that if I accept this scholarship, I go back to B.M. the next year on scholarship and take my degree. I don't want the fool letters, but, in fact, it seems the only sensible thing to do, for then I could get a position in a college where I would not mind teaching. As it is, I seem to be doing things like Kemper Hall, and the end of last summer I really wanted a position but could not get one. In other words, my training seems to be just at the stage where it means nothing to me. You know it isn't as though I had had awfully good undergraduate training and a saleable *B.A.* I don't know what I am going to do. The thing that seems to combine most of what I want to do and what I ought to do is stay in England next year, and go back to Bryn Mawr in fall of 1910. However, that involves so many possibilities of borrowing money, chances of winning a foreign fellowship, etc.—my head reels to think of it.

I have just come back from Thanksgiving dinner at the Club—a big affair about seventy-five girls, and such a good dinner. As usual I overate. Mrs. Austin of the "Land of Little Rain" was there and made an awfully nice toast. She told the girls there if they were to become great and do great things, they must do them at home, and not here; that all the great men had done their greatest work at home. I was particularly pleased with it because there are so many girls here who need just that sort of talk. They seem to think that just being here will make them great and famous.

Louise continues in a letter dated December 10, 1908:

You would be perfectly disgusted with me if you knew how I am spending my time. It is so funny to stand off from one's self, and say, "the thing she thinks is so important is not important at all, but it is better for her to think that it is." Of course we all say it about the other person, but am I the only one who says it about herself? How long does one continue in such a state of mind, at what age does one find things really worthwhile?

But what perfect nonsense! What a pity Billy is not here to give me a loud *Brrhhf!* It will give you something to do when washing dishes: For, settling the problems of the universe, after one has pigeon-holed one's own, of course, is the proper philosophical use of the time spent in washing dishes.

In more sane language, I am living a very quiet, uneventful life. I go to the library every morning as early as I can get there, and, unless there is something special to call me away earlier, I work as long as it is open (4 p.m.), or more usually, as late as I can see. Then I go around to the Sorbonne to a lecture, if there are any I care about hearing, or go somewhere to tea, or often just wander around the streets looking in the windows, or ambling around in the big stores. . . .

My evenings are spent very quietly here at home, in fact, I am usually too tired to care much about going out. When one does not have dinner until after seven, there is not much evening left. Three mornings a week I exchange lessons with the young Frenchman Mlle Puthod introduced me to, and these events are about the most spicy of the week (not real spice, rather K.H. variety) for he is quite interesting both as a man, and a Frenchman. The other day I said something about a "boulangerie"* when I meant "boucherie,"† and

*Bakery.
†Butchershop

after we finally got things straightened out and I had discovered the word I wanted, I said, "O well, boulangerie and boucherie are almost the same." "Not at all," says he, " 'chérie' and 'lingerie' are not the same!"

Henry Van Dyke is an exchange professor at the Sorbonne and people (chiefly Americans, I believe) are literally fighting for places to hear him. His subject is "Spirit of America," and so nearly as I can judge, he is giving them their money's worth of hot air. I have only been to one lecture and five minutes of another, where he said this: "the people in America do not take manners very seriously; the average American does not feel very badly if he commits a breach of etiquette, but he will feel very badly indeed if he really hurts you, or if you really hurt him. The streetcar conductor does not tip his hat to you, but he does not expect a tip, etc." I do hate for a person in a position like his to talk to and for the Americans entirely, when he could so easily, and is supposed to, tell the French something about us and our ways.

I went to tea with Gertrude Schoepperle last Sunday, and whom do you suppose I met there? Winifred Hawkridge![8] She was with another Wellesley girl of your class. They had just gotten to Paris, and are to be here some months, I believe, have just come from Italy, and are having a grand time all the way around. I saw her later at a lecture at the Sorbonne. She asked me to give you her love, and tell you she was going to write.

Don't worry that I am alone. I am very content. I have decided that I had rather be alone unless I could have you or one of my immediate family with me. If I stay next winter in London, couldn't you come over? I am much alone now, for when I go to the library, I do not come back for lunch, and I often do not see a soul to talk to between breakfast and dinner. I believe it is a sign of age, but I don't mind if it is. Aren't you glad it was too dark for me to go to the library this a.m., and don't you think I have made good use of my time?

Best love from
Louise Dudley

BIG BEAR [Florence Risley]
Wellesley, Mass.,
December 9, 1908

Ethel P. Waxham
1364 Marion St., Denver, Colo.

Miss Little Bear, belovedest as was and is and ever shall be, what under the shining heavens are you doing on a white iron cot with "an awful apparition in blue and white stripes?" Little Bears aren't legs for fat babies and should not ever need to rest—at least not more than a bear should.

What a sophisticated point of view Louise Dudley is getting, all from hearing the American abroad! How I should delight in finding out for myself that the English attitude is unspeakable and all the rest, instead of spending the days in writing notices for the bulletin boards, or putting perfectly futile reading lists—handed in weekly by 120 seniors whom I have nothing against except their lists—in alphabetical order; or running to the bookstore to buy a quarter's worth of stamps. Ah well, it buys my bread, so I can "acquire merit" by being the industrious poor [graduate] student who does anything for the sacred sake of learning—and then I have no time left for the learning. Do you suppose that is part of the eddication?

Did I tell you about the horrible tortures of a seminar with Mr. Young? It is on Emerson and Transcendentalism, and the only thing transcendental about it is the idiocy of taking it. For three solid periods—not ever changing chairs to shake off the yawns—we, four graduates including Laura Welch and B.B. and 2 seniors sit in rebellious and gnawing silence, fighting off sleep with disgust only, while that precious man paws around in the air for a better word, generally cribbed from Emerson, and says in every forty minutes the same thing some half dozen times that any sane creature could say better in a single short sentence. And this, oh this, is eddication! . . .

B.B.

SANDFORD MILLS
Red Bluff Ranch
Dec. 12, 1908

Dear Ethel,

This morning I started to answer your nice letter of the twenty sixth of October, which was here to greet me on my return from a grand hunting trip. We returned the twenty-first of November. I am very naughty for not writing to you before, but Tom Bain is here and Mr. Bruce, so there are card games nearly every night, dancing and playing the phonograph. But what are dances and card games to me compared to a nice letter from you.

We spent the day breaking horses. Tom has father's horse "Topaz," Mr. Bruce "Big Enough," "Sandy" for myself. Sandy is going to be a good lazy all around horse, very easy to ride, Big Enough is balky, and Topaz behaves like a lady most of the time. You can have Sandy to ride next time you come to Wyoming.

Must tell you about the hunting trip. We left the first of November, with a spring wagon and four horses. The first day we stopped in Lander for supplies. Next day we went to Fort Washakie; got there about seven o'clock at night. All the third day we traveled through a barren country, and saw nothing but Indians, we reached Bull Lake Creek late in the afternoon, made camp and went fishing, but with no luck whatever.

We traveled up the river three more days. The sixth we went through Dubois and camped on Wind River for the last time, on the seventh we went up Crooked Creek, left our wagon and packed over the mountains—past Fish Lake— crossed Warm Spring Creek. Next day we reached the head of the Gros Ventre, where we camped and hunted. The first two days I was sick with a cold, so Tom did the hunting, the first day he shot a spike bull [elk], the day after we brought it into camp and ate two frying pans each of meat.

The weather was very cold and frost was falling every

night and sometimes in the day, every time I wanted to take a picture. On the eleventh I followed three Elk all day but couldn't get one; when I returned to camp about dark, Tom told me he shot another about five miles from there.

Next morning when we were packing up, Harry Baldwin and some more men came, looking for the Forest Rangers' camp. They were the only persons up there that we knew.

On the sixteenth we started for home. I had not been on quite such a satisfactory hunt, even if I didn't get a shot at anything, I had just as good a time. I shall send you some pictures pretty soon. Wish I could see you some afternoon in your nice blue dress.

Very nearly forgot about a dance that there is to be here on the twenty-ninth. Miss Howard, Miss Poling and George Poling are to be here. Wish I could have the pleasure of your company. The dances are not what they used to be when you were here.

Thank you again for the pictures. It is three o'clock, so good bye,

remember
Sandford Mills

ETHEL P. WAXHAM
Denver, Colo.,
24 December, 1908

Moneta, Wyo.

Dear Mr. Love—

Here is a letter that meant to reach you by Christmastime, but has only its good resolutions to recommend it.

The tree is waiting in the parlor, all silver and white, and the presents are heaped up beneath it. In the kitchen are the boxes of candy which we've been busy with for several days. The table is set for breakfast—and deary me, I'm so sleepy. Eyes ought to have props to keep them open. Things are done so thoroughly that Kip's back and my arms are sparkling with artificial snow and one is in danger from holly at every turn. Vera and her babies, and Mr. and Mrs. Shattuc, and Miss Little are to be here for the tree at nine. Dinner is to be at one—six courses. If Pearl grows religious, we never can manage it.

Here are some Christmas and New Year wishes for you, and a tiny bit of snow! Goodnight

E.P.W.

8

DENVER: 1909

The year 1909 began much as 1908 had ended, with Ethel still in charge of housekeeping for her father, sisters Faith and little Ruth, occasionally working as a substitute teacher, and often enjoying the best of Denver's social and cultural attractions. The same good friends continued to give her glimpses of their worlds and their lives. John Love continued, patiently, in his endeavors to win her hand.

ETHEL P. WAXHAM
Denver, Colo., 1 January, 1909

Moneta, Wyo.

Dear Mr. Love,

A fine large basket of chocolates came to me on the day after Christmas with your card. Faith says to tell you that we have all been enjoying them—which is perfectly true.

Christmas is long past, now. Ruth's horn is broken, pillows for her doll's bed lost, Christmas book cut into pieces by her Christmas scissors, foot departed from a strong wooden dog, and the hair gone from her doll's head. Fortunately some indestructible dishes and blocks remain. I rescued Kippy only day before yesterday. Ruth said that she was going to take Kippy's "peeling" off to make a muff! My glasses are the last sacrifice—yesterday morning.

I have just had a painful interview with a Sugar City [Colorado] principal who wants me to come down with him and teach. "Brr," said Little Bear to herself, "if the work doesn't kill me, I couldn't live on the salary." Pater is urging

263

me to look for a school in Arizona or Northern California, because the cough that started in Kenosha is beastly.

Pater and Faith are off for the theatre—Pearl has been at Vera's all day. Pearl's belief is about the most overwhelming that I ever heard of. She does not believe that the world moves, or is round, because Joshua gave orders to the sun; does not believe in evolution, of course, because man was made of "dirt," and woman of a rib; does not believe in doctors, operations, and so on, because we are all children of the Lord, and he made us the way he wanted us to be. She knows people who have seen demons—dozens of them—so she is careful, very careful. It seems incomprehensible that she could believe things so implicitly.

Tomorrow I may go to Boulder for a day or two, so I wanted to write "thank you" before starting. I have not made any good resolutions, and need a hundred.

Goodbye, good luck and a good new year.

Ethel Waxham

GOLDYLOCKS
[CAROLINE HOLT]
Wellesley, Mass.,
January 11, 1909

Dear Little Bear,

Ain't lost, ain't drowned, ain't 'sploded. Just laboring so hard for daily bread don't have time to do anything else at all.

Went home for Christmas and helped Santa Claus all first week just every minute. And second week made new gown. Little Bear would laugh to see how stylish Goldylocks is getting. Not that she has reached Big Bear's height of rats and long corsets (here is secret mustn't mention, but Goldylocks has persuaded B.B. to give up rat and she does look so much prettier!)

Do you know that Big Bear is wearing Katherine Lee Bates'* teaching shoes and they really seem to fit her very

---

*Katherine Lee Bates, beloved professor of English literature at Wellesley, and advisor to the Scribblers, whom Florence Risley was replacing as a graduate assistant.

well? The Bear family ought to feel very proud to have one of its members lecturing six hours a week to Literature 9 and I guess we are. She is doing wonderfully good graduate work besides her "official labor" and the Lit. people are all so pleased with her!

I go up to College with B.B. every morning and usually come home with her at night. Sometimes we go places together. Went once to Symphony and to Isadora Duncan. 'Spect B.B. wrote you how wonderful she was. I just hold my breath when get to thinking about how beautiful her dancing was. Oh, Little Bear, when she comes next year, you must be near and we'll go see her together. You *are* coming in June, aren't you?

How are eyes? I can imagine how my Little Bear looks with four eyes. Will you have to have four eyes always or just for a little while?

Write me all about the family 'specially the babies.

The watch clock is striking eleven and my landlady is snoring till house trembles—guess she must have bad cold for never heard her before. Think maybe better go bed and let Little Bear have rest. Goodnight and write me very very soon.

Carrie Maude

MARY B. MILLS
Red Bluff Ranch
January 15, 1909

My dear, dear Girl,

With such a dear dainty Christmas box and such a lovely fat letter, I feel that I have waited long, too long in writing.

It has been a very busy Christmas season for me; all the time I was on the watch so as not to give out at some ridiculous moment. Tonight there are only Mr. Mills, "Bill" Bruce and myself at home, a good opportunity for letters, you see.

We had our usual happy Christmas. The house looked very Christmasy with ropes of evergreens and red bells and holly.

The afternoon of Margaret's birthday, Mr. and Miss Howard and Louise Poling came over for two days. The dance in the evening was a great success. The floor was like glass, the new music fine, luncheon at twelve and to bed at 2:30. Riding the next day, cards in the evening. Then came New Years. Next day came a big big washing and Monday, yesterday, the four went over to the Howards for a last good time before the Polings move to the Schlichting place next week.

Can you realize dear that we are going to have *real* neighbors? After living without them twenty-one years and living beside the Ehlers for twelve, the Lord is going to be good to us, I think.

Mrs. Poling is Mr. Howard's sister-in-law and seems to be a very lovely woman, and we like Mr. Poling, too, although we have not seen much of him. Louise is almost nineteen, five feet nine, weighs a hundred and thirty, would be a *very* pretty girl if it wasn't for her teeth, full of fun, too. (Doesn't this sound like a teacher's agency blank?) George, the son, I'm a wee bit afraid I'm not going to like, but can tell later.

Mr. Howard said to me, "I want the boys (Sandford and Tom Bain) to get George over here, give him a good trouncing and get some of the conceit out of him. He's been spoiled."

The Schlichtings have about finished moving. They are to live in town, for a time, at least. Fancy those boys.

I can just see the happy time you had at Christmas with the children; it takes little ones to make a gay time. They are always so excited. Robert is perhaps too young for the full enjoyment, but little Ruth must have been amusing.

You certainly do get hold of curios in the way of kitchen-maids. You rather enjoy it all I know. You always did see the funny side of everything, happy girl.

Mr. Love came up in this part of the country before going to Denver to tell everyone how badly his teeth needed attention. Of course they couldn't have been finished in one time, but he'll be around soon again and tell us all about it. It's too bad, with the start he has, he doesn't pay a little attention to business, but I suppose that's his affair, only one can't help being provoked with such foolishness.

We have had so far what might be called a hard winter, very much more cold than usual, not such a great quantity of snow, but no wind to blow it off. They have been feeding the cattle for a month and as a general thing, we do not commence until February. Fortunately there is plenty of hay. We bought all of the Schlichting heifer calves the other day. Dan Hudson took the rest of the cattle.

Oh, by the way, the 15th of December, a new bank opened in Hudson and Dan is *president.* Can't you see him sitting at the head of the table when a meeting of the directors is called? Little Deane is going to school and doing very nicely. There are ninety pupils in the Hudson school, so you can see the town has grown some. A regular coal mining town. I should not like to live there. The Hudsons are in the suburbs which makes it a little better, but the school is very rough.

Dear me, child, if anyone else gets a letter tonight, this one will have to come to an end.

A Happy New Year to you and every one of you and oceans of love for your dear self.

Mary B. Mills

ETHEL P. WAXHAM
Denver, Colo.,
29 January, 1909

Moneta, Wyo.

Dear Mr. Love—

It seems that I am convicted of an obscure style; often suspected it! When I mentioned the delay of my last letter, I had in mind your words to the effect that you were not gloomy whether people remembered you at Christmastime or not.

"Some must follow and some command,
Though all are made of clay."

267

Longfellow did not include potters who are commanded and don't follow. My "palm tree" pot came safely through the firing, but the color of it would strike woe to the heart of a dog. It shines; it is exactly the color of the bowl that I make muffins in, which is to say, a sick yellow-brown. I am just on the point of giving up clay forever, as I have done every time that I ever came back from a potter. Who are we that potters should shake our faith in humankind? Haven't we just as much right to illusions as other people? Brrr!

My ten days in Boulder were delightful. Margaret Tanhart, two men, and myself climbed Flagstaff [Mountain] by sunset and moonrise, had a fire near the top, and came back in the evening.

That was just before the Wellesley luncheon when Miss McCaulley was toastmistress. I had to make the toast on "A Few Impossibilities" myself. It was appropriate, wasn't it, considering our discussion of impossible things? I laughed afterwards to myself when I thought of my point, that impossibilities turn into possibilities, and then probabilities, and then, voila!

Fountain pen has run dry. I thought it would last—Can't be replenished tonight, however, for during my absence yesterday Ruth spilled all the ink over herself and the parlor.

She has been comparatively good of late. Drank some kerosene one day, without any damage, and at another time took a pink pill which she found in the alley where she is not permitted to go. The consequences of that were disastrous. I doubt whether she takes any more pills. Almost all of her Christmas presents are gone. The big doll has been broken, mended and broken again. Pater bought her two new ones to take its place. The new girl doll has the name of the old one, Mary Jones. Can you see anything particularly fascinating in the name *Jones?* I can't. But Ruth does. Either she or I must be Miss Jones most of the time, as well as the doll.

This Miss Jones did a little more teaching at Miss Wolcott's last week or week before. It was German. Pure bluff. I live in constant dread of the German teacher's illness. If I go south, it will be teaching. I am ashamed not to have any sparks of enthusiasm to be aroused. K.H. must have put them out. Family affairs have been going from bad to worse ever since I was nine, "wonder what will become of us"—not a very good battle cry, is it?

You are very kind, Mr. Love, to care to make things easier. But you saw, I think, that your proposition is among the impossibilities—really, would you not be surprised if I should accept it?

"Oh dear my," as Ruth says, I wish I were in Venice at twilight, in a gondola—or watching northern lights in the land of midnight suns—or seeing moonrise from a Swiss chalet among the Alps—or enjoying the early morning bustle of a harbor in Algiers—can't you see the sails?—or wish I were a lizard lying on the hot rocks in New Mexico, a gold fish swimming around the South Seas—or anything in the world but this with cold in throat.

Best wishes—
E.P.W.

"BILLY" WILLIAMS CHANDLER
Tucson, Arizona,
February 13, 1909

Dear Ethel—

Meant to write a moon ago, but have been "teribal" busy getting vegetable garden started.

Ethel, those females who did such marvelous stunts while doing cooking, sewing and housework, *I* think are myths, so there! To be sure we have their books, but I'll bet they were awful housekeepers and I'll wager too that they didn't darn every hole nor sew on every button. I'll bet they used pins. I've tried to learn Spanish while washing dishes and making beds, but it's a sad affair.

And now it's Feb 24! That's the way it goes. Since last I wrote, Harry has been with three other men on a forty-mile jaunt across the desert and into . . . Feb. 28!—This letter is doomed, I clearly see. And, little 'skito bite, not for lack of thought but time. I'll begin where I left off . . . into what, I wonder, I've forgotten! Oh yes, into the Mountains. They had a glorious tramp and I had a glorious time here, for Miss Aldrich came and stayed with me and we spent the time in riotous living. She certainly is mighty fine, and we're very fond of her.

Had a long grand letter from Laura {Hibbard} yesterday. She misses the K.H. "family." Wish she could come here and bat with me a while. Yesterday I had the best day. Saturday is always set aside for bake day and I baked cookies and bread and 3 mince pies and beans and pot roast and doughnuts. I'm just in my element when I've got my fingers all stuck up with dough and am generally be-floured.

Flower garden is doing marvels. And you should see my vegetable garden. Lettuce, radishes and peas are up and onions are just cracking the ground. Ethel, I'm hopelessly domesticated, and like it better every day.

No, I didn't tell you, did I, of the grand exhibition I gave at the art craft society? Yes, I took my "tools," upon request and showed 'em how I did it. I started a sconce and have it almost finished, all except rivets.

I'm going to wind up lest I get side-tracked again. Have had callers this afternoon several times while I've been writing this. Harry went for a twenty mile walk today, so I expected to have lots of time to write, but it proved otherwise.

'Scuse awful jumble, but my heart's in it. Don't wait as long as I have to write to

> Your devoted
> Billy

ETHEL P. WAXHAM
Denver, Colo.,
21 February, 1909

Moneta, Wyo.

[Forwarded to Wolton, Wyoming.]

Dear Mr. Love,

It is not a month this time! Your letters have reached me, and only a hundred and one things have kept me from replying as I should have done before.

In the first place Faith has been under the weather, out of school and all abed with rheumatism of the neck; masseur is still coming, although she is now better and has been to school. Little baby Hugh has been ill ever since Christmastime when he had a bit of bronchitis. Now, no kind of food seems to agree with him, and the little fellow has lost five pounds—a good deal at his age. Vera is busy and worried about him. Robert grows and prospers. Yesterday I left Ruth with Pearl and spent the morning with Vera. Just had to clean things up—couldn't resist.

I'll write again soon—Can't finish tonight. Tired.

E.P.W.

A week later she was rested enough to write again:

I wonder whether you had a share in our last storms? Blizzards, the papers called them, though they had little effect here, except keeping us within doors for a while, and making walking difficult for a while afterward. It happened that on the worst nights of each Pater took me to the theatre! First to see "The Virginian," which I had never seen before. It was good—but whom do you think that Virginian, standing against the door, giggling, made me think of? No one else than poor, hysterical George Ehler! The second time we saw Lotherno as Lord Dundreary. Faith saw him in "Hamlet" yesterday afternoon.

Faith is to leave Grand Avenue School and come to Emerson, only a few blocks from here, where the Assistant is to be married next month. She is very glad to change. The teachers in the school which she leaves have been entertaining for one another, and she wants to have a luncheon for them soon— near St. Patrick's day—as a formal farewell.

Ruth is getting to be quite a society bird. She has been out twice alone to dinner. She behaved beautifully the first time—ate nothing and said nothing. The second time she talked and ate, so she must have disgraced herself!

I am planning to plant some flowers in the back yard this spring. There is a strip of ground by the fence perhaps a foot wide to be divided among the four apartments of our building. Mrs. Kingsland is going to have poppies and nasturtiums. I have selected about twelve different kinds of flowers from Burpee's catalogue—chiefly experiments! Probably will get about six of them; some to climb over the ugly back porch, and some to look at and some to smell of.

Kathryn sent me a long letter full of news this week. The Howards and Polings seem always to have come or be coming or the Mills children to be going. I asked her about Tom Bain. Her description was as enthusiastic as yours was the opposite. She credited him even with ambition. Everyone who knows him likes him and has a good word to say for him. What I do not like about the matter is that the people I like so much don't agree! Can't all be right; next best thing is to have you all a little wrong.

You do not think that the only reason for teaching is the salary? One does it for one's precious self-respect, and the exercise of one's faculties, and for half a hundred reasons not included in the salary—which nevertheless one accepts and spends very quickly. To Pater, the whole matter seems to be salary. He doesn't know the grind and the pettiness and— but that was all Kemper Hall. It was fine in Boulder, though it was hard.

If we were all better than the social rules and regulations, there would be no need for them. I can imagine circumstances under which I would accept your offer gladly and in the same spirit in which you make it—but those desperate circumstances[1] are at present nonexistent. My next teaching will not be before fall—possibly not then.

You may outlive me by from one to fifty years, Mr. Love. I sincerely hope that you will, for I do not like the thought of benefitting by your misfortune. You are always "on the list," as Burns said in the verse you quoted.

With best wishes, I remain
                              Sincerely yours,
                              Ethel P. Waxham

JOHN G. LOVE
Moneta, Wyo., March 3rd/09

Dear Miss Waxham,

I just got home tonight from the sheep camps and found your long looked-for letter awaiting me at the ranch. I am off to the camps again in the morning, but as a team is going to Wolton, I will write you a few lines even if I am tired and sleepy.

I was very sorry to learn of the sickness in the family. I sincerely hope that you are *all* well again, especially yourself.

The sheep are all looking well, but we are moving up to the foothills for snow. Feed is practically a thing of the past, but if the weather stays fine, all stock will come through in good shape. While I was away at the camps, I had the men put up ten tons of ice.[2] It might come handy; it might all melt and do no one any good.

The men went with two four-horse teams for more posts today. I really wish you were here for at least an hour to tell me how to finish the house as it should be done. I have a carpenter here now who is going to work at his trade, as well as look after the house. He will also feed my horses when I am away, which will be quite frequently from now on. I am expecting some men to come round up some horses and I will be ready to go at any time they come. My four running horses are in fit condition to run for their lives. If I am only in as

273

good trim, there will be no cause for complaint. I am actually losing my nerve in the saddle.

When I got the mail on the 24th, there was no letter from you. From then until tonight I could have ridden day after day and never noticed badger holes or gulches, absolutely blind to everything but the bunch of horses in front of me, straining every nerve to get round them with never a thought of self. Tomorrow, I would see all kinds of badger holes and gulches, although I never yet have failed to do my share of the running. When a person begins noticing holes when riding after horses, it is time for him to quit. With you here, I would never get the blues at all and would be worthless to chase wild horses, so I must either break them or sell them this spring once they are caught.

It has only been a little more than two months since I saw you but they certainly have been long ones for me. I surely will never be tied here another winter without you.

This has been a very warm day and the frost is going out of the ground very rapidly. I have sent for vegetable and flower seeds in order to have them here in plenty of time. Hoping that you are *all* well, I am with best wishes,

Yours Sincerely,
John G. Love

LOUISE DUDLEY
3 Rue Vavin, Paris,
March 24, 1909

Dear Ethel—

Your last letter is so generous it really frightens me, though to be exact I am terribly pleased to find someone taking an interest in my letters. My own family has successfully buried me a long time ago. I hear from them, but in an extremely impersonal way, and for all the answers I get to them, nine-tenths of my letters might have gone to the dead letter office. Mamma's "I have heard from all you girls this week and you were all well" is a complete answer to a proposition that she come over for a few weeks next fall, a long description of the Latin Quarter as one lives in it, and several postcards of Notre Dame!

I am going to the country next Tuesday for two weeks. These blessed people close the Library for two weeks' vacation before Easter so I am going out for a spree. I don't know where I am going. I am tired of the city.

Got a postal from Dr. Furnivall the other day saying he would print the B. & S. thesis in the Early English Text Society Publication.

The night your letter came, I had been dining (here in *pension*) with a large Russian woman, rather dirty and greasy, who played the piano, smoked many cigarettes, and who begged the gracious favor of the stamp off your envelope!

I was forcefully reminded of Kemper Hall yesterday at Mlle Puthod's when she was telling about some friends of hers here who weighed their bread to be certain they did not over-eat, and who ate only little fish because big ones were meat! I am not certain but what that will get tacked on to my tales of K.H. itself in course of time; it is so appropriate.

I am going to give a party Monday night in honor of the fact that G. Schoepperle has left me her pictures and tea set.

Now that I have written off my bad temper I am sleepy. You seem to be coming out the little end of the hour in more ways than one.

Goodbye,
Louise Dudley

JOHN G. LOVE
Moneta, Wyo., March 28th/09

Dear Miss Waxham,

Everyone else is in bed sleeping the sleep of the just, but as I am not sleepy, I will write you a few lines before I go to bed.

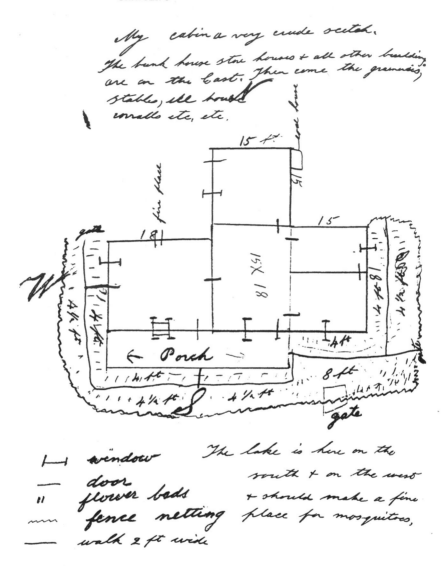

My cabin a very crude sketch.

The bunk house store houses + all other buildings are on the East. Then come the granaries, stables, ice house, corrals etc, etc.

⊢┤ window
— door
" flower beds
∿∿ fence netting
— walk 2 ft wide

The lake is here on the south + on the west + should make a fine place for mosquitoes,

Enclosed in this letter was this sketch of John G. Love's ranch house. "The house had been under construction for 4 years, and because of its size, roof design and remoteness from source of materials (the logs were hauled by team and wagon 100 miles from the Wind River Mountains—and each round trip for 20 logs took two weeks), was still far from completed.

"The roof was so unusual that a word about it may be of interest. John Love had designed a type of roof which was new to this country. It had a low pitch and was underlain by horizontal conventional rafters to which ceiling board was

I ache in every bone and muscle tonight, but it is my own fault. Like a fool, I was trying to renew my youth by riding a horse that my bronco twister absolutely declined to mount. I rode him first in the corral and then turned him out and rode him sixteen miles. I have one crippled finger on my left hand and as I went to swing into the saddle, my grip in that hand failed me. He lunged ahead, I landed behind the saddle. I certainly know better than to mount a horse that is not absolutely gentle. Now I am paying the penalty of my folly, but I have the satisfaction of knowing that I can still ride when I have to, the knowledge that the horse was ridden, and ridden to a finish.

We have been having beautiful weather of late, but tonight it is snowing heavily. The snow will not stay long now as the frost is all out of the ground. All hands for the last five days have been making flower beds around the house. It is rather slow and expensive. If the flowers do not grow after all this labor, if you are not here, I will be sorely tempted to cuss. If you are here, it will not matter so much, for we can go to the mountains or "the Park" and forget the flower garden until next spring.

The wagon is at last finished, except for the inside painting or staining. I do not know what that should be, so I will

---

nailed. A second set of tilted rafters ran from the eaves to a lower ridge pole. To these were attached hundreds of 2 inch poles tightly fitted side by side to form a solid slanted pole roof. The poles were covered with burlap and then heavy canvas, then 6 inches of clay in which a second set of 2×4 rafters was imbedded. These were joined to an upper ridge pole. To the upper rafters and ridge pole was nailed heavy corrigated sheet iron which was then coated with black asphaltum. The house was always cool in summer and warm in winter. It did not leak for many years, and then only where the sheet iron was improperly joined.

The living room had formerly been the hotel dining room, a separate log building, at Old Muskrat. It was now joined to the west wall of the big house and a wide doorway was sawed through into the dining room."[3]

call a halt and wait to be enlightened. The bows and slats are stained with cherry.

I have been having quite a time of it with herders this winter. It has been worse of late and now I have gone to hiring Mexicans.

I do want to get down to Denver to see you for a few days before lambing commences on April 20th, but it is now very doubtful unless I just say "the cow is in the hammock" and come regardless of losses.

I just looked out. It is clear now and very little snow has fallen. I will have all my sheep in the corrals in a few days and sort them all over preparatory to lambing. Then I will know just what my winter's loss has been. I set a goose today and a hen two days ago. Hoping that you are all well and happy, and that I will hear from you soon, I remain with best wishes for you all,

> Yours Sincerely,
> John G. Love

> ETHEL P. WAXHAM
> Denver, Colo., 3 April, 1909

Wolton, Wyo.

Dear Mr. Love—

It is not nearly a month yet, dating from the time when you read my last letter. *"Que voulez-vous?"** as the French say. There are reasons galore why I should not write so often. I'm a beast to write at all. It makes you—(maybe?)—think that no is not no, but perhaps, or yes, or anything else.

Brrt! Bears are beasts of course. This little one is all, all alone this evening, feels gregarious, and someone else has to take the consequences unless a caller interrupts. Pater and Faith are taking their familiar outing to the Orpheum. They wanted to go last week. I said to wait and see Nazinova in

*"What do you want?" or in this context, "What do you expect?"

278

something really good. They saw her in "A Doll's House."
Pater said that he had to go to the Orpheum to get the taste
out of his mouth. Doesn't like Ibsen. Thinks people like
Torwald don't exist. Marcia came in from Boulder to see
Mme Nazinova today with me, in "The Comtesse Coquette."
I was disappointed in the play; it is as bad as a decent, clean
play can be—empty, frivolous, etc.

The other event of today was putting in the first of the
garden. The devil must be against us. (Did I write you the
story of "The Devil and the Cherry Pie"?) Well, the devil
made the "Gods' ground" as hard as the sidewalk; and he
kept the landlord forgetful about fertilizers, and dulled the
minister's spade which we borrowed, and today he finished
the hose. I tried to sprinkle newly-planted seeds. Will draw a
picture.

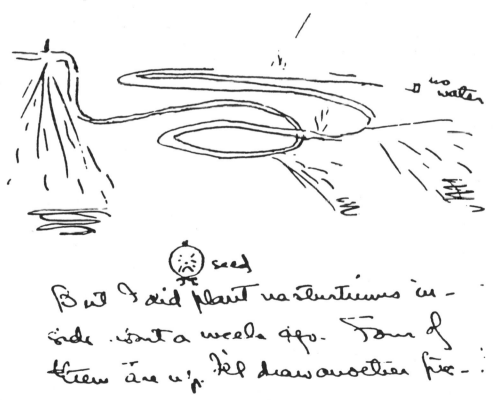

But I did plant nasturtiums inside about a week ago. Four of them are up. I'll draw another picture—

life size, ivy leaved, pale green hopeful things. I . . . waste half my time carrying the pot from window to window to give it sun.

The devil must keep away from those nasturtiums. I brought home from K.H. charms blest by the priest so he better had!

All reasons pro and con about teaching next year I've been considering, and have about decided to take a position. It would not be bad in Honolulu I'm quite sure. Who knows? It might be heavenly (●. dear—'scuse blot. Pen rebelled at last word, and I haven't any more paper.)

Good wishes for your busy season from
E.W.

P.S. I like you very much. E.W.

9

DENVER: 1909

Numerous advertisements in the *Rocky Mountain News* and the *Denver Post* suggest that fortune telling was very much in vogue in the early 1900s. Ethel Waxham and a number of her friends had their fortunes told on several occasions, either from idle curiosity or as possible solutions to personal dilemmas. In her letter of September 16, 1906, Ethel Vaughan remembered that Ethel Waxham had written down a fortune reading done in Salem, and asked how much of it had come true. That fortune was not preserved, but a more recent one—perhaps more pertinent—told by a Miss Bueler, written down as Ethel remembered it, remains.

Fortune
6 April, 1909

Choice of profession—do better in dealings with men.

Stage—place in serious drama, emotional work especially in character work; would not do well in vaudeville; anyway dislike the publicity. Would make a fine singer and dancer; do anything with fingers and toes.

Decorative work would be best for me, do anything from designing hats and clothes to china painting etc. Have a talent for music, esp. stringed instruments.

Literature would pay; repertorial or other work, I pay attention to details which others miss. Plot struck me excellent, start stories & poems.

Teaching *avoid* because of drudgery, have patience and love of children but it makes me too nervous.

Health—improvingly good. Troubles—nerves, heart, & perhaps left side or disposure to fall. Live to be 60.[1]

Items—Valuable present to be soon received. Many papers soon to sign. Money to be left by deceased elderly relative. Residence soon to change, house, town, state. Trip to both coasts; one soon, spend much time in Los Angeles.

Husbands—love matches, both. No, one is poor, but family rich, son meets fatal accident. Two is rich & lives long. Both come before 29th year.

Disposition—Impulsive, quick to act & quick to make friends—or acquaintances. Friends are few; do anything for those I really care for. Few confidants. I'm sensitive; once hurt by a friend never get over it. See faults in friends & virtues in enemies; grow tired of people's mannerisms, get along best with people born in November & April. Never put myself out for men; go halfway in a friendship but no farther; in case of trouble can't write for reconciliation. Whatever I do, do thoroughly. Over-do on everything. Unfit to take care of myself & don't,—like nice things & enjoy spending money for them.

Miss Bueler

JOHN G. LOVE
Moneta Wyo, April 9th/09

Dear Miss Waxham,

I got home tonight very tired with a worn-out horse, but nonetheless triumphant. I corralled a horse that on five different occasions has shown me a clean pair of heels. I found your letter awaiting me and the world once more looks good, so the horse will not be ridden for some time to come.

Thank you very much, "little girl," for the P.S. in your letter. You say "There are reasons galore why I should not write so often. I'm a beast to write at all, etc." Now, "little girl," you cannot expect me to agree to anything like that. Until another claims you, "little girl," please let me be as happy as possible.

I am indeed very sorry to learn that you are meditating

teaching again. No doubt you think it very foolish of me to care whether you teach or not, and that I should look at it in the light of "what care I how fair she be if she be not fair for me." Another winter like the one when you were at K.H. and I will worry myself grey completely. I will be only too glad to hire you *not* to teach at double any salary and never breathe a word of it to mortal. I just won't stay here and fret and worry over you like that again, but will have to do like Mahomet of old.

I expect before fall to have a family installed on the ranch to see to things and have my sheep all let out to other parties to run, although I still expect to own nine thousand. The others I will put on the market. The extra money that I have perhaps foolishly spent on this house and garden will never be missed by me. It may do you or someone else some good sometime when I am done with it. When I leave the ranch I will lock up this house and also the wagon. Then I will know just how I will find them when I get back.

I greatly fear that I will not get to see you until June. I have horses to gather, cow ponies to get in, colts and calves to brand, the crop and garden to get planted, extra men to hire, supplies to get etc., and any amount of other work. And lambing begins on the 18th. The weather is fine now and the grass is growing nicely. The lake in front of the house is full to the brim and running over. I have two of *your* ponies in now and I heard today where the other one was. I broke them especially for you and you do not have to be burdened with me to get them either. In the meantime, they can eat grain and grass until you want them. They are pretty little fellows, but too light to carry my weight as fast as I generally want to go.

You did not write me the story of "the cherry pie and the devil"; please do so. This letter will leave in the morning and I wish that I were going with it; but after staying away all winter, I had better stay a little longer and not see all my winter's work go for nothing. Now, you dear little sinner, be good and write often—the oftener the better. In spite of myself, I look for a letter every time I get the mail and cannot help being disappointed when there is none. With best wishes for you all,

Yours Sincerely
John G. Love

ETHEL P. WAXHAM
Denver, Colo., 16 April, 1909

Moneta, Wyo.

Dear Mr. Love—

And did you ever try Anglo Saxon? I've been doing a little because I ought to have done it before, and didn't, and need it in the business. It is like German, and Scotch, and Dartmoor dialect and French and Latin, but not enough to help! It shows, or seems to me to show, some common origin to languages, or else strong early cross-influences. Some of the early laws that I read were amusing. If a stranger meets you, and doesn't shout, or blow a horn, he is a thief! And thieves are fined some sixty shillings. Fighting is prohibited in the king's palace, and at banquets . . . and so on.

Now here is a fallacy. You say that writing to you will exercise the faculties as well as teaching. Needing exercise, I wrote Big Bear a letter in Esperanto some two months ago, and she has not answered yet. I'm fearful even to talk about Anglo Saxon, thinking that the result may be the same with you.

Pearl and Ruth are safe vents—I'll tell you about the devil and the cherry pie. Faith had a sewing woman that week; I was helping, when Ruth rushed in calling, "Oh Sis'Ato. Poil made a cherry pie and Poil dropped it on the floor!" I knew that Pearl was making a pie; I had fought that pie for weeks, then submitted. "Poil picking it up now!" In a few minutes she was back again. "Poil wants to see you." I went into the kitchen. Pearl sat in the middle of the floor, and bits of pie were every where about. Pearl was almost in tears. She loves pie. "The devil is always up to something," she said. "I was just taking the pie out of the oven, and it was a beautiful pie; the dishcloth caught on a knob of the stove, and the devil knocked the pie right out of my hand. I guess he's over there in the corner now, laughing at me."

"Don't give him the satisfaction of making you miserable," said I.

"I just mopped up the floor, and there ain't time to make any more dessert."

Pearl hasn't said pie since. It was cheap. But was it the devil or a guardian angel, or mere chance?

I have a large pot full of nasturtiums up in the house. The news of the week is news of the nasturtiums. Monday—one appears. Tuesday—another. Wednesday—nothing. Thursday—a third. Friday—the first nasturtium has a new leaf. Saturday—Ruth breaks the tallest. Sunday—Robert completes the disaster. Monday—a new plant appears, and puts forth two leaves in one day. Tuesday—new plant is tired, turns yellow, and droops. Wednesday—two of the nasturtiums get their fifth leaves. Thursday—nothing happens. Friday—nothing happens. "And tomorrow and tomorrow and tomorrow," says Macbeth. The garden outside remains in the ground. I sprinkle it with a sauce pan and a pail. The new hose is one of the things in "the all encircling good." TÒ πEPIÉXN* is the Greek equivalent I discovered in one of the early philosophies. New thought as old as that!

Have you seen my hostess Miss Davis recently? The Mills people seem caught in the toils of money making.

I suppose that you will be busy night and day, now for a while. Good wishes to you from

Ethel Waxham

JOHN G. LOVE
Moneta Wyo, April 28th/09

Dear Miss Waxham,

Yours of the 16th received yesterday. Needless to say, I was very glad to hear from you. I never understood the study of

---

*"That which surrounds or enfolds."

285

Anglo Saxon, but I am willing to if you will be the teacher. I have no doubt but what it would be rather an interesting study. Poor Pearl! Is she to be pitied or envied in her belief? I guess the Mills people have been enjoying the winter from what I can hear. I have not enjoyed myself overly well since Christmas. I expect to some day, but not with poverty staring me in the face. Even with no one depending upon me, I absolutely could not enjoy myself doing nothing at all as long as I was in debt. To keep up my insurance policies costs me twice as much every year as the entire Mills family earns.

I met Miss Davis in Lander on the 19th and she looks just about the same as she did. As well as being County Superintendent of schools, she is librarian in the new Carnegie Library in Lander. I saw in the paper that she had been granted a life certificate to teach in any school in the state and had the certificate framed and was justly proud of it. Wyoming is making great strides educationally.

The day after answering your last letter I came very close to being crippled by a horse falling with me. I had driven six horses all day on the disc harrow putting in oats for two days running. The evening of the second day, I jumped on Brownie to corral a workhorse and was galloping along when, without warning, Brownie, for the first time in seven years, took a header and caught me underneath. Fortunately no bones were broken, but I was rather badly bruised up and limped around for several days. If that had happened on a Sunday I might have thought that the devil had something to do with it.

I have a dozen saddle horses now at the lambing camps and my four saddled. Even your saddle is in use. There are a special saddle, bridle and two blankets that go with your ponies. Your stirrups I cannot use as they are too small. They are small heavy steel safety stirrups that I gave four dollars for, guaranteed to throw the foot out of stirrup in case a horse should fall or throw you.

We are having miserable lambing weather now: cold,

windy and snowy, and there is a heavy loss amongst lambs. Tonight is bitterly cold. The grass is very slow about growing and food is scarce. We may raise a good crop of lambs yet, but I have already lost over four hundred. I think that I will at least manage to raise enough so that I will be able to winter contentedly in Honolulu (if the Fates decree that I must.). I telegraphed one hundred and seventy-five dollars the other day to a family in Oklahoma to come up and run the ranch.[2] I have three men picked out to take the sheep off my hands next fall.

There is not a bit of use my staying up here grubbing along alone when I could be comparatively happy where I could just see you once in a while. I will cheerfully agree to double any salary "little girl," if you will only agree not to hire out to teach again. Say "no" to me forever, "little girl," if you must. There is reason and sense in that, but I fail to see any reason or sense in your wearing your life out teaching.

It is late and I have to be up early, so I will close for this time. Hoping to hear from you soon and also to see you in June, I remain, with best wishes for you all

Yours Sincerely,
John G. Love

LOUISE DUDLEY
27 Rue Nazarine, Paris, France
23 May, 1909

Dear Ethel—

It is only your scorn of postals which has kept you from knowing I was going to move a week ago. I have not had time to snatch a letter in edgewise lately.

I took my work to the man whose books I have been using all winter, and he was so pleased with it he asked me to come live with him, so I took him up immediately. Unfortunately this one is like all the stories one tells after one has been in Paris a while, the tale is more exciting than the truth. The whole family really live in the country, but the mother and two children are existing in the city this winter for the sake of the girl's music. Papa lives out in the country with the books and comes in only on Sunday, because he has to give his courses at the university Monday a.m. Madame takes one *pensionnaire* to help out, and the room happened to be vacant at the time I turned up so he said come here and he could give me much more time. (Not good English, but maybe you can snatch at the truth.)

It is quite interesting. They are one of the good families of the country. I don't mean good in the sense of aristocratic, but the good farmer type who have had lots of sunshine and rain and hard work in their make-up. The wife does the cooking, and "fears you have not made out a meal" when you have twice as much as necessary. The husband I shall probably write you more about another time, for I have not exactly made up my own mind about him yet. Externally he seems just the masculine of his wife, endowed with a mighty brain. But his books show a fineness of sentiment which is inconsistent with that, and just now I have found out that he has a taste for music which goes to support the impression from his books.

I am so glad I did stay in Paris until spring; it is entirely different from Paris in winter. In fact, it seems as though it were made for the summer, and people just drag along through the winter, without taking the trouble to fix up or do anything for the comfort of the winter. The little tables on the street where one sits and drinks coffee or beer are not even taken in, and sit there through rain and snow so desolate, but now they are full all day long. The same is true of the statues of poorly clad muses and inspirations: they are lovely when the leaves are out, but in cold weather with no background—ugh! The environs are fine now; there are so many pretty parks which one can reach by boat or streetcar.

I went out to Versailles the other day, but one day is not nearly enough. One gets quite a nice sense of the old kings at Versailles in spite of the fact that the château is used as a historical museum, and too many of the rooms are decorated with pictures of Napoleon, and Napoleon III! You have no idea how hard it is to get that impression of the kings here at Paris. The fool Republicans have carefully scrubbed out all the footprints of the Louis's and written "Liberté, Egalité, Fraternité"* instead. Granted, there would be a lot more for a person who had more knowledge of the history of France, and more imagination; the history of France for Paris is at best a poor thing. Whoever thinks of the Louvre as anything but a *musée,* † the Palais Royal is used for little jewelry bazaars and second-class hotels! While for the Place de la Concorde, they sought something that would have no reference to the past horrors of the place, and landed on an Egyptian obelisk! Very suitable indeed for the purpose, but when one is skidding across it (Place, not obelisk) avoiding 25 autos and 16 carriages amidst countless bright lights, and gayly-dressed ladies, who has time or imagination to think that people waded across it, knee-deep in blood! The best one can do is to say when scooting by on the top of an auto-bus, "I wonder just where the guillotine stood!"

Versailles though, is a place which could not have been except for the kings, and one feels the difference. However, I will spare you a description of it this time.

Some things are worse than Kemper Hall. This boy here, 16 years old goes to school from 8–12, then 1:30–6:30, nine hours every day! and has one hour of gym a week! Of course he is too exhausted to do anything but flop when he comes home in the evening, and he holds himself so poorly; a man of eighty-five should be ashamed of his shoulders. When he lies down on the floor, he cannot make his shoulders touch the floor. I have started in making him do arm exercises with me every evening, but naturally he hates it and begs off every time he can. I cannot understand how parents will permit a thing like that. Miss Reid (the American I was with at 5 Rue

*Liberty, Equality, and Fraternity.
†Museum.

Vavin) says that is what comes of having an Egyptian obelisk for a father.

I will be here until the end of June, possibly longer.* I am awfully disappointed in a way, for I was getting ready to move, and if I go to Oxford for the winter, I will have very little time left for London this summer. Sometimes I feel as though Paris were a kind of wire I had gotten into, and it is not only harder to get out the longer I stay, but that pretty soon it would be impossible.

Warm kisses! (That is what the French say, and I rather like it, it means something still in English.) from
Louise Dudley

CARRIE HOLT
[GOLDYLOCKS]
Wellesley, Mass.,
May 24, 1909

Dearest Little Bear,

I suppose you wonder what has made me silent all these weeks. Ethel, I never kept so busy in my life I think, and yet have not accomplished very much.

Big Bear was sick in the hospital for a week with tonsilitis and I had to go down and keep her mother cheered up and run errands and that kept me so well out of mischief I have had no time for it since.

How is Boots [Little Ruth]? I want so much to see her! And the other youngsters too. I suppose they are much funnier to hear about than they are to care for, but luckily you have a strong sense of humor.

You'll be 'stonished when you see how we've grown. The new dormitory is nearly finished on the outside. They have two sets of workmen—one set begins at four in the morning and works till twelve and the other begins at eleven and works till eight and meanwhile the inhabitants of the hill go nearly crazy. The library is not growing so fast. One reason

*She had some work to finish for her mentor/landlord.

seems to be the fact that the workmen are distracted by the Shakespeare and Senior Play rehearsals in the Hollow and the Tree Day dancing across Longfellow.

Little Bear, I have had most astonishing Botany experience. Have had an asparagus fern for three years and at Christmas time it died. I cut it down and kept the pot of roots sitting round hoping that they would send up new shoots but none came. While I was home for Easter something wonderful happened, for when I came back there was the pot full of lovely hyacinths tied up to a nice little stick for support. Now the hyacinths are dead but the stick is growing beautifully. It already has twenty-three beautiful glossy leaves. Now what do you suppose will happen when the stick dies? For I suppose it will die, don't you.

Evidently my lamp was not filled today. At least it has very suspicious symptoms. Guess must stop writing and get it filled. Write me "by return mail."

Goldylocks

ETHEL P. WAXHAM
Denver, Colo., 4 June, 1909

Moneta, Wyo.

Dear Mr. Love,

Are you wondering how my garden is getting along? I do, myself, almost every day, and sometimes I think that it would discourage a Christian Scientist. Pater's radishes are doing nicely; this weather is good for them. Other things dip and droop and drop. I chose seeds to plant in a dry, hot, sandy place—and this has been a drizzly English spring.

The National Education Association meets here in Denver from July fourth to eleventh, and Faith has persuaded me to join. She has invited a friend of hers from Greeley, a big country girl, to stay here for the week to go to the meetings. Won't we have a pedagogic time? The only relief is that friend is to be married in August, and of course she will be interested in trousseau and wedding frivolities. The summer session of the University closes for the N.E.A. and it is rumored that all the clubs will entertain.

Our last few weeks have been redolent of paint, varnish, and stains. We have, so to speak, walked on the walls and ceilings, and merely looked at the floors. We have had breakfast in the dining room, dinner in the parlor, and supper in the kitchen, all in one rainy day. Kippy has learned to walk a plank, and as for Ruth, we have found her in paint from her hair to her shoes. Her chief joys have been scattering putty, hiding the painter's hat, and falling off what she calls his "climb up." The painter and his climb up left marks all over the garden, as well as in the house. Calcimine spattered all over furniture, walls, wall paper, windows! Floor filthy; doorknobs even, unspeakable, and housecleaning just over. Well, housecleaning isn't in it. Use liquid veneer!

Painter told me the last day in confidence that he was married to one of the best women in the world; he "couldn't do as well a second time!" He was really very nice though he looked like an overgrown Brownie. The others, the papers, calcimines and especially the "boss" are worse than potters. Could I say more than that?

Good night—Are you planning to have the work on your teeth finished in June?

Ethel Waxham

CARRIE HOLT
[Goldylocks]
Wellesley, Mass.,
June 11, 1909

Dear Little Bear,

Looks as if your letter came by return mail so Miss Haytop (Goldylocks' new name because I'm getting to be such an old woman) can't even stop to get her breakfast before she answers it. You blessed Little Bear! I just laughed and laughed till the old ladies thought I had had a spell. Tomorrow is Tree Day so when I get four shirtwaists washed and ironed and dress sewed up and beautiful *crimson* and *rose* silk Fauver made for 1903 and twenty-five notebooks corrected, I have all the rest of the day free till three o'clock, when Tree Day exercises begin.

Big Bear is buried in the garden now. She lets me come down and pick potato-beetles and plant-lice and dig cutworms and grubs and kill caterpillars and have the loveliest time. C.M.H. has laughed up her sleeve till it got a rip in it. You know B.B. and B.B.'s mother never saw a garden before and they thought you just had to put seeds in the ground and they came up and bore fruit a hundredfold and all they had to do was pull up a weed now and then and eat the fruit. So each new colony of bugs and beasts that moves in gives them a fit of blues and they decide they'll keep hens instead of having a garden. Haven't dared tell them 'bout the beasts that spoil the hens less you watch out.

And—now, you mustn't even pretend you ever heard of this—but mother of B.B. planted potatoes "any old way" and B.B. made her dig them all up and plant them over with the eye up. "Eke," said she, "they will all grow *into* the ground instead of up." Then they planted seeds of pretty tall red stuff—can't think of the name—round the front lawn and they all came up cabbages. They planted nicotiana[3] along the side of the house and when it got about two feet high, someone told them it was mustard! But they are having such a good time in spite of it all.

Must make bed, eat breakfast and go to work. With more love than you can guess.

C.M.G.H.

ETHEL P. WAXHAM
Denver, Colo., 12 June, 1909

Moneta, Wyo.

Dear Mr. Love—

No fault committed—nothing wrong. I was very sorry to read of your trouble with the sheep. Does it take a whole family to care for you, or do father and mother assume the responsibility?

School is over at last. Faith is going East after the N.E.A. for the rest of the summer. Little Ruth Harper is back from California, much to our joy, for her substitute, Dorothy Isabel has brought our Little Ruth to grief many a time. Day before yesterday it was an ant hill and mud on clean clothes. While Ruth was screaming and the ants were biting and I was trying to get them out of her hair and off of her anatomy, Isabel cried joyously, "It hasn't stopped hurting yet, has it? It hurts awfully, doesn't it? It won't stop for a long time! They didn't get on me at all!" Yesterday, bare feet; today a can of fermented maple syrup and tobacco. Tomorrow—?

Garden is doing well, in spite of three hail storms in two days. Why is it that nothing grows as fast or as easily as a weed—say lamb's quarters? I have had several crops of them already.

Baby Hugh is a tiny bit better, and we hope that it may be a turning point. He is more like a baby, though still only about as large as a doll.

It's late and eyes won't stay open, so goodnight from
Ethel Waxham

JOHN G. LOVE
Moneta, Wyo, June 16th/09

Dear Miss Waxham,

I am in Moneta looking after the shearing and although it is now after midnight, I will write you a few lines with a lead pencil as that is all I have. I am doing this upon a Montgomery Ward catalogue and in my own light, so it may be a trifle worse than usual. I was certainly glad to get your letter three days ago and pleased to get another one tonight.

I will be through the shearing in three days if it does not rain. The sheep will then start for the mountains and I will go back to the ranch and get things in shape to leave as soon as I can. I must brand some of the calves before they scatter again, but the cattle that are away off and straggling horses will have to go until I get back. It seems ages since I saw you. I have fought my inclinations all winter and attended strictly to business, made money, and then watched eight thousand dollars of it go in forty days. If I lose no more, I have still made money for the year. I want from you what money cannot buy, so there is no object in my piling up money.

The "whole Oklahoma family" have very little to do with me and have no especial care of or for me. Their house of about four rooms is about ready, and it will be a relief to get back to my old den again. They can run a road ranch[4] or do as they please. When I or the hired men eat there, I will pay for the meals. I had to have a family there to do the work and see to things. Even with you here, the work would have to be done by someone else. You would not be able to do the work and would not be permitted to if you were. Had I been looking for a slave or a drudge, "little girl," you would have been about the last one I would have picked upon.

Poor little Ruth certainly does have her trials and troubles. At the close of your last letter you say, "Baby Hugh is a tiny bit better, etc." You never before mentioned his being sick. I sincerely hope that he is all right once more.

We have had several showers during the last few weeks and the grass is good all over the range. Today was very warm and this is a beautiful night. In just three hours and a half, I will be standing at the dodge gate working sheep, so I had better get to bed. Please write soon, "little girl," for I may not get away as soon as I expect to. With best wishes for you all,

Yours Sincerely,
John G. Love

LOUISE DUDLEY
Paris, 28 June, 1909

Dear Ethel,

It is two weeks since I told you I would write again in a week, but I have been so busy I have not had the time. I think I have been working too hard; I am dead tired all the time and thoughts are a thing of the remote past. (P.S. Am better now that I have had my dinner. Despise not all "cuisine.")

It's all very well to talk about the saving loneliness that makes life possible, but I am getting to the point where I could stand a little steady company of someone I liked.

I went to an exhibition of pictures this afternoon, and as I thought about you a good part of the time, shall have to tell you about it. There were a hundred portraits of women of the 18th century of the French and English schools. The French pictures I did not care for much, but the English ones were lovely, Sir Joshua Reynolds particularly, and Sir Henry Lawrence, and Gainsborough. I almost wished I was a man for the first time in my life. The best of them were such *perfect* women, and all of them so calm in their beauty, or their attempts at it, and none with any sense much, and only some few—chiefly among the French portraits—with any sense of humour.

Why do we have to go puttering around making ourselves miserable by trying to have sense? I looked at the pictures of those women, calm, noble, simple in pleasures, submissive to their husbands, but not servile, and I looked at the women looking at them, with white gloves, suits and hats to match, etc., and it seemed to me they filled their place in the world much better than those of us who go buzzing around after things called higher. If I were a man I wouldn't want a woman like myself; and yet inconsistently, or is it consistently, I think I had rather have a proposal than anything else on earth now. Not that I am in love or anything of that kind, but I never have had one in my life, and it would be kind of a secret title, or degree, as it were, certifying that Louise Dudley is not an entire failure as a woman.

While I was looking at the pictures, too, I began thinking of your remarks about Matthew Arnold and Pater. No, I don't think Pater found at all "the things that make one realize one's existence most passionately;" he realized the lack of them and that is how he knew their value. Those who do realize their existence most passionately are not the ones who think that at all—if indeed they have the time to think about such things. It is like Stevenson's saying we must not look for happiness in this world, but our first duty is to make our neighbor happy. It looks as though it were a premium set on the unthinking, doesn't it. The comforting thing is that we would all rather have but a little gold, or none at all, and know that it is valuable, than be surrounded by it and not be able to tell it from the common dust.

Enough of those platitudes. I am going to London! I hope to get off next week. Expect to find some of my Bryn Mawr friends there who have scholarships, etc., and wish I had some more clothes, for coming right from America and Bryn Mawr, they may be shocked at me.

Am going to start you a little book before I leave Paris. You must like it because of the two engravings, and because I picked it up in one of the boxes along the Quai, and paid 10 centimes for it.

Goodbye, lots of love,
from Louise

JOHN G. LOVE
Moneta, July 2nd/09

Dear Miss Waxham,

Everyone else is in bed and I should be, but as I am going to Moneta in the morning, I will write you a few lines.

I have dipped all of my sheep in cresoleum dip and finished hand-doctoring them this morning for leg and lip ulceration. I used sulphate of copper, sulphate of mercury, pure carbolic acid, iodine and a host of other things, and my hands are in beautiful condition. I start dipping again on the 7th. I have had a veterinary surgeon from Washington here for the past eight days superintending the doctoring and holding post mortems on dead sheep. The sheep still continue to die and he acknowledges that he cannot tell either the cause or the cure.[5] His present opinion is that they eat something that by the time the plant or plants reach the fourth or true stomach, they or it has formed hydrocyanic acid which causes a very speedy death. Sometimes they die a very few minutes after we first notice them. From one to fifty per day join the silent majority. It is rather hard luck, "little girl," but as I cannot help it, I have to take my medicine and look pleased. Not a calf or a colt has been branded yet and although I have twelve hired men, I am crowded with work. I planned to be in Denver long before this, but as Burns says "The best laid plans of baith mice and men gang aft' agley."

The days are very warm, and this is certainly a beautiful night, calm, clear, cool and almost a full moon. My garden looks very good, but some of my oats are suffering for water. It is very discouraging, "little girl," to lose from ten to four hundred dollars every day. I suppose that it will just be my luck when I do get down to Denver to find Dr. Hepp gone for his vacation. At present we are getting the benefit of all the ice that I put up last winter. We are not going to have enough of it, but what we do have is good.

I will be at home even on the "Fourth" if it is Sunday. The teams and saddle horses will move along just the same as if it were Monday or any other day. They can play and do nothing when I am away, but they will move while I am here.

Two four-horse teams go to Wolton in the morning for grain and supplies, and come home on Sunday the 4th. On the 5th we start towards the dipping plant, and then home again to my own corrals to work and doctor the sheep again. I am enclosing a list of drugs that I want and if your father will kindly get them for me and ship them at once by express to Moneta, I will appreciate the favor. Have him send the bill along and unless I am coming right down, I will at once send check for same. Please write soon and often, "little girl," and cheer my drooping spirits, but please do not write any "impossible" letter. With best wishes

Yours Sincerely
John G. Love

CARRIE HOLT
[GOLDYLOCKS]
Woods Hole, Mass.,
July 6, 1909

Dearest Little Bear—

Commencement seems one long nightmare and I am glad Little Bear is coming some other time 'cause had so many things to do. Only I'd have brought Little Bear down here to Wood's Hole and it would have been very lovely.

You'd like Woods' Hole, it is such a queer place. This part of the place, where are the Laboratories and the Fish Commission, looks as if someone had gone over the country and bought up odd lots of houses at bargain sales, little houses and big ones, of every shape and color—and then taken them up high in a big air ship and tumbled them down. Some landed right side up and some wrong—some on the water's edge, some *in* the water, some in midst of green fields and some on sand heap. And everywhere, filling the queer spaces between are roses—lovely fragrant wild roses and honeysuckle and bay. There are three little houses just alike on the side here by the eel pond—one just a little above the other and every one calls them "do" "re" "mi" and I live in "re." I can see the ocean and the sunset from my window and nothing else because window is so high up, ledge is on level with my chin.

Everything so clean and such funny signs everywhere. In my mirror is the polite request "Please do not bathe from this room." What do you suppose that means? There are no bathrooms in Woods Hole and out behind the house is the most shining place all with a new coat of blue paint with a coat of varnish you can see your face in, and up on the wall a neat card with "Please do not soil the seat."

Little Bear, I really got to go to sleep. Want to sleep all the time and not eat. Goodnight,

Goldylocks

ETHEL P. WAXHAM
Denver, 12 July, 1909

Dear Mr. Love,

Pater sent you the drugs you wanted, he said, and I certainly hope that they will prove effectual. Of course you will not plan to come down until the sheep are getting along better. Denver, and Dr. Hepp and I will probably be here a month, or two or three months, from now about as surely as we are here this minute.

Garden is discouraging. During the N.E.A. convention, there was a hail storm every afternoon or evening for nearly a week. This week the poppies were stripped of every leaf and beaten down until there seems to be nothing left. Now I am getting some nasturtiums, sweet peas and a few cornflowers every day. Some great beast—I suspect the janitor—broke almost all of my cosmos. Do you know of an oasis in the desert for rent, one surrounded by a high wire fence, charged with electricity, warranted to keep away lions, tramps, and painters? If you know of such a place, it will save my advertising. Pearl says I'm always "fussing" with flowers; "You're a great flower somebody."

It is really astonishing what a host of unexpected relatives a convention brings. That is one of the advantages, or otherwise, of living in a convention city. Haven't seen so many distant relatives since the D.A.R.* Some from Detroit whom I never even heard of came, calling me by first name, telling all the history of my life, and claiming to be cousins twice removed, or something of the sort. It's uncanny. Some are coming this morning, called "queer" because they have strange ideas, live very much alone, although they are burdened with this world's goods, and are not clannish. Relatives just left—ever so nice. Wish everybody was "queer."

Faith left last week for Rockford, where she was due yesterday morning. Her Greeley friend wrote at the last

*Daughters of the American Revolution.

moment saying that she was unable to attend the N.E.A. and must forego her visit here; wedding exigencies, I suppose.

Before she left, I had a three day visit to Empire up in the mountains. A High School friend of mine whom I met by chance in the street, after having neither seen nor heard from her in three years, asked me for a little visit. She too is preparing a trousseau. Seems to me all the world is to be wed.

Days are hot, hot. Miss McCaulley, Dean of Women at Boulder whom I met at the N.E.A. reception, told me that she was going to take to the hills, with a baby Irish terrier, and a woman weighing two hundred pounds. Asked me if I thought it was safe, at her age. How many people of any age would really do it? Here's to Miss McCaulley!

Marcia's in Idaho, with husband, gold mine, lawsuit. Comes back the first of August. That is all the news except that Hugh is better, better every day.

Are there any sheep left? Don't get the blues. If you stay away much longer, you'll have two surprises instead of one when you come to Denver.

Sincerely yours,
Ethel P. Waxham

Two empty envelopes from John G. Love, dated September 2 and September 30, 1909 show that he replied.

TWILIGHT

Twilight of floating silver veils
*   Between the earth and darkening sky,*
Softly and closely upon the dales
*   Prisons the fragrance drifting by—*

Locust, hedgerose, and tansy weed;
*   The chiming of the bells floats down,*
Stilled at the level of man's need
*   With all the noises of the town.*

The mother of All at her wild wood hearth,
Crooning a song to him who aspires,
Hushes and calms with the beauty of earth
The thoughts that wander, the soul that desires.

Ethel Waxham   Denver, 1909

LOUISE DUDLEY
Oxford, [*date illegible*]

Dear Ethel—

I moved up to Oxford yesterday. My! but I wish you were here! It is lovely! Nice old crumbling college buildings with bright window boxes, and perfectly smooth, green lawns, walks under the trees, seats by the side of the river, boats all along the river, with nice youths in shirt sleeves drawn up up in the shade smoking and reading, family parties going out for the day, and every now and then a perspiring German rowing along; all the others are paddling or punting. Did you ever see anyone punt? You have a very long pole which you stick in the ground and push yourself along with. The "punter" stands at the end of the boat and punts standing, very graceful when one does it well, something like I imagine the "gondoliers" in Venice.

I am living here in Oxford with two women I knew at Bryn Mawr and a B.M. girl who has been there since I left, and it is disastrous when it comes to using spare time. I spend it all talking to them.

Think I shall go to Cambridge for the month of September maybe, if a man there will let me work with him. Have not told him of the honor about to be done him yet.

Will write again next chance I get.

Love,
Louise

ETHEL P. WAXHAM
Denver, October 10, 1909

Wolton, Wyo.

[Forwarded to Moneta, Wyoming.]

Dear Mr. Love,

Your letter came to me about two weeks ago; this time I
am following your good example and answering first.

Bertha did not improve; in fact she departed in less than a
week, and I, having learned to spell w-i-n-d-e-r, like the
immortal Mr. Squeers, immediately proceeded to wash it.
That lasted until the gains, which would have been Bertha's,
obtained a tiny little Hamedan rug for the hall. Then the
giantess came. History outdoes itself, you see. Pearl weighed
a hundred and forty, with about my height. Bertha, with the
same height weighed a hundred pounds more; and the giantess—but she must be six feet four, so she does not look very
large. She's a widow with a son of seventeen—intelligent,
pleasant, and comparatively capable.

I was very glad when she came, for I had just begun
tutoring a tutoreen, to turn an honest, but very diminutive
penny. Tutoreen is in High School, in the ways of Caesar,
Physics, History, English and Algebra. She is ill of a myste-
rious disease which puzzles the wise-heads; a red spot appears
and disappears on her ankle, then the foot swells and she
pops into bed.

Another reason for joy in the arrival of the giantess is that
she could make two of Ruth's three birthday cakes. For Ruth
had a party of twelve children and about six grownups to
celebrate her fourth fall with games and cake with candles,
ice cream, candy and presents to be fished for with a string
and pole.

Little Robert has been having a number of mishaps and
illnesses, all directly due to his appetite. Once he was the
victim of a grasshopper whom, in a moment of hunger, he
tried to devour. Another time he tried rock salt from the ice

cream freezer, and again the baby's medicine. Down, up, both of them. Hugh is trying to destroy this letter this very minute, for I'm holding him and writing at the same time and he's cross.

It is a queer, queer world, isn't it? And at the worst, one would always like to know—but somehow when it is best, the answer does not so much matter. Same old bee has been buzzing in my bonnet—teaching. Perhaps it is the fault of this first cold weather, or tutoring, or some High School friends I met for the first time in a good many years, or because Pater wants me to teach. Anyway the spirit is willing at last, and if job comes, goodbye E. P. W. I'm sure it can't be as bad as it was. Who knows? May become desperately enamoured of the profession.

Did I write you about my day with Marcia to serve at the reception for her brother and his bride? Her house is lovely. It does not seem as if Mr. George could do enough for her. Their trip to Alaska you may be glad to know involved no walking. It was only a sea voyage of several weeks to look at the Skagway—a glacier.

Speaking of glaciers—the garden is a sad sight. The first frost came on the eighth of October, and it was a hard one. All the gay green leaves are black and crinkled, and the sturdy marigolds look as if a fire had blackened the stalks, and left just a little flame at the top where the blossom still shines. I went out in the snow storm and picked the last of the sweet peas.

Haven't touched the piano for weeks. Perhaps now I can, while the giantess does the dishes! This is a volume, isn't it? Time to say good night, and sign myself

Yours, very sincerely,
Ethel P. Waxham

JOHN G. LOVE
Moneta, Oct 12th/09

Dear Miss Waxham,

   Away over a month, "little girl," since you last wrote.

   I have been in the saddle all day and am rather tired, but I must be up and off by daylight in the morning to look for Punch. He got away tonight from one of my men with a new saddle on. After I get him, I must go to Moneta to see about dipping the sheep. There is nothing the matter with them, but the federal government backed up by state officials has ordered a general dipping of sheep and I must obey. The loss was heavy this summer, but I start in the winter with eleven thousand, five hundred sheep, two hundred cattle and a hundred horses besides cats, dogs, chickens, geese, etc. I am once more in debt, but if my season of bad luck has come to an end and the winter is not too severe, I will come out with flying colors in the spring. From Oct. 1st, 1908 to Oct. 1st, 1909 I figure that I have *lost* over four thousand dollars. Yet on April 1st, I could have sold out and cleared ten thousand dollars. I hope 1910 will see things on the right side of the ledger once more.

   Your picture nicely framed now adorns the wagon along with a rather nice water color painting that was given to me by one of my favorite girls a few months before she was married to a drunken sot last fall. I have a nice coal fire burning in the wagon now as the nights are rather frosty. I can hear the wild ducks quacking on the lake as I write. They really should be asleep and so should I instead of burning the midnight oil.

   I have most of my potatoes in the cellar and will start the teams plowing until it freezes up. Then I have twelve hundred cedar posts to haul seventeen miles and sand to haul to make a concrete cellar next summer. Then I must haul sand and rock for the chimney to the fireplace. No end of work to do, but still I am not contented. We have had two little "skiffs" of snow already, but they soon melted and we are now having beautiful weather.

The Oklahoma family are all well and really keeping themselves cleaner than they were. I am seldom in the house—only at meal time. They are very good cooks. The girls are very good girls, but they know very little and I don't like them for some reason. Write soon and often.

Yours Sincerely,
John G. Love

MARY B. MILLS
Red Bluff Ranch,
October 18, 1909

Dear little Housekeeper—

It seems strange enough to sit down quietly this afternoon and write. First time I've been able to do so this summer, which has, indeed, been a busy one. I've jellied, jammed, pickled and spiced until I'm tired, but it's a satisfaction to have it all in the cellar.

Monday night we had a dance to celebrate Sandford's birthday—the house looked pretty, the girls looked pretty, the boys looked nice, the midnight supper was fine, (so they said) and altogether everything a success. A boy is twenty-one but once you know. Friday, the eighth, we all went over to Red Canyon—the delightful house is just completed—and danced a farewell to Louise Poling. You would love Louise—very simple but so artistic—nothing jars when you enter a room—something so unusual in this country where one usually must use whatever they happen to have.

I've had the loveliest roses this summer—real roses—picked the last lovely La Francesca for Sandford's birthday dinner—the sweet peas, too, have been lovely. The year did not start out very finely in the spring, but fruits and gardens have been a great success—great quantities of tomatoes, cucumbers, watermelons, etc. This afternoon they are gathering in the winter vegetables.

I expect those dreadful threshers will be here next week.

You don't know how cosmopolitan Lander has grown—cement walks and autos everywhere—the poor horses have rather a hard time.

Haven't seen the Charlie Halls this summer. The new oil town of Wyopow is located on part of their ranch—above the house on the hill are two immense oil tanks. They have piped the oil from the oil well near Dallas to the railroad at Charlie Hall's. Of course, Charlie has wild dreams and I only hope they will come true.

I think Rosie Hart is at St. Joseph's Hospital in Denver—at least, she is to go there and become a nurse. Nursing makes me think of the babies. We were so glad to hear of little Hugh's improvement—does he still continue to laugh? Robert must be exceedingly interesting—and what of Ruth—does she go to school?

We hear a great deal of the Denver kindergartens when Mr. Love comes up—he seems greatly interested in them. We hadn't seen him for ages until two or three weeks ago.

The shadows are getting long and this housekeeper must see about filling the inner man—not having an English giantess, she must do it herself.

I am writing at a new desk—my birthday present— lacquered oak in the mission style. It came knocked down and unstained, so it was lots of fun finishing it. Everyone likes it very much.

Ever most lovingly,
Mary B. Mills

Ethel P. Waxham
1364 Marion St., Denver
17 October, 1909

John G. Love

Dear Mr. Love,

The time did get ahead of me last month when it came to writing letters. I thought, however, that it would not make much difference, for you were so busy that *you* did not write for about a month. I had a long letter from Mrs. Mills, telling of the company there and the children's good times. I wondered if you were one of the guests mentioned only in numbers—not named!

Uncle Ernest has been in town this week. Pater has had some company and Faith has not felt equal to doing anything more than her kindergartening. Weather has been beautiful. Every time I look out at the trees—yellow now—I think that perhaps the next day I can get out. Pater hopes for an automobile, and I for a horse! Tutoreen is in small difficulties. If she were only ambitious and thorough, she could do fine work, for she has a good mind, and a fine start. But she is destined for a muscial career. Her mother has all the ambition for her that she lacks, and will make a musician of her, whether or no!

When is your Oklahoma family going to cease troubling you, and move into their own house? You see I have an interest in your welfare!

Sincerely yours,
Ethel P. Waxham

[Scrawled at the top of this page: What you can't read, guess at.]

JOHN G. LOVE
Moneta, Wyo., Oct 25th/09

Dear Miss Waxham,

Your letter of the 10th received on the 21st, forwarded from Wolton, and yours of the 17th received on the 25th. If your letters would continue to come that often, "little girl," I would indeed be happy. I am camped now at Ed Merriam's ranch 2½ miles from Moneta. The lamp is about out, also the fire, and it is almost midnight. I must be up at four in the morning. I have just come from the engine house where I am fireman, engineer and dip mixer. My sheep are all dipped and gone, but I have to help others for three days yet before I can go home. I am writing this in the cold with my feet on the table and the tablet on my knee and have neither ink or any other paper here. If I do not get a letter off to you, it will be ages before I hear from you again.

After September passed and you did not go to teach, I heaved a sigh of relief. Now you say you may yet do it if you can get a job. If your father wants you to teach, that shows clearly that he does not particularly need you there. I need you up here, "little girl," very much if you will only come. To give you the luxuries of life or a European tour just at present would cause me to sacrifice some of my livestock, but I would ten times rather sell off everything than to have you teach and have anything happen to you. What good would my livestock be to me in that event? At all hazards strangle that teaching bee as regards others, but please decide to come and teach "poor me."

Lamp going out so I will have to close for the present, but will write from the ranch when I get home again. Please write at once, "little girl," and tell me that you really will not hire out to teach this winter to set my mind at rest on that point at least.

P.S. Not being permitted to sign myself other than the above, I always leave the rest to be understood and you understand.

He continues in a letter dated October 31:

I am once more back in the wagon. The weather is very nice and I am hustling every day to get as much as I can done before it freezes. We started a new ditch today,[6] but broke the "go devil" and had to quit. The plowing is getting along nicely, but still it is sure to freeze up before I am ready for it.

I can look up as I write and see your picture on the wall of the wagon. That fills a long-felt want, "little girl," but I long for the original of it. The family are still in my house and I do not know just at present when I will have them move. I can manage first rate with the wagon if they will only keep the phonograph still when I am eating.

There is no use in my fixing up the house anymore, papering etc., until I know how it should be done and I won't know that until you see it and say how it ought to be fixed. If you never see it, I don't want it fixed, for I won't live here. *We* could live very comfortably in the wagon while *our* house was being fixed up to suit you if you only would say yes. I have a paperhanger and painter herding for me whom I could use to advantage in case of need. Now, "little girl," there are two things that I especially want you to do: say *yes* and write often. And two things that I especially wish you would not do: please do not teach and please do not write any "impossible" letters. If you will only comply with those wishes, I will be supremely happy and we will live happy ever after. Hoping that you will do so, "little girl," I remain

Yours Sincerely,

John G. Love

ETHEL P. WAXHAM
Denver, 14 November, 1909

Moneta, Wyo.

Dear Mr. Love,

News from Wyoming has been plentiful this month, with about five letters from the Mills people. For you know Sandford has had a great celebration on his twenty-first birthday, and is now, I suppose, a grown man. Wonder if he has the same unquestioning belief in what he is told or sees in print that he had three years ago. Misrepresentation of any motive for good reasons or bad was quite beyond him. Mrs. Mills wrote that you seemed much impressed by the excellence of the Denver kindergartens, and she wondered why.

Speaking of kindergartens, Ruth has started at Emerson. Ask her if she likes it, and she will probably answer "Naw!", but she does.

The kitchen has been all too empty of help for a long while. Even the washerwomen were incompetent and slow. Really, I think that I might compete with the Fat girl in the number of "pieces" ironed in a day, but I trust that that knowledge of the art will always be superfluous. I've been tutoring another girl, from Miss Wolcott's school. She wears me all out, because she is nervous, and doesn't study, and thinks she knows. I told her that she did not need me. Suppose you never wished that you didn't have to be grown up, but would rather live with Peter Pan in the tree tops.

You really don't mean what you said about my teaching you? I'm sure you would not like it, after a few weeks. Besides, it is harder to teach one than twenty, often. If you try to do it without being suspected of trying to "improve" someone, that someone is blissfully unconscious of any gentle influence. But if you say, "Pater, when you say 'there is two,' you are using a singular verb with a plural noun, which is incorrect," Pater says, "Oh that's all right!" (Because he does it, forsooth!) Or, "My grammar is better than some," which is perfectly true but unsatisfying. Or, "That's good enough for me." There the would-be reformer is obliged to consider herself a busybody, and knows better than to continue her thankless efforts, but adjusts herself to the lower standard.

How are Jack and the nurse doing together? Have they come to the adjustment period yet. I wonder if they come to grief over religion!

The children are comical little beggars. Hugh sits on the floor and says, "How 'te do?" and Robert, talking in his sleep a few nights ago announced, "Santa Claus loves Sister Ethel and Aunt Faith and is going to bring Grandpa lots of toys." Ruth suspects a white bearded gentleman across the street of being St. Nick himself, and asked him about it. "He says he ain't Santa Claus, but Santa Claus is a friend of his." Pater is already telling Ruth and Robert that Santa will be present in person to take gifts from the tree.

It is late for me, and I am tired, so I will bid you good night.

Sincerely yours,
Ethel P. Waxham

10

Pueblo: 1909

The opportunity for a change presented itself. Ethel, encouraged by her father, ignored John Love's entreaties not to teach again, and accepted a position at Central High School in Pueblo, Colorado. Constant as before, he now had concern for her welfare as a teacher to add to his growing list of problems with the ranch. Ethel's widowed sister Vera and her two small sons returned to the Marion Street apartment to share the household responsibilities of caring for themselves, Dr. Waxham, Faith, and young Ruth.

Ethel P. Waxham
206 East Orman Ave.
Pueblo, Colo.,
29 November, 1909

John G. Love

Dear Mr. Love,
    You won't like what I have to tell you, and I'm sorry. But please, kind sir, I won't do it any more, or at least not for a long while. On the evening of Friday last I was advised to ask Mr. Barrett for the place of the Latin and Greek teacher, who was suddenly taken ill here. On Saturday I did; came [to Pueblo] Sunday; went to work at eight ten this morning. It really is not so bad; seems like the millenium after the Dark Ages of K.H. Mr. Barrett suggested a rooming house near the school, landlady suggested a boarding house quite near (both are yellow) and the High School teachers have all been

313

as cordial as could be. In fact, last evening when my trunk was unpacked and I was almost ready for bed, landlady announced that Mr. Barrett was in the parlor! Position may be only through January if Miss Powelson recovers sufficiently to return. If she does not, I shall stay until June. She is to be married in the summer, so Mr. Barrett has already suggested my filling her place in the fall, even if she does return for the spring months. Spite of the prestige and remuneration the allurements of the life are few! Pater is the only one who seemed very glad to have me teach. But I am glad; for Vera will be at home now, and won't have to work so hard over the babies. She has been all worn out and half sick.

The day I decided to go was surely exciting. Telephone call came at noon. I began packing at once. Then made the discovery that Mildred had been appropriating things. She tried to bluff for a while, and then broke down and confessed, promised to make reparation and so on. Company came in the midst of the tumult.

Mrs. Signor and Edith came to Denver a few days ago, to get treatment for Mrs. Signor. They expect to stay over the holidays. I invited them to supper Friday night, but that was the only time I had to visit with them since I left so suddenly. Mrs. Signor said that Mr. Young had built some sort of a lodge or road ranch for Jack and the nurse, whom she considered "quite a cute girl."

It is very late for a "wage slave" to be up, so I will say goodnight and write again soon.

Sincerely yours,
Ethel P. Waxham

JOHN G. LOVE
Moneta, Wyo., Dec. 10th/09

Dear Miss Waxham,

Your long looked-for letter just received and I am indeed sorry, "little girl," to know that you are once more teaching. I have troubles enough without having that to worry about. I can't explain why even to myself. It must be because you are such a dainty little mortal and do not look strong enough for the work. Please write often even if it is only a few lines saying that you are well and happy, but do not take time from your needed rest to write long letters.

I have lots to worry about here and I confess, "little girl," that I am glad that you are not here to share my worry. The past twelve days have been the hardest on livestock that I have ever seen on the range at this season of the year. The snow is deep and the weather has been bitterly cold, 30° below zero, and lower part of the time. It moderated last night and today, but for the past twelve hours, there has been a heavy driving snow from the northwest. Now at midnight, the storm is as bad as ever. My teams got in yesterday with eleven thousand pounds of corn and oats to feed the sheep. In the morning I start for Wolton with four four-horse teams for more corn. We will have to take shovels to dig through the drifts.

I knew that the Signors were in Denver for I saw Eli Signor in Lander. I got a livery team in Lander on Thanksgiving day and drove out to see Jack and his better half. I only saw them for a few minutes, drove back that night to Lander, and came home on the train next morning. I failed to see anything "cute" about the nurse. She is a rather tall, slender, very neat and very sensible, nice girl. I did intend to get them down here, but I have decided to run bachelors' hall until spring at least. This tribe that I have here now will leave in a few days, bag and baggage for their home in Oklahoma and I certainly will be glad to see the last of them. The man is a fine fellow and a good worker, but the others are wasteful, dirty and lazy, and all around fools.

It is entirely beyond my comprehension why your father wants you to teach. I sincerely hope that the teacher whose place you are filling, recovers and still yearns to teach. I also hope that the fellow to whom she is to be married has no better persuasive powers than I have, and that she will insist upon teaching in spite of him.

I don't know just when I will get to see you now. I had planned to tough it out here until the 6th of January. Then I was coming to Denver for the livestock show to stay a whole week. I thought that would be better than coming during the holiday season. My plans may change yet. The weather may prevent my leaving at all. Write soon and often.

Yours Sincerely,
John G. Love

ETHEL P. WAXHAM
Pueblo, 16 December, 1909

Moneta, Wyo.

Dear Mr. Love,

Your letter reached me a few days ago, and I was indeed sorry to learn of the hard weather that you are having. Now I shall have to worry about you, as well as about the family in Denver, and my own work here. Pater is very much discouraged because times are hard and practice poor.

Miss Powelson has been operated upon for appendicitis, and is rapidly recovering. She expects to return in the middle or last of January. One drawing card, I imagine, is the fact that the man to whom she is engaged lives here, and another is that she wants the salary for pretty wedding clothes and household linens!

There is just a week of vacation for the public schools. I am hoping to get to Denver for most of that time. Vera and babies are at home, and Pater and Faith write that she is looking better, eating better, and seeming happier than she was.

The weather here has been cold and wretched. The thermometer has registered seventeen below, and there has been snow on the ground almost ever since I arrived.

Mr. Barrett, the principal, I suspect is trying to see what I can do. On Monday I reached school at eight, and left at five-thirty. On Tuesday he gave me thirty, eight-page essays to read and grade—not even in my department!—and a class belonging to the history teacher. On Wednesday it was eight to five-fifteen again, and today an enrollment room and an English class for an absent teacher. Experience *gratis*. Time to get ready for supper; will have to tell you about study hall in next letter.

    Best wishes for you and the sheep

from

Ethel Waxham

DONALD MCLEAN
Monte Vista, Colo.
12/18/09

Dear Ethel—

    It was 23 below last night and all day the mountains, usually clean-cut like strong men's chins, have seemed pale and feathery. Colors have ridiculous names, sometimes, which they get from trying to be fashionable, such as Alice Blue (which should be juniper berry blue instead) and cerise. Well, this sky was "Elephant's breath" shade and the mountains, the same color, and merged into it without any distinct outline just as though you should draw something with a white charcoal and smear it.

    So now I have to sit in a bottomless chair by the stove, as I shiver by my table, and write with a pencil (or go to bed). The pencil seems homelike and old timesy, anyway, so you won't mind. The fire seems that way too, and I'm getting to like my bunkhouse quarters very much. The work is just what I want and all my animals have become personal friends. It seems, though, I'll have to change my range soon. I'm not very successful and it's not my fault this time. My boss isn't square, and a man can't keep his work a-bubbling when that's true.

    You're right about "you used to try. I'm ashamed of you." Am I degenerating? I do not own. Sometimes I think I am and sometimes I'm sure I'm not. The must-be's press pretty

317

close these days, and as to stories, I know I'm getting a more sensual way of feeling them without trying to express them. They're there just the same and I see them and enjoy them just as much as ever, but the must-be's keep me from concentrating or trying to express them. Expression is a matter of practice, isn't it? And I'm keeping a long silence these days. I've talked so much all my life, without being accurate, and without knowing what I said.

Tell me! Do you think I'm degenerating? I'm losing much timidity, I'm getting somewhat more forceful—manly (some would say, whatever that is.) But I'm forgetting some details, losing some art, but not the feeling, I hope, if that is possible; some refinements too, and I'm not nearly as particular, so straight-jacketed as I was; I'm a positive backslider in some ways, and I'm much looser—not nearly as "substantial" as I was. Should I get married as some people suggest I should? I don't seem to be nearly of a marriageable age yet. Besides, I've decided I don't know what love is. You promised me some "philosophy of life" in your last letter. Come now! what is love, or what should I have to get married? Must I have an "absorbing passion,"—something that makes me ache and grieve when I'm not near her, makes me restless at night, and is honestly an awfully sensual desire when dispassionately analyzed? And isn't this necessarily a matter of contact, and how am I to go courting in this business and at my age when life is business and I've got it to do? Should I have married at 18 when I had time to court?

Or should I ask one who I know will stimulate my best, and help me to grow where I'm weak and at the same time keep all these finenesses which I say I'm losing? One who raises no unquenchable thirst in me or passionate desire, but who, I'm sure will grow apace and keep me growing, and one whom, I think, my present affection for, will grow to a great love—common version—when there is everyday contact? This seems much more intelligent. Or should I wait till I find an ideal, a combination of both?

Is it necessary that I get into such a mess that I'll say "no man ever loved, as I love you, my own."?

Please give me some good solid advice from your store-room on this. And I'd like it if you'd ask for some of my philosophy on your life. You don't say much about yourself. I don't need entertaining by discussing myself—at least, not always. I still philosophise if I don't tell stories.

For Christmas, I got you *Inspired Millionaires* which says a few things I hadn't thought of, and a lot I had in a way I like. It's ordered from the publisher's and will be coming along soon without card to your Denver address.

And as for Christmas wishes, you're stupid if you don't know what they are without making me be trite.

Donald

UNSUCCESSFUL

Some few I dreamed of in the haze of fall,
  Bound by earth's loveliness to reverence
All that we see ensphered by the immense
Blue jewel of the sky; bound too, by all
Earth's cruelty and sin and untold wrong
    To suffer pain—though pain itself was young
    When many thousand thousand winds had sung
Through tropic forests beauty's ageless song.
I dreamed of those whose hearts could faithful be
    To dreams of beauty aging with the years
That men call old, to dreams of liberty
    Unfound, of truth unknown, and conquered fears—
Which we dare hope must come to pass, since they
Through falling empires keep their quiet way.

Ethel P. Waxham   1909

ETHEL P. WAXHAM
Pueblo, 22 Dec. 1909

Moneta, Wyo.

Dear Mr. Love,

I'm ever so sorry about your bad weather. It has been the worst here for twenty years. The poor people on the streets

look wretchedly cold, with their worn out clothing. It has
been bad enough, and hard enough for people as prosperous
as school teachers to keep warm. The school thermometers
have registered between forty and sixty-four all week. That is
cold, for sitting still all day. Then on Monday the pipes burst
so we had a holiday, tra la!

Miss Powelson continues to improve, but there is a va-
cancy in a rival High School on the North Side. I haven't
applied for it, but probably will.

Will this letter reach you about Christmastime, I wonder?
It will be in time to wish you Happy New Year, perhaps, if
not Merry Christmas. Here's hoping that Fate will make the
year to come a good one for you.

Sincerely yours,
Ethel P. Waxham

She wrote one more letter in 1909, with a P.S. added January 1, 1910:

Dear Mr. Love,

Santa Claus forgot to bring me any stationery, and I did
not provide myself with any, so I will have to ask you to
pardon the typewriter paper. I do want to write to you,
however, to tell you about a large, round, leather covered
box of candy which came to me last Thursday at home. There
wasn't any name with it, but I did not feel at all in doubt
about the sender. I only wish that you were here tonight in
Pueblo to help with the last of it, for the candy was splendid,
and we all enjoyed it immensely.

Suppose that you have heard from me again? I wrote as
many as three notes to you after leaving Denver; this makes
four, and perhaps I will write another before very long, for
Pueblo is a very lonely place, and I want some letters myself.

The weather has become very spring-like and warm both
in Denver and here. I am hoping that the cold has moderated
in Wyoming too, and that your losses will not be very heavy.
Only a stray postal or card have come from the Mills people,

but that did not tell how they are faring. Sandford did write me a long letter, but that was full of nothing but his hunting trip.

What think? Everyone at home was just beginning to recover from grippe or something else when I came to Denver for the vacation. Little babykin was quite ill with high fever and indigestion, and Ruth was pale and cross from earaches. We had not any maid, and the house was a mess. We managed to enjoy the little Christmas tree all the same, and you ought to have seen the toys for the youngsters. The State Teachers' Association met in Denver during the holiday week, so I had the pleasure of attending several of the meetings—though it made me miss a night with Marcia in Boulder. Dr. Brackett and a few others from the University lectured before the Association.

Since you are not here, I'll have to tell you about Mrs. Butler, in whose house I have the northeast room. She is a little war-horse of a woman with a long, thin husband. I'm telling you about her, because she has been improving him for about twenty years, and it is beginning to tell on him. He never ventures an opinion except to support hers; he always stands when a lady enters the room, and he always does what he is told. Besides, he has hardly a spear of hair on his head. Of course he is very fortunate to have a wife of such sterling qualities, one who took care of him for years when he was ill, but I can't help feeling more than a little sorry for him. As for Mrs. B., you bring a storm of words upon yourself if you venture to suggest that it is better to own a home than to rent one, or that there is anything good about the D & R G* railroad, or that Mrs. Stickney's boys or rubbers might be improved. She makes boarding more interesting even than fat Mrs. Wilson, who serves meals a block away, and tells the poor people who eat her lumpy bread—in a loud voice from the kitchen—if they have any fault to find to come out and settle it with *her!* Of course I don't tell anybody here, but her

*Denver & Rio Grande Railroad.

good is the worst I ever saw. Guess I'm too particular for a poor school teacher, about greasy plates and half cooked rice, and such things. Yet everybody says that Mrs. Wilson keeps the best boarding house on this side of town.

Time to put an end to letter. Tell me, is "Hope" dead?

Sincerely yours,
Ethel P. Waxham

P.S. Suppose that you lost everything that you have and a little more; and suppose that for the best reason in the world I wanted you to ask me to say "yes." What would you do?

E.

11

PUEBLO: 1910

Winter struck with a vengeance. In vain, John Love and his neighbors struggled to save their livestock from the elements, and some lost their own lives in the effort. Ethel's friends' letters had reflected their own choices for further study, or marriage, or careers. They, combined with her own situation in Pueblo, and that of her family in Denver, may have influenced her decision in the waning weeks of 1909. Possibly no one could have been more surprised and gratified than John Love when Ethel, like Marpessa, chose to take her shepherd's arm.

JOHN G. LOVE
Moneta Wyo., Jan 4th 1910

[Postmarked January 9, 1910, Moneta, Wyoming; received in Pueblo January 11, 1910, 9:00 A.M. Another stamp on the envelope says: TRAIN LATE, MAIL DELAYED.]

Dear Miss Waxham,

Your short note of the 22nd just received tonight. I am in Moneta with three four-horse teams after corn. Another four-horse team went to camp today with more. I certainly will try hard to save all the sheep that I can. Last night I was in the saddle *all* night and drove a four-horse team all day today. The weather is bitterly cold. One of my herders is lost and I am afraid that he is frozen to death. He failed to get in to camp on the night of January 1st. We have found most of the sheep, but have failed to find a trace of him or the dogs. I was in camp and saw the old year die and thought of the night

323

four years ago when we came home from Lander in the snowstorm. It would do me a world of good, "little girl," to just see you for even one day, but the Fates decree otherwise just at present.

We had six inches of snow (on top of the snow we already had) on January 1st and the night of the 2nd was the coldest of the winter. At the camp where I was that night, we lost by freezing to death fifty-one sheep. I am too sleepy to write, "little girl." Please excuse the scrawl. This paper, pen and ink are a startling combination. Hoping that you are having a far better time than I am and that you will write soon and often, I remain with best wishes,

Yours Sincerely,
John G. Love

He continues in a letter dated January 11:

The train finally got through once more and brought your letter, and one of my corn teams brought it from Moneta today. It is late, or rather early, but as the team goes back to Moneta in the morning, I must at least write a few lines to you. *Hope* is far from being dead yet, "little girl." I have lost over twenty thousand dollars in the last forty days. If I lose another twenty thousand, hope will still live and not even be very feeble; yet another twenty thousand and it will not be dead. If it went very much beyond that, hope *should* gradually begin to get smaller and more feeble. You propound the query in your P.S. "Suppose that you lose everything etc. etc., what would you do?" Not a hard question, "little girl." If I were with you, I would throw my arms around you and kiss you and wait eagerly for the kiss that I have waited over four years for. Later, common sense and sound judgement might come to my aid. So you see, "little girl," hope is far from being dead yet.

The cattle and horses are wintering far better than the sheep and there is no loss to speak of amongst them. My herder that was lost on January 1st was found on the evening of the 3rd with both feet badly frozen, his nose very badly frozen also. I took him to Moneta and did everything that I could for him, but he died on the train yesterday on his way to the hospital. He was a big, strong, good-natured Irishman and leaves a wife and two daughters in Iowa. He had not lived with his wife for years, but had left her well provided for and educated his daughters.[1]

Four letters duly recorded from Pueblo in a month and a half. When you get twice that many in the same time, it will be still better. Two days more and it will be four years since we went to Hailey and I fell into disgrace. Is your memory as good as mine on that question?

Too bad that you have such a poor boarding place as you eat little enough at best. You may get some valuable "pointers" from Mrs. B. that will help you in your task of training and improving me. I will not, however, either become long or thin during the process even if, as I hope, it will extend over a period of at least fifty years. Write soon and often. With best wishes,

Yours Sincerely,
John G. Love

JOHN G. LOVE
Moneta, Jan 25th/10

[Postmarked January 27, 1910, Moneta, Wyoming. *Additional stamp*: TRAIN LATE, MAIL DELAYED.]

Dear Miss Waxham,

Everyone has been in bed for hours and I should be. I have a rousing coal fire in the wagon and as three four-horse teams go to Moneta in the morning, I will write a few lines to you. The passenger train from the East was expected through Moneta tonight for the first time in thirteen days. There should be at least one letter from you. Owing to the trains

The first passenger train from the East to arrive in Moneta, Wyoming, in thirteen days, 1910.

not being running, I still have the Oklahoma family with me, but I expect to be rid of them in four days if the track is once more clear.

I have not room enough here in the wagon for all of my plunder and it will be a relief to me to get back into the house again. I may get a man to do the cooking and see to things around the place. If I do that, he will have the other house. *Our* house, I will vacate no more. If I knew how it should be done, I would begin fixing it up for you as soon as the family move out. You see, "little girl," hope is far from being dead. I am a selfish wretch to want you to come out here to this lonely place. Still, I actually think that you might be happier here than teaching school and having to eat what you did not want, or go without.

If the weather moderates and I get the sheep in shape again and the trains get to running regularly once more, I will come down to see you if only for a day. If you are still teaching, I will not visit the school. For pettie's sake, "little girl," please do not emulate Miss Powelson and teach "for the sake of the salary to buy pretty wedding clothes and household linens." I endure more misery every week that you are teaching than will ever be counterbalanced by the pleasure that you and I will ever derive from the pretty clothes and household linens. I simply have an absolute horror of something happening to you. Best wishes, write soon and often.

Yours Sincerely,
John G. Love

ETHEL P. WAXHAM
Pueblo, 29 January, 1910

Moneta, Wyo.

Dear Mr. Love,

I was just thinking that it was about time for another letter to you when your letter came telling me so. The days have been so full of schoolwork since Christmas that a number of my presents have not yet been acknowledged! Miss Powelson is doing nicely, but the doctors say that she is not strong enough to start work again, climbing the stairs at Central High. So I suppose that she will spend the spring embroidering fat P's on towels and table linen. Mr. Barrett asked me to stay with the English work if she did come back, so that I would be here anyway. Mrs. Butler says that I am an "expensive little piece," because she made a sleeping porch for me—a fine one, screened with canvas curtains. But she need not have done it if she had not wanted to; I did not urgently entreat her, or threaten her either.

Several teachers have been absent the last week from illness, and about sixty new pupils entered. That made extra work for the teachers who were there, since no substitutes are provided. The German teacher has also struck for shorter hours. She is a joyous rebel. I only wish that she had been at K.H.

Nothing is happening to me. The Fates are partial. Pater writes that Faith is going to the hospital for an operation on Monday.

You did not answer my "query." The crucial question is about what you would do next.

Best wishes for yourself and the sheep

from

Ethel P. Waxham

JOHN G. LOVE
Moneta, February 5th/1910

Dear Miss Waxham,

Your long looked-for letter arrived in Moneta on the 3rd. If there had still been no letter I would have caught the train at Moneta in the morning and come down first to Denver and then to Pueblo.

I really thought that I had answered your "query" sufficiently, but here goes to complete the answer as to what I would do "*next.*" I remember exactly where I left off and word for word what I said. If you leave it to me to decide and we were in a county seat at the time, I would marry you in less than an hour and "live happy ever after." I can start with *you* and less than nothing financially and soon pile up another stake, if you could only be happy in the meantime. I am feeling very good over the outlook at present.

Your thinking that my answer to your "query" was not complete leads me to think that you thought that I was laboring under the delusion that I could strangle "hope" unaided. I know better than that, "little girl." I know that I would have to make a mighty and prolonged effort and you a still mightier one and still we might fail. There could be only the one answer to your query. The one that for over four years I have hoped for, lived for and worked for. They have been long, long years for me, Ethel, but I could not take "no" for an answer. I will wait four more years if you make me, but I will not stay away from you.

While you are teaching, wherein lies the gain? Think of the munificent salary you get. The sum total would not pay my losses and expenses for a single day through January or December. I do not think that you can say that you even enjoy teaching. Better give it up and let someone else try their wings. You have tried yours and found that you can earn an independent living. You will probably ruin your eyes so that you will always have to wear glasses. Better let Prof. Barrett get someone else in your place so that you can come back to this wilderness with me. Please do not say "impossible," "little girl."

I got back from Moneta today with more grain and must go to the camps in the morning. Fourteen° below zero this morning, but not nearly so cold tonight. Have you noticed the comet yet?* I watch it every night.

February 8th

Still lots of snow on the ground, but the sheep are doing well and the weather is not very cold. The comet is no longer visible. The hens are laying from five to eight eggs per day and I keep up one milk cow. I also have a fireless cooker.[2] I had it before the Oklahoma family came, but they never used it even once. The one thing that bothers me in cooking is the yeast bread. I am quite an expert at making baking powder bread, but I hate the stuff. I am going to get a bread mixer and try it, for I do hate to get my hands in the dough. I have not quite decided whether to get a man cook or a man and his wife on the ranch. I could get Jack and "the nurse" if I want them. Never again will I be saddled with such a family as the one that I have just gotten rid of. They were certainly the limit for dirt and slouchiness and greasy cooking. Many a meal I cooked for myself out in the wagon.

If Mrs. Mills had heard that I came near to being burned up rather than frozen to death, she would have been nearer

*Halley's comet.

the truth. About a week ago I was fooling with the fire in the big coal heater when all at once the gas exploded and a sheet of flame flew out in my face. My moustache (I had too much anyway) surely got trimmed, likewise my eyebrows and eyelashes. No serious damage, however. I moved everything in out of the wagon today. I brought in the "two elephants" out of the cold and put them back in the bottom of the trunk once more. I do wish that you had them with you or, what would be far better, that I had you here with them.

I suppose that instead of doing all that I can to persuade you to give up teaching, I should rejoice to think that you were earning money while I am losing it. I can put sentiment, affection and peace of mind to one side, however, and still see from a cold-financial standpoint where we could lose ten times the amount of your six months' salary. If we are going to live here any length of time, I would not lose that 320 acres below me for ten times your salary for a whole year. I have the posts cut and hauled down to the ranch to fence that land, but dare not make a move until it is filed on. I have been dreading someone else filing on it for the last year.

I am trying to get things in shape to leave for a few days at least, so that I can come to Colorado. One of my bridges has been loose for months and really should be attended to soon. A fine excuse is it not, "little girl?" Two of my best work horses died, "Bill" and "Reno." Do not know the cause; they simply dropped dead.

I was sorry to hear that Miss Faith had to go to the hospital. I hope that she is up and around once more. I am getting sleepy now, but if I get time I will finish this sheet as I hate to see good paper go entirely to waste. Hoping to hear from you soon and often and expecting to see you before very long, I remain, with best wishes,

Yours Sincerely,
John G. Love

LOUISE DUDLEY
Bryn Mawr, Pa.,
February 16, 1910

Dear Ethel,

I protest. You used to write me two-page letters, then you dropped to a single sheet but when it comes to a single sheet of answer,—party-invitation size, it is time to open my mouth in protest.

Your letter went to London, then to Georgetown, and at last wandered in here. I sent (to Denver) your Christmas present a week or so ago; did you get it? It is the imp which sits on one of the capitals in Lincoln Cathedral, and it is always spoken of as the Lincoln Imp.[3] The story goes that this imp and the wind were at odds, and one day the wind was about to get the imp when he said: "Just wait a minute until I go in the Cathedral to see my friends the Dean and Canons." Then when he got in he did not come out, but the wind is still waiting for him just outside the Cathedral. Did you know the story before?

I hope you are saving your money to come to Kentucky this summer. Mamma wants you to come, and I have made up my mind that you shall. You can stay several weeks in Georgetown; then I want to take you up to the Kentucky mountains and show you what we can do in the way of primitive humanity. Won't you come?

I am working like a slave here, with no chance of any let-up before June. It looks, now, as though I were going to get my degree then, and I do hope I can push it through. My professor and the president want me to, and that is the chief point after all.

In addition to my other woes, I have to be worrying about a position for next year. Do you know of any? Is there a good Normal School in Colorado? They quite often pay good salaries, and have advanced work, too.

It seems that I have been here for ages; my passage [on board the *S.S. Laurentic*] is so far back I remember it, but vaguely. It was a very nice one, though we were delayed two days on account of storms. One gets the most delightful hodge-podge of people on a boat; my friends included two men of about forty, one a married Englishman, the other, an unmarried Jew, an Englishwoman who takes in washing, another Englishwoman, a trained nurse who is own cousin to several Lords and Ladies, but delightfully unconventional. In between times I played with children until one of the old men asked me about the little ones I had left at home!

It is after twelve, and I must stop. Goodbye, best love and good luck to you

from Louise

ETHEL P. WAXHAM
Pueblo, 22 February, 1910

Moneta, Wyo.

Dear Mr. Love,

The news of your being frozen did not reach me until you wrote of it yourself, I am glad to say. But of the two, burning or freezing, I think that I should prefer freezing.

Faith is still in the hospital, but she writes that she has been sitting up an hour a day, and hopes to leave soon. I wish that I could have been with her these last few weeks.

Wonder whether I have written you the news since the tragi-comedy of Marshall, Miller and Tooley, the wreckers, was completed? Marshall was the "boss" of the three, who took meals at the boarding house. I took a dislike to him at the first, although I suffered no more from his attentions than some others there. For a while I stayed away from suppers entirely to avoid meeting him. About two weeks after his arrival, he became engaged to a Miss R. here at Mrs. Butler's. On payday, he telephoned a story about his daughter's illness (he said that his wife had died several years before) and disappeared. But he did not go East as he said, but stayed here in Pueblo. Miss R. did not hear from him for two weeks. News came at last in his own request for a pass, that he is married, and is bringing his wife West—etc. etc. Such vulgar stories one hears every day in this horrid place.

I've changed boarding houses. Couldn't stand hearing Mr. Wilson have convulsions in the next room at meal times. The new place is much better, although it is half a mile away. Mrs. Spencer, who keeps it, is an old Englishwoman who used to cook for Governor Adams. The house is decorated with Scriptural mottoes from hall to dining room, and deaf old Mr. Spencer regales us with religious verse, "Railroad to heaven," and so on. As Miss Hoellischer, the German teacher says, I am "making a strange experience."

Miss R. gave a birthday party last week for some of her married friends, about ten couples. She wanted me to tell their fortunes before they began to play cards, so I dressed in Mrs. Butler's oldest clothes, blacked my face like a beggar woman and came to the front door to sell buttons and pins. It was great fun. They did not guess at first that I wasn't a beggar, until Mrs. Butler gave it away. Then I told their fortunes by palmistry, and although they were nearly all married and some had children almost grown, they were very anxious to have their palms read. Even after the beggar woman had left, and I had come back in *propria persona*,* I told fortunes. One man, a big, homely, smooth-faced, clean-handed fellow was a little too much interested. He had a little, nervous, much-adorned wife, and I told him in every other sentence that she was not well, and that he ought to take better care of her. It was perfectly true. Hope that he takes my good advice.

"Bohunks and Pollacks," Miss Hoellischer calls these people. Only once in a while I meet one who is much more than a curiosity.

The latest news is that Mr. Barrett has given me a French class. "What next?" said the tadpole when his tail fell off. It is really not very hard, but if I had not been forced into taking the class, I should be conscience stricken for teaching

---

*In this case: in her own clothes.

them with so little preparation as I have. What matter? Classroom French? Nobody here knows whether they learn French or Yiddish.

I'm tired and tomorrow comes very soon, so I'll say good-night, with best wishes.

Sincerely yours,
Ethel P. Waxham

She continues in a letter dated March 1:

The weather here, since the cold snap at Christmastime has been generally warm. It is hard to think of its being much below zero where you are, or of there being much snow. Pueblo makes up in wind and dust for everything lacking in snow and mud, however. And the mud is bad, when there is any. A story is told of a lady who lost a rubber at a crossing and in trying to find it discovered fourteen other rubbers before her own.

Faith writes that she has not yet been able to leave the hospital. She gets out on the porch now for about an hour a day, but it tires her out.

As for my query, I thought that there might be two sides to it or I should not have asked it. You think that only one answer is possible?

The hour is late—for me—and I am tired, so I'll not write more, except to tell you that if you stay with the sheep and let me hear the news regularly, I'll write oftener.

Best wishes from
Ethel P. Waxham

JOHN G. LOVE
Moneta, March 4th 1910

Dear Miss Waxham,

Your letter of the 1st received tonight. It was good of you, "little girl," to write and I surely appreciate it. Even if your letters are short, it sets my mind at rest regarding your welfare and that is the main thing. Warm "chinook" winds have been blowing steadily since I last wrote and the snow is all gone except in the gulches. The frost is all out of the ground and everything is spring-like.

If I possibly can, I am going to scheme to be in Pueblo next Friday. I know that you have not much time, but Friday evening, Saturday and Sunday would do. I have just come in from the sheep camp and the sheep are doing well now. The ground is too wet to plow and the roads are too muddy to haul over, so if nothing unforseen happens I will come and you will have barely time to forbid my coming. I will telegraph you from Denver.

I found a dead herder on the range today about four miles north of the ranch. He was lost in the January storm. I will telephone for the coroner tomorrow from Moneta.

I am very sorry to learn that poor Miss Faith is having such a long siege in the hospital. Still it might be worse, for it might have been you. I laughed at your account in your other letter about Miss R. She certainly must be a fool to ever dream of marrying a man that she had only known two weeks. She may get wiser in time.

I see by the postmark on your letter that it left Pueblo at 12:50 on the 2nd and got to Moneta on the night of the 3rd. According to that, I could be with you Friday night, Saturday and Sunday, and only be gone from the ranch six days. I will try to catch the train at Moneta next Thursday morning, get to Denver Friday morning, see the dentist and come down to Pueblo Friday afternoon.

Hoping to get a letter from you at Moneta next Wednesday night and hoping to see you next Friday. I remain with best wishes,

Yours Sincerely
John G. Love

ETHEL P. WAXHAM
Pueblo, 8 March, 1910

Moneta, Wyo.

Dear Mr. Love,

Your note saying that you may come to Denver and Pueblo this week has just arrived. The time you speak of would be very bad for me, because I have engagements covering that Saturday and Sunday, and would probably be able to see very little of you. Ordinary engagements might be postponed, but this I made some time ago with a man whom I knew at Harvard, who is on his way north from Mexico.[4]

Spring vacation begins about the twenty-fifth of March. Why not come then, and you may not have to come farther than Denver which would save half a day at least.

Things are going fairly well in school, but it has been hard to keep the boys and girls at work during this fine weather. I'll write again soon.

Sincerely yours,
Ethel P. Waxham

Either John Love did not receive this letter in time to change his plans, or he ignored it and went to Pueblo anyway.

NORMANDIE HOTEL

One-half Block from Depot

European Plan

JOHN BROWN, Prop'r

Steam Heat

JOHN G. LOVE
Cheyenne, Wyo.,
March 12th 1910

Dear Miss Waxham,

Just a few lines to let you know that I am this far on my way home. I will reach the ranch in the night tomorrow. I did not have five minutes to spare catching a train out of Pueblo and got in to Denver in time to catch the "Overland Limited" for Cheyenne. I did not get to see the dentist, but it does not matter. I am glad that I got down to see you, "little girl," but it is going away that is the hard part of it. I will scheme to get down for two days during your vacation, but I may fail. Please write soon and often. With best wishes,

Yours Sincerely,
John G. Love

ETHEL P. WAXHAM
Pueblo, 16 March, 1910

Moneta, Wyo.

Dear Mr. John G. Love,

Somebody is tired, and somebody is sleepy, and somebody has had what would rightly be called a "divilish" week. The divilishness began with Teachers' Meeting which was unusually long and prosy, and where somebody was appointed Secretary to and Language Member of a Committee for the revision of the Course of Studies and required work. The divilishness will probably last through next week when marks go in, and flunkers lose hope. 'Spect those are about all of somebody's troubles, except that she wishes that she was a jellyfish and didn't have any back.

Your two letters came yesterday and the day before, with one from Harvard friend. He left Sunday night because I told him that I was too busy for the theatre on Monday evening. There were ever so many interesting tales about Mexico, and two gifts which could not well be refused—an idol-head from the pyramid of Chalorba, and a lovely silk scarf or mantilla, the kind that the ladies wear in Mexico.

Here I have yawned about a hundred times. Perhaps it isn't polite to tell about it, but it explains my not saying anything else, but goodnight.

I hope that you found things running smoothly at the ranch, and are more contented to stay than you were—

Sincerely yours,
Ethel P. Waxham

She adds on March 26:

> Vacation has begun! On Monday morning, at five-thirty (notice the time) unless the train is late, Miss Hartman, the English teacher, and I leave for Denver. We stop over for most of the day at Colorado Springs to visit the Van Briggle Pottery, and to see the mountains. I want to find some anemones, which Miss Hartman regards with scorn. We expect to be good travelling companions, however, and are planning to run about together a little in Denver.
>
> Will you be down, I wonder? I hope that your affairs will be in such good shape that you can if you wish. Faith writes that she is about the house, though not strong, that the babies are better and that there is a new cook—all just as usual. I am tired; want a long, long sleep, so here's a good night to you
>
> from
> Ethel Waxham

Between March 26 and April 4, John Love paid Ethel another visit, which was to change the course of their lives.

ETHEL P. WAXHAM
Pueblo, 4 April, 1910

Moneta, Wyo.

Dear Mr. Love,

The kaleidiscopic end of a kaleidiscopic vacation has come! Trunk is unpacked, ready for the attic, Latin and Greek for tomorrow have been looked over, and experiences exchanged with Mrs. Butler and other roomers.

Only this morning I showed the elephants to Faith.* Wouldn't have done it if she had not had the blues. You should have heard her exclaim in horror when I said "Yes," in

*One of the "elephants" was a Tiffany-mounted diamond solitaire engagement ring; the other, a sunburst brooch of gold and diamonds.

answer to her question, "Will you go up *there* to live?" And she was equally horror-stricken when she asked about the house, and I said that I supposed we should live first in the wagon. "Will you be awfully poor like Vera and Will?" she asked next, and then all sorts of questions which I could not answer about you and the ranch and weddings. She is very anxious to tell her friends and the family, but I told her that it would not do until the time was set. Wish we had talked more about that.

All day I have been wearing the ring—to become accustomed to it! It certainly is beautiful. Perhaps if the elephants were not so lovely I could thank you for them.

I've been making all sorts of vague resolutions which will have to become distinct soon, in the next few months. Won't work too hard, will get clothes ready, so as not to be dependent on drygoods stores next summer, will find out about house furnishings and so on.

Hoping to hear from you soon, I am

Sincerely yours,
E.P.W.

JOHN G. LOVE
Moneta, April 5th, 1910

Dearest Ethel,

I am once more seated at my own desk, everyone in bed long ago and not a soul in the house but me. On the desk are my latest magazines unopened: *Harpers, Scribners, Outlook, Hamptons, World's Work, Review of Reviews, Everybody's, McClures, Success, Country Life, Woman's Home Companion,* farm papers and newspapers galore. On all sides are papers, letters, bills, accounts, old clothes, new clothes, etc. Up to my left in an oak frame amongst six polished buffalo horns hang my three pictures of you. If you could see my two rooms now, "little girl," you would wonder how on earth I managed to get in here and wonder still more how I could find what I wanted after I got in. You would laugh to begin with, for you just could not help it; later you might look solemn and give me a serious talking to and sage advice upon neatness etc., etc. Things will change later. It may be bad enough when you see them, but they will not be anything like this. After working all day, I do not feel much like fixing up things in the house. I have a good deal of writing and figuring to do that I cannot get out of and that is all done in the night after everyone is in bed.

Supper tonight was at eight o'clock and breakfast will be on the table in the morning at 5:30. I always get up, but seldom eat then. The men did as well as I expected while I was away, but I am behind with my work and will have to crowd things all I can for the rest of this month at least.

Two four-horse teams went after wood today whilst the ranch boss and I worked four more horses getting the garden ready for seed. We expect to have it ready tomorrow and the wood teams will be back also. Next day three four-horse teams go to Moneta for hay and supplies. Then I have to go to Wolton after potatoes. There is more ground to plow and seed, ditches to fix, brush to grub, trees and currant bushes to get and all *should* be done at once, but will not be. This is the busy month on the ranch and lambing begins on May 1st.

The weather is beautiful, but a rain or snow would help the grass a good deal. Please write often and never wait for me to answer, for I often get the mail without having a chance to mail letters.

Hoping that you are well and happy, I am with love and kisses

Ever yours,
John G. Love

ETHEL P. WAXHAM
Pueblo, 11 April, 1910

Moneta, Wyo.

Dear Mr. Love,

A good letter from you to me; and now a good letter from me to you. Be sure to write me from the ranch some of those interesting things that you promised; write me about the ranch, too, and the horses. It will seem good to belong somewhere again, and to say, "This is home"; and after a while perhaps you won't laugh when you say "There's no place like home."

It has been a hard, tiresome week, and I have lessons to look over, still, tonight. But what do you think are on my table and bureau? Apple blossoms! I don't mind even Latin prose, with them near.

Goodnight. I am going to love you if you are always as good to me as you have been.

Ethel

John Love's next few letters are missing, but Ethel continues:

April 16, 1910

Dear Mr. Love,

Your suggestions as to what I should have told "Miss Faith" will be acted upon tomorrow—including the hint about embroidered towels. I am wondering whether you have an aversion to tablecloths as well as to sheets. Some things, man, are necessary in any house.

If *when* is to be this summer, had you not better write Pater and ask for the hand of one of his daughters?

Even a tiny little home wedding, if the lady does not have "six of everything" from facecloths to stockings, as the good book says she should, takes some time. *Ach, Himmel!** And two weeks or ten days before, invitations have to be out, and announcements must be engraved, and books have to be packed. Can't send invitations without giving the date and time o'day, and can't send announcements without a card saying: "At home after September first—" Where? You see, you will have to have a little to say. At Moneta? Or at the ranch? Or "at home in a sheep wagon down by the garden"? And how many invitations and announcements must there be for your relatives and friends? And what time are we to leave for

*Oh heavens!

Wyoming? Suppose that the ceremony should be just a little before train time, to avoid the dreadful drop in spirits that comes to people waiting for something to happen.

You will write to Pater at once? You do not know Faith if you think that she would intentionally tell what she was asked not to tell. But you would not know her either, if you thought that she could not be persuaded or entrapped into telling, all inadvertently, what she was trying to conceal. You must not call her a sinner, however, even in fun.

Best wishes for the third elephant from the other two, and from

E. W.

26 April, 1910

Dear Mr. Love,

It seems a long while since I last wrote you, but that can hardly be because I have not yet received an answer to that letter.

Those resolutions are more vague than ever. I have had to undertake to give tutoring lessons to a girl, and a boy has asked for them, too. But what a boy who has finished school wants to do with private lessons in beginning Latin, I don't see. There is a lady here, though, who would be glad to have him take lessons of her—I'll recommend her! Then on Sunday last—please don't be shocked—I planned to sit quietly on the back upper porch and hem two blue and white dishtowels and think about the wagon. Was I right in thinking that there were not any blue and white dishtowels in it? But Mrs. Bullen telephoned asking me to take a trip to Canyon City with them in their machine. Of course I went. The day was glorious, and the machine went perfectly. Mr. Bullen said that he had not had a single thing go wrong since he bought it in December. We reached Canyon City about noon, after wasting an hour at Mr. Bullen's new fruit ranch. Then we had dinner at the hotel, and walked about town for a while. The place is very pretty, in the middle of a fine fruit section. Apple trees and gardens were already in bloom. We came by Florence on the way back, making a ride of more than a hundred miles.

Since then, of course, work has been harder than usual. Tests, committee work, tutoring. Brr, this Little Bear has not hemmed those two blue and white dish towels yet. Sometimes she thinks that she can't possibly be ready to leave civilization before September. What does the white elephant think?

Home won't be happy unless the people in it make it so. That is a terrible consideration, isn't it? Sends the shivers down my backbone until—ff!

Write to me soon?

E. W.

John Love wrote to Frank Waxham to ask for his daughter's hand in marriage and received the following reply:

F. E. Waxham, M.D.
323 Jackson Building
Denver, Colo.
April 29, 1910

My dear Mr. Love:

Yours of the 21st caused me no little surprise, and you must realize what it is to me to give up to another's keeping one who is so dear to me as Ethel. She is as pure and good as refined gold and you are fortunate indeed to have won her love. She gets her rare qualities of heart and mind from her sainted mother and is one whom any man might proudly worship. I am glad to say that I have confidence in your ability to care for her tenderly and to promote her happiness in every possible way. I am sure you will not find her demands unreasonable, and that you will find her a good, true, faithful helpmeet. I am sorry that you are to take her away so soon for I fear that it will be impossible for me to do for her as I would like and as my heart prompts me to do at so early a date. You probably know that I too have learned what financial disaster means.

Can you forgive me, Mr. Love, if a father's anxiety prompts

343

me to ask you for references? I feel that you will not take offence or think less of me for the request. Your letter rings good and true and I have great confidence in you, but I feel that I will not have done my full duty as a father without taking this step.

With assurances of high regard, believe me
                              Very sincerely and truly
                              F. E. Waxham

P.S. Kindly let me hear from you at once.

Unfortunately John Love's reply was not preserved.

ETHEL P. WAXHAM
Pueblo, 30 April, 1910

Moneta, Wyo.

Dear Mr. Love,

It won't be such an ordeal! We shall have it quietly at home, and if you wish, there will not be any invitations. Of course, we would not invite many people within a thousand miles of Denver, for if they came, the furniture would have to be moved. We have about seven families of aunts and cousins who are so clannish to feel hurt if they have no share in any such public event. Marcia and Big Bear and a few best friends would have to be asked. Don't trouble yourself about importing a best man. We don't need any. A Stetson would be just the thing, though I think that it is hardly necessary for the ceremony. I am even thinking heretically of omitting a wedding cake! Would you miss it? It was thoughtful of you to write about bringing the trunk. Bring a large one! My desk, and probably books, will have to be sent by freight.

Is September first early to be at home? 'Spect home will have an unsettled look even then, if we spend part of the summer in the Park. There will not be very many people dropping in for five o'clock tea to see us anyway. You will really have to tell me, though, where we are to be at home;

do you tell people whom you really want to see to come to Moneta, or do you give the name of your ranch?

There will be a few lunch cloths, but no tablecloths at first, for they have to be suited to the table, and I suspect that you will soon be getting a new table. Is that correct? Faith took the hint about towels, but said that she had not time for embroidery. She is going to try to finish something which she promised for me long ago—a sofa pillow with the Leach coat of arms.* Useful? I did not tell her that I should really prefer towels. We may demonstrate the problem of the irresistible force and the immoveable body, in the question of sheets. I was never without them in my life; wool prickles my neck and feet.

Pater wrote me today that he had received your letter and was about to answer it. Just had a contract for next year's position given to me to sign, too. Haven't told anyone about not coming back, but there is a rumor about that I am to marry a Denver doctor in the fall!

Tell me which saddlehorses are going to the Park, if we go. Must say goodnight for I am tired and feel wretched.

Ethel

Life was growing more complex in the Waxham household in Denver. Ethel's widowed sister Vera was setting up a notions shop to earn a livelihood. She was unable to return to her profession of teacher, but it is not known whether it was due to regulations discouraging married women from teaching, the charge of her two small sons or her precarious state of health. Faith was also there, sometimes teaching, sometimes not. Ethel's father, Dr. Waxham was courting Helen Welles, his second wife's sister, whom he married shortly after Ethel married John Love.

ETHEL P. WAXHAM
Pueblo, 7 May, 1910

Dear Mr. Love,

If you were not a barbarian, I should suggest that you might write me, for it is a very long while since I heard from

*Leach was the maiden name of Ethel's mother, Elizabeth.

you last. But I know that you are busy, and well cared for, so I am not worrying about you personally.

School is more interesting and absorbing than ever. The cooking class gave a ten-course banquet to the teachers last night, and asked me to give a toast, along with the mayor, school superintendent, principal and several teachers. Tell it not in Askalon, but the banquet was better than the toasts. Miss Wilson leaves for several days to attend Miss Powelson's wedding in Boulder. Of course, that makes extra work, although Miss W. asked Mr. B. if she might not get a substitute, and he *refused*. Gives us her work.

Vera and Pater have both written me this week. There seem to be difficulties in the way of starting the penny shop business but Vera hopes to have the matter settled somehow soon. Faith seems still undecided about her place.

I am a *tertium quid.** The man pretends not to know that the girl is frightfully jealous.[5] It is perfectly ridiculous because she has not any reason to be, and has a sign of their engagement on her fourth finger. After the grind all day in school, the comedy is very entertaining.

What think? Thursday I did not have school from eight until nearly six. Friday was two hours better, but the banquet took all evening. Sometimes the sight or thought of school makes me weary.

Three blue and white dishtowels are ready for the wagon. They have loops sewed on to hang them in the sun. Three are enough to begin with, aren't they?

Won't it be terrible?

E. W.

She continues on May 14:

Dear,

Surely you have heard from me, or should have heard, twice since the sixteenth of April. The days are full, to be sure, but not so full that I cannot write you at least once a week.

Aren't you glad that you are not doing anything with the

*Third party of an ambiguous status.

house, in addition to farming, gardening, lambing and finding horses? It will be a sudden change for me from Greek roots to potatoes, from French verbs to scrubbing brushes, and Latin prose to making bread. You will need to have broad charity for a long while. Never made bread but once, when I was in High School, and took cooking lessons once in two weeks.

Miss Powelson was married last Wednesday. One of the teachers went to Boulder for the wedding, and told us all about it, even to the telegram which Mr. Wilson sent, "Fifty miles out, and still sowing rice."

Mr. Barrett has been talking to me again about coming back. I don't like his contract. Will you let me write my own contract for my next position?

There has been rain here for three days; too much like Wisconsin for me. I have missed getting out for the two possible walks—to Lake Minnequa and to City Park.

The day that your letter came, there was one from Sandford, too. He said that a crab apple tree was budded; also that Margaret was going to Lander because of toothache. That was all the news!

The postman ought to come soon now. I hope that he will bring a letter from you. And listen, you will have to tell me where we are going to be at home, before I can tell you when we are going to start.

Ethel

Having obtained Frank Waxham's consent, John Love was officially welcomed into the family.

F. E. Waxham, M.D.
323 Jackson Building
Denver, Colo.
May 17, 1910

My dear Mr. Love,

Yours came yesterday and I give it prompt attention. I am very glad to tell you that I am convinced of your goodness and sincerity. I hope you have not misunderstood my motives in wishing references. It is not worldly possessions but the real worth of the *man* that concerns me. I would not have Ethel marry a man with millions if his moral nature was corrupt and crooked. Yes, I am convinced that you will care for Ethel beautifully and tenderly, and I do not believe that you overestimate her worth.

It is only natural that I shall miss my Ethel more than I can tell you, but in giving her up, it is a pleasure to know that it is to a good, honorable upright man whose worth insures happiness and contentment. You certainly have waited long and patiently and I sincerely hope that your reward in happiness will be equally great. You are to be congratulated in winning Ethel, (pardon a father's pride) for she is as *good* as she is *brilliant*. Care for her tenderly and may God bless you both.

Sincerely,

F. E. Waxham

F. E. Waxham, M.D.
323 Jackson Building
Denver, Colo.
May 17, 1910

My dear Ethel

I received a splendid letter from Mr. Love yesterday and have just finished a reply which I think will make him very happy. I am fully convinced of his *honor, integrity,* and *goodness* and I am sure he will make you happy and contented. My prayers and best wishes go with you, my dear. I am so sorry that I cannot do for you as I would wish.

I am very glad and happy in the firm belief that you will be very, very happy and contented. It will be a sore trial to give you up, my dear, but I feel that your future will be a very bright one and safeguarded by a splendid man with unblemished character and who loves you more perhaps than you can ever know. Can you not come home for Decoration Day so that we may plan and talk matters over? I will stand the expense if you will do so.

Did I tell you of Ruth's and Robert's pranks? They are fun-

nier than a pair of monkeys. They had me for a camel the other
evening, and Ruth was a monkey riding on my shoulder and
Robert was the organ grinder and followed up with his little
red chair on his arm and grinding away at a great rate. They
have a sand pile now under my bedroom window and have
great times. Well, dear, we all send lots of love to you.

> Ever fondly,
> Pater

P.S. Your letter to Faith came today and we were all glad to
hear from you. Vera thinks she has secured a location that she
likes, a little store and five rooms in rear opposite the Web-
ster school on the North side. Try and keep well and do not
work too hard.

> VERA WAXHAM SHATTUC
> Denver, May 17, 1910

My dear Mr. Love,
    It will seem strange to call you "brother" and will take a
little time to become natural, but I assure you that you are
nonetheless welcome in the family.
    While I know that both you and Ethel are looking to "the"
day, I'm sorry that the delight of preparation is to be so short.
    Little Robert and Hugh will welcome you right heartily
and I am glad that they are to have such a good uncle. My
heart is full of congratulations and best wishes.

> Sincerely yours,
> Vera (Waxham) Shattuc

> FAITH C. WAXHAM
> 1364 Marion St., Denver
> May 18, 1910

My dear Mr. Love,
    A letter from Ethel has just come giving me permission to
write to you. You surely are a most fortunate man to have
won Ethel's affection, and I feel sure that you will take the
best care of her. She loves your kind of life, the outdoor life so
much, and I feel sure that she will be very happy with you.

You have the qualities which make a *man* and I am sure that anyone would trust you even if they knew nothing of you.

I am sorry that we did not know of the happiness in store for you while you were here.

The time seems so short that Ethel will be at home with us. She says that she is to leave us the last of June.

I wish that I could do a whole lot for the dear girl, but my strength and time as well as money is limited and I cannot do what I would like to.

She suggested that I embroider some towels, but I fear she will have to wait a little for that.

We will be glad to see you and welcome you into the family as one of us.

Most sincerely
Faith C. Waxham

JOHN G. LOVE
Moneta, May 19th, 1910

Dearest Ethel,

Yours of the 14th received tonight and as Danny Shehan is here and will be in Moneta in the morning in time to catch the train, I must write you just a few lines.

The main thing that I see requiring answering is where we are going to be "at home." Easily answered on my part and I think that I have done so a time or two already. Wherever and whenever you say, "little girl," suits me—"savvey?" Yes, little pet, you may write your own contract for your next position and I, as party of the second part, will agree to live up to it before reading it, providing you leave out a few things such as scrubbing brushes and other heavy manual labor that are nonessential to your happiness. You are not adapted for hard work. Furthermore, you will not be allowed to do it, so you may just as well give up all idea of any such, or you will be kissed into submission. The wagon is about your size and will not require much scrubbing, so you can scrub that to your heart's content. The house is different. It will be fixed as you want it, but you will not do the work.

A letter today from your father says he is willing to trust you to my care. I won't betray his trust, but will care for you the best that I know how. I will be proud of you, little pet, and justly so, and will do everything in my power to make your life a long and happy one. Do not worry about the bread-making or cooking, "little girl," for you will get along famously. If you do happen to make a failure of something once in a while, or even every day, what does it matter? You will have no one but me to please and you can easily do that.

It is a little stormy tonight, but it may not amount to much. I sent you a picture of your little black pacer, Kentucky, wearing your saddle; also a picture of the house and part of the wagon, and one of my two favorite collie dogs. Mrs. Williams took them that Sunday that she was over to visit, and I just sent them on to you. Please write often, little pet.

> Yours with love and kisses,
> John

ETHEL P. WAXHAM
Pueblo, May 22, 1910

Moneta, Colo.

Dear John,

I received your long letter, and was very glad to hear from you. Really, it would be a waste of time to wait until September, but if you do come in June, it will not be before the twentieth. Faith has engaged a dressmaker for me, for the week after school is out, though I'm sure I don't know what to have her make.

We won't have any invitations. I can write to the aunts and ask them to come, and you can write to your sisters and anyone else whom you wish to invite. 'Spect I'd better ask Pater to speak to Dr. Bayley about performing the ceremony;

if Dr. Bayley can't, I'd just as soon have a justice or an alderman, or anybody. This is the question about the "at home" cards: ought the name of the ranch to be there? Unsuspecting college people might expect to find us within two hundred yards of the Moneta Station . . . and we wouldn't be there. You want to have people come, don't you? I know a dozen people whom I should like to have come by two's or three's when the wilderness begins to pall. May I ask them when I tell them the news?

Today I wrote to the man who came to see me just before you did, and told him that I was going with you to try to make the desert blossom like the rose. I think that he ought to know.

I don't want people here to be talking about it, though, for I have not many good friends and prefer not to be asked questions by semi-strangers. A Boulder girl who is going abroad this summer just said that she would get some table linen in Germany for me; not a present, of course. I asked her to get it. Then it will be here probably about the first of September. I hope to featherstitch two dusters this week, one for the wagon, and one for the house. One has pink roses on it and one has blue. Tell me the size of the pillows, so I can get some pillow slips. Aren't these domestic details? And here is a worse question. I tried to see whether I could get a riding suit here to save time in Denver later on. The only suits in town are khaki—don't like them, do you—and one, a lovely brown silk-corduroy, with a satin-lined jacket, very warm and serviceable. I remembered what you said about my other corduroy. This is much nicer, but I hardly like the color; it does not match sand or sage brush or rocks! What do you think? I don't want to get anything which you may not like.

It is a matter of form, I think, to ask for references, unless they are offered. I'll wager, though, that Pater never looked them up. He has had occasion more than once, but once especially, to distrust his judgement of humanity.

"Won't *what* be terrible? And you yourself said that we should be subjects for charity and sympathy. Making bread—eating canned things and condensed milk—talking to no one who ever heard the difference between the use of shall and will—I, living with a barbarian, and you with a domestic tyrant. I know that I am going to be a tyrant, or else a slattern. Heaven help us!

There is something which I can do for you, perhaps. Typewrite your business correspondence to save some of the time that you will waste with me. But when I think of packing that typewriter, my courage fails. I'll do it, of course, but it is a worse task than packing books.

Before very long I'm going to write Mrs. Mills and tell her that I'll accept her invitation to come to see her this summer—with you! I do hope that we can go to the Park, even for a short time. A month would surely be long enough. In fact it would be longer than a good many wedding trips. Then I could begin to scrub in the kitchen or the parlor to get ready for the people who won't come in answer to the "at home" cards. Did you plant the sweet peas? Be sure and tell me when the garden comes up.

Ethel

P.S. Mrs. Butler thinks that the best part of marriage is before the wedding. I forgot to thank you for the pictures. One looks like a village street.

Her next letter is dated May 29, 1910, still from Pueblo:

Dear John,

Your letter of the nineteenth reached me on the twenty-third. Now I am sitting on my porch on Sunday morning to answer it, while a house-finch close by is singing madly, and a doleful hymn sounds from the little church across the way.

Part of the morning I spent working with a pair of bookends which I have been making for a friend's commencement on the eighth of June. This afternoon I have been invited to spend with some girls whom I knew in Boulder. Then I must begin to write and tell some of my friends what is going to happen in June.

In 1905 when the Chicago & Northwestern Railroad pushed westward from Casper to Lander, it passed 15 miles north of the Love Ranch. Stagecoaches were now superfluous, so John Love bought for almost nothing the soon-to-be-abandoned stage station town of Old Muskrat, 18 miles downstream. He moved the entire town to his ranch with horses and wagons.

The ranch development was spread out in an arc 300 yards long, concave southward, sheltered in the lee of a south-facing terrace. Farthest east were eight barns, sheds, and other buildings, all connected. The largest had been the saloon at Old Muskrat, and the scene of many a lively party, but was now a respectable hay house. Corrals and hay enclosures were attached to the south side of the building complex and from there one extended all the way to the creek, which provided a maximum of shelter and close access to hay and water. Next, to the west, was the "long building," formerly the hotel at Old Muskrat, consisting of four large rooms in a row, used for saddlery, grain, kitchen for the ranch cook, and storage. To the west of it was the large bunk house, the social hub for the working men in the adjacent 1,000 square mile area. Between the

354

Last week I wrote to Pater, trying to persuade him to make Vera give up the shop idea. I think that if she felt that she was really needed or wanted at home, that she would not go. Besides, she does not seem well, to me, and she has enough to do now, caring for the two children. But a postal came from her yesterday, saying that the matter was settled. She seemed very glad. I have not said anything to her in disfavor of the plan, except that if she did keep shop, I should call her Hepzibah for the woman in Hawthorne's *The House of Seven Gables*.

The two dusters with blue and pink roses are almost finished. Before very long you will see me using them and you like to have things clean, too, don't you?

Have you had the cattle and horse round-ups this year? Or won't there be any? Think how much I'll know about such things in just a few months. It will be quite as bad as Marcia's suddenly acquired fragments of geology. Wonder if you will learn anything, too?

As ever,
Ethel

---

bunk house and the big house were a blacksmith shop, buggy shed, and store building, all connected, moved from the abandoned Golden Lake stage station southwest of Old Muskrat.

The big house was shaped like an inverted "T" with the stem pointing north, but with additions sprouting off in various directions. It was about 55 feet long and 40 feet wide and eventually was split up into 11 rooms. North of the big house was a log ice house and west of it was a large two-room sod cellar and chicken hatchery with 3-foot thick walls, built into the south side of the terrace. On top of the terrace, 150 yards downwind to the northeast, were extensive sheep pens, marking chutes, wool sack towers, and racks for sheep wagon bodies. In the front yard was a hand dug water well about 12 feet deep with 4 feet of water in the bottom and a wooden windmill tower straddling the pit. Muskrat Creek ran from east to west, 150 feet south of the big house and 10 feet lower.

JOHN G. LOVE
Moneta, June 1st, 1910

Dearest Ethel,

I received your letter when I was in Moneta and mailed one to you. I got home today and the cattle round-up is here tonight, about twenty men and one hundred and twenty saddle horses and *ten* head of cattle!

This ranch has no particular name and yet it has several, but no distinctive one.* Any of your friends will be welcome here and I will do my best to entertain them and be proud to know them. Ask any whom you wish, but not for the reason you give "when the wilderness begins to pall." I do not intend that you shall make a martyr of yourself, "little girl," and when you are tired of living here, we will move. If you think that you won't like it here, little pet, we won't go to the expense of fixing up a home here.

I do not know the size of the pillows as I have them in all sizes, but do not worry about pillow slips. I have them and for a wonder they are clean. Queer idea to give me credit for having pillows but no slips.

I do not think that I would like to see you in khaki or yet corduroy, but still I might. For summer riding, just common pretty shirt waists with a dark, nicely made, long (that is not *too* short) divided skirt of good material, I think, would be the thing. I have seen very fine tailor-made riding suits of good material, and comfortable, no doubt, that I would hate to see you wear. I hope never to see you wearing short mannish-looking clothes even if they are comfortable. I always want to see you looking just what you are, the dearest little girl on earth. Your taste in dress I have found to be very good and what suits you is very liable to please me; if it does not, you will never hear me utter a harsh word, but the garment might accidentally be lost.

Is it possible, "little girl," that I was so nearly asleep that my pen wrote "*we* should be subjects for charity and sympathy?" If I did, it was surely a glaring error. I am to be

*It was most often called the Love ranch.

congratulated first, last and all the time. I desire none and will never get any sympathy, "poor me!" You living with a "barbarian" is all right enough, but you may improve me a little in time. I won't be living with either a "tyrant" or a "slattern" for you will never develop into either. You will be just my little pet, the dearest, best and happiest little wife that a man was ever blessed with.

I did not know that you had a typewriter or that you could use one. You will be a regular treasure and I will surely appreciate and care for you as such. I will not object to your doing some typewriting or bookkeeping for me. That will be a far bigger help to me than cooking.

It is true that I will spend a good deal of time with you, but I will "waste" none. Again you mention scrubbing. Forget it, little pet, for that and washing and all heavy manual labor for you is "taboo." If you really object to getting the fragments of your clothes back from the steam laundry, I will agree to compromise on that hand by doing the hard part of the work while you superintend and do the finishing touches.

I planted quite a few sweet peas, but they are almost a mile from the house. Most of the things in the garden are up and doing very well so far. You say "if you come in June it will not be before the twentieth." Will it be the *twentieth?* I do not think that there is any danger of our not going to the Park this summer, as all of my plans have that end in view.

The last two days have been very warm here. I start shearing again on the 5th at Moneta and expect to finish on the 8th. The wool market is very dull and there is no sale for the wool. Too bad, but it cannot be helped, although I need the money to pay my debts. I went into debt very heavily last winter, saving what sheep I managed to persuade to live. With you, little girl, and no bad luck, I will soon make it back again. I am getting sleepy. You may hear from me once more before you leave Pueblo.

With love and kisses,

              Ever yours
              John G. Love

ETHEL P. WAXHAM
Pueblo, 5 June, 1910

Moneta, Wyo.

Dear John,

In less than a week, now, I'll be back in Denver. Commencement is on Thursday, and the receptions and social events following have no attractions for me, so I will probably leave here on Friday morning.

The time seems shorter and shorter, and more and more things appear which ought to be done. But if you would like to have me come without "six of everything," and rest after getting to Wyoming instead of before, we might make the day June twentieth. If not, about the second week in July, or the first in September. It makes no difference to me; but I should like to lose no more time, now that I have told you that I will come. June twentieth is Monday. We might have the ceremony about five and leave soon after. Isn't there a seven o'clock train? If this suits you, and if you have any friends whom you wish to invite, write to them, and send me their names, and I will write, too. Might any of your sisters come? I think that I'll ask aunts only, and Mrs. Kingsland. Perhaps one aunt may come from Rockford. There would have to be decorations and refreshments if many people were asked. And in the unsettled condition of things at home, even that would be hard. Besides, *nihil nisi bonum,* which is being interpreted, "nothing except the best." (That is why I'm taking you!) You won't need anything for the wedding except clean clothes, if you have a pretty good suit.

I am not getting any "finery"; leave that until we go to Paris! If things are plain and substantial and look well, that is enough. Still the trunk will be useful for us both. Is there anything which you would like to have me get for you while I am getting things for myself?

Ethel

JOHN G. LOVE
Moneta, June 10, 1910

Ethel P. Waxham
1364 Marion St., Denver, Colo.

Dearest,

Yours of the 5th received yesterday and I am glad that the time is near at hand when I won't have to depend upon the mail. Very good of you, pet, to make it the twentieth instead of making me wait longer.

You can rest here all you want to and be out in the fresh air, but I greatly fear that you will not do much resting until we get on the road in the wagon. I will see that you are comfortable, "little girl," and that you do not overwork yourself.

I intended to get a new black suit from the tailors who have been making my clothes, Dresher Bros. of Omaha, but they have lost or mislaid my measurement. The clothes I have are better than a ready-made hand-me-down suit. I will probably be in Denver on the 18th as I have some business to do. I will try and not be in the way, although I will be up to the house some of the time.

I will not have things in as good shape here as I would like and as I intended to have them before you come out. One of *our* wagon wheels is gone to the blacksmith shop, likewise one of my buggy wheels, but we will get home somehow on the night of the 21st. I am draining the lake preparatory to fixing it over, so you may see only an unsightly mud hole to begin with. I have grave doubts, little pet, about getting my two rooms cleaned out before you get here, much as I would like to. Too many irons in the fire. It keeps me hustling to keep them from burning.

I am very glad for your sake that refreshments and decorations are to be left out, for you would have been completely worn out with all that work and worry.

Thank you for the compliment, pet, but I well know that I am far from being "the best" and will never see the day that

359

I am worthy of you. I will see the day, however, that I will win all of your love and affection. When once won, I will hold them while life lasts. I wish it could be forever, for I would be as near heaven as I would wish to be and perhaps nearer than I will ever get otherwise.

You may find it a little dreary out here in the wilderness trying to train up a savage like me in the way that he should go. One thing I must try and get in Denver is tablecloths for the wagon table, for even if we do eat from aluminum dishes, we want tablecloths. I may get time to write to my sisters to ask them to come to the wedding, which they won't do. They have been very good sisters to me but are very unlike me. With love and kisses,

Yours,
John

ETHEL P. WAXHAM
1364 Marion St., Denver,
10 June, 1910

Moneta, Wyo.

Dear John,

This is probably my last letter to you for some time, so it is a very important one. First, are you coming to be married on June twentieth at five P.M.? Please say yes, if you are, and then we can order and address the announcements. I am worried for fear that you may not get here until the fourth of July, and I warn you that not even for you will I be married on the fourth. That is Independence Day. Guess I'll change my mind about being a tyrant if you keep on talking about the things which I shall not be *allowed* to do, and what will happen to my clothes if you don't like them. I'm not a spoiled child quite half the time. *Verbum Sap.* *

Secondly, is your middle name Galloway or Galway?

---

*A word to the wise is sufficient.

Scotch or Irish? We'll take chances on the first for the announcements; if it is wrong, 'spect we'll have to be married over again to get it right.

Thirdly, there is to be a cake. I suggested to the family that there would not, and cries and lamentations arose immediately. "But the cake is baked already!" they remonstrated in one voice. Then I could say no more. An old lady patient of Pater's presented *him* with the cake. It is his cake anyway, not yours or mine.

Before leaving Pueblo, I told Mrs. McHarg about you, and she was kind enough to be delighted. She is Scotch— somewhat. Something she offered shows that friends are better than pure gold. "If you are disappointed in going to Yellowstone, come and use our shack in Beulah!" The "shack" is their summer home. Mr. McHarg took us to the station when I left, in their machine, even as early as eight-thirty in the morning, and you should have heard him wish me joy, as if he and Mrs. McHarg had it all and he were giving me a glimpse of it.

Here's to you &
E.W.

If this letter is delayed in reaching you, perhaps you had better telegraph about the date. The announcements must be ordered by Tuesday, the fourteenth, the saleslady says. E.W.

MARCIA CHIPMAN GEORGE
Boulder, Colorado
29 June, 1910

My dear Mr. Love:—

May I offer every possible good wish to you and Ethel on your marital way, and tell you how glad I am to realize that you have each other, and life together.

I am an enthusiastic advocate of the home life with all that it brings and have even longer been an ardent advocate of

Ethel. It is in atrocious taste to talk to a man about his wife. Whatever I might say would undoubtedly appear to you utterly inadequate to express my appreciation of her character and of *herself*.

Perhaps it will be more excusable to quote from a letter written by my friend Miss Sawyer, who visited me in March.

"I shall always rejoice that she came to Boulder. What an exquisite combination of strength and the gentlest charm—welded by that flashing mind!"

If you are given to learning quotations, it might be well to commit that one.

With every kind thought toward you both.

Very Sincerely Yours
Marcia Chipman George

They were married on June 20, 1910, in the bride's home in Denver. One mud-encrusted, peeling photograph of this happy occasion survives. It shows John in a white tie and shirt and a black suit, but wearing the "Old Indestructible," the Rancher's Stetson hat that was his life-long trademark. Ethel is in her "going away clothes." Distinguishable are a high-necked blouse and a huge broad brimmed hat. She looks like a little girl, with her sweet and slightly wistful smile.[6]

EPILOGUE

Initiation to the rigors of life in Wyoming began immediately. Bad weather and the straying and disappearance of the horses that were used to pull their new sheep wagon combined to cut short their honeymoon to Yellowstone. Although specific details were rarely given to their children, subsequent mishaps and misfortunes during John and Ethel's next thirty-seven years together on the ranch produced a wan smile and the comparison, "Just like our honeymoon." They didn't actually see Yellowstone Park together for nearly twenty more years.

Little could have prepared Ethel for life on the Love ranch, not even the seven months she spent with the Mills family.

> In contrast to the verdant, beautiful, well-watered Mills Ranch on a mountain flank, Ethel was now faced with a landscape that was rolling, treeless, immense; the only water was in Muskrat Creek. Mountains were on all sides, but in the shimmering distance. The closest neighbors were thirteen miles away; there were no cars, railroads, or highways. As she wrote to a friend, "The sheer alone-ness of it is unique—never a light but one's own, at night. No smoke from another's fire in sight."*

During the next two years the Fates hurled death and disaster in the face of the dreams of the couple: a miscarriage, the death from a stroke to Frank Waxham, the difficult birth of their son Allan in 1911. Much of

*J. D. Love, "A Part of Your Heritage," p. 9.

363

what they owned was destroyed when torrential rains burst both of John's earth dams, and the ranch house was flooded. After a series of disastrous winters and a dull sheep market, a crowning blow came when a Lander bank foreclosed on John's livestock loans. The bank confiscated his remaining livestock, cattle, sheep, dogs and—most difficult of all— his beloved horses, leaving him only his land. He was forced to let go all of his cowboys.

As the last dust cloud from the departing visitors and their loot dwindled and disappeared over the horizon to the north, a deathly quiet seemed to hang over the ranch. The bustle and noise and industry that had involved each day for the last two years, the sounds of the stock, the wagons, the pounding of hoofs, the shouts of men, all had ceased almost abruptly. Dad and Mother were very, very much alone. They stood, side by side, on the hill looking out across the ranch, across a quarter-mile, flood-devastated, empty, creek bottom, across the rolling hills with no moving specks on them, and close at hand the sodden ranch house. Years later, in brief, sentimental reflective moments, we learned bit by bit what they thought and what they said during this crisis in their lives.

Dad put his big arm gently around Mother's thin shoulders and, in a soft voice with the Scottish burr more pronounced than usual, said, "Lass, you were not born for this kind of a life. You can make your way better in the world you knew in the past. It might be better for Allan, too. I don't want you to leave me, but I won't blame you if you do."

Mother knew the effort it must have cost him to say this. She knew also something of the agony he had just gone through, because to her had come the realization that all these things and these emotions were very important to her, too. With complete honesty she looked him straight in the eyes and said slowly and distinctly in little more than a whisper: "I've thought a lot about leaving you and leaving the ranch. I didn't know if I could bear to live here any more. Now I think I can. My place is here with you and with our son. We're not quitters. We still have the land, we owe no money, and we can still have our dream. Remember, only two years—two almost life-time years—ago, we vowed to each other, and we meant each word . . . for richer, for poorer . . . in sickness and in health . . . until death us do part."*

A year later a second son, David was born, and the Love ranch began its slow recovery. A short note in 1915 from Ethel to her classmates via the *Wellesley College Record* only says, "I have been busy trying to get some raw material in shape for you teachers, and this report is late because the raw material has been teething." In 1920 she wrote again to the *Record:*

> I've been vainly trying to dig some forgotten adventures or attainments or travels out of the last five years, but nothing comes to light. Yes! Four years and a half ago I spent six weeks in Denver with my two boys. Ever since then I've been here, just living. We live the ranchiest kind of ranch life.
>
> Our virtues and vices date back to 400 B.C. We keep open house for all who pass, and they are always men, men of all kinds and conditions from murderers to geologists. "When did you eat last?" is the correct greeting. More than one man has come in who has been out all night in a winter storm without supper or breakfast, lost.

Their third child, Phoebe Elizabeth, was born in 1924, to the delight of the whole family.

The Love household never boasted such luxuries as electricity, indoor plumbing, and a telephone. However, Plato and Proust and the *New*

*J. D. Love, "A Part of Your Heritage," pp. 18, 19.

York Times were just as easily enjoyed by kerosene lantern, and the Loves' two older children learned their lessons at a high, round, felt-topped gambling table (complete with a brass slot for the dealer's wild cards), a relic of a pioneer stage station, transformed by a bright red and white India print cloth into a proper dining table. Their main link with the rest of the world was the written word. Despite her many duties as a ranch wife, mother, and teacher to her children, Ethel wrote—to friends everywhere, observations and stories about her family, visitors, her life on the range, poetry in the margins of her days. As her little boys began to talk, she took detailed notes about the sounds they made, at what age, and the development of their vocabularies. Nothing and no one was unworthy of note, not even the family pets or "Murderers I Have Known."

When the days became less busy, the notes were there to be pieced together again, chapters in her unpublished story "Panorama" describing ranch life along Muskrat Creek. The following passage, written much later, was found among Ethel Waxham Love's papers.

If I were to embroider a sampler showing life on the Rat [Muskrat Creek], the center would be a log house surrounded by trees and garden. Barbed wire fence would circle the sampler. A man in a Stetson would stand beside me on the porch. Next to him would be a small girl holding a cat, and a collie before me. We would be looking at the sandy banks of Muskrat Creek in half flood before us. A broken dam would be lower down the creek—bones of cattle in the lower corner. Sheep would cover a hill on the top left; on the top right, cattle and horses. Rising from behind a hill would be an oil rig. There would be a glow behind it. Two small boys would be sitting high on the windmill polishing buffalo horns. Beyond them the corral would be at the side, full of range horses, where a man would be leading a gray horse to drink; another man would be looking out a sheep wagon door.

A light wind would be blowing the tree branches;

wild roses pink against the house, a cedar tree at the corner, hop vines over the gate. College towers would show faint outlines at the base of the sampler. So would be drawn some of the people, animals and background of this story.

NOTES

PROLOGUE

1.   William DeWitt Hyde, *The Choice of the College Woman, Address Delivered at the Twenty-seventh Annual Commencement of Wellesley College,* (Cambridge: Riverside Press, 1905).

2.   Stephen Phillips, *Marpessa,* "Flowers of Parnassus—III" (London and New York: John Lane Publisher, 1902), p. 38.

CHAPTER I

1.   Alice Welty had reached middle age before she left the civilized world of the East Coast behind. Yet she took up the life of the pioneer West. In her obituary, it was said of her: She liked to ride, loved to hunt, was a good markswoman, and had no difficulty in getting her game. She often whipped the streams for trout and took delight in bringing home a string of fish that would be the pride of any angler. She traveled alone on the stage, making trips to Rawlins where she took the train for journeys back to the East. On one occasion, the stage encountered a terrific wind as they crowned Beaver Hill. It blew the stage over. It was just another incident in her interesting experiences.

Her granddaughter Gladys Welty Hawley relates that "Grandmother was no slouch when it came to riding and roping and was even able to shoe her own horses. There wasn't much in the line of outdoor work that a woman of that day in the West might not be called upon to handle. Grandmother was fiercely independent . . . although always a lady. One story of an outing in the mountains tells of Grandmother coming out of her tent to find a bear in camp. Brandishing a stick, she shouted, 'Shoo, you ugly beast!' " (Tom Bell, " 'Doc' Welty Left a Legacy," *Wind River Mountaineer,* vol. IV, no. 3 [July–September, 1988], pp. 5–6.)

2.   Actually these were the Ferris Mountains, named after the same Ferris as the Ferris Hotel in Rawlins. The Seminoe Mountains are farther east and not as conspicuous. (J. D. Love, personal communication, 1989.)

3.   The soldiers were from the U.S. Cavalry, which established Fort Stambaugh in 1870 to keep peace among Indians and whites. (J. D. Love, personal communication, 1989.)

CHAPTER 2

1.   J. D. Love, "A Part of Your Heritage," (unpublished paper, 1968), p. 3.

2.   Kathy Robinson, "Interview with Sandy Mills," (unpublished paper, Lander, Wyoming, October 2, 1967).

3.   J. D. Love, personal communication, 1990.

4.   Miner's Delight (also called Hamilton City), South Pass City, and Atlantic City sprang up in the late 1860s when gold was discovered in the area. The claims were greatly exaggerated, however, and the towns slowly died and were abandoned. (Todd Guenther, "God, the Cariso, & South Pass City," *The Wind River Mountaineer,* vol VII, no. 2 [April–June, 1991], p. 5.)

5.   Actually Major Thomas T. Thornburgh and thirteen of his 150 soldiers were killed. Marshall Sprague, *Massacre: The Tragedy at White River,* (Boston: Little, Brown & Co., 1957).

6.   Some legends say that Washakie, chief of the Shoshoni, defeated the Crow chief on top of the butte, cut out his heart, and ate it himself.

7.   Ethel Waxham Love, "At the Twin Creek School," Alpha Xi State Delta Kappa Gamma, *Let Your Light Shine, Pioneer Women Educators of Wyoming* (Sheridan, Wyoming: Wyoming Print Shop, 1965), pp. 95–96.

8.   First published in *Writing at Wyoming* (Laramie, Wyoming: Department of English, University of Wyoming, 1958), p. 12.

9.   J. D. Love, "A Part of Your Heritage," p. 4.

10.   The Mills Ranch never had less than thirty-five horses, often more, which they pastured on the open range. Sometimes Gardiner Mills provided horses for the U.S. Army. (Robinson, interview with Sandy Mills)

11.   Mary Alice Davis was born in Schuyler County, Missouri, in 1872. After teaching in the Missouri school systems for several years, she developed what the doctors pronounced "consumption" and was

given only six months to live. Her family physician advised a change of climate as a means of combatting the disease, whereupon she selected the higher altitude of Wyoming. In 1898 Miss Davis filed a claim on a homestead southeast of Shoshoni. This was home to her through the remaining years although she was away at intervals when she taught in such places as Lander, Shoshoni, Lost Cabin, and Atlantic City. For some time she was principal of the Shoshoni schools and she held the office of county superintendent for a number of years. She also served as Fremont County librarian.

After her retirement her sister wished to take her to California, but Alice preferred to stay in Wyoming. Allie Davis was exceedingly proud and did not wish to have it known that she was receiving an old-age pension after her retirement from active duty. In her declining years the Boy Scouts of Shoshoni assumed the responsibility of paying her a visit each evening to see that she was amply supplied with the necessities of life. It was said that "the world was a better place because Miss Davis lived here." (Anne Wright in *Let Your Light Shine,* p. 46.)

12.   To prevent scurvy, the Hayden Geological Survey Party planted watercress at every fresh-water spring they passed during their trek westward toward Yellowstone. Watercress is abundant to this day in the spring at Red Bluff Ranch. (J. D. Love, personal communication, 1988.)

13.   Grain was harvested during the late summer and stored in bundles until threshing crews could come to winnow it or separate the grain from the chaff. These migrant workers of the early 1900s were a source of concern for the parents of young ladies, and Mrs. Mills often sent her daughters to stay with friends while the threshers were at Red Bluff Ranch. (Jack Corbett, great-grandson of Gardiner and Mary Mills, personal communication, 1989.)

CHAPTER 3

1.   Also known as Worlin Well, drilled in 1902. This well was probably a landmark. (J. D. Love, personal communication, 1990.)

CHAPTER 4

1.   Ethel Waxham wrote with it for the rest of her life. (J. D. Love, personal communication, 1989.)

2.   "Box and Cox," a lively play in one act was written in 1847 by

John Madison Morton and produced at the Royal Lyceum Theatre in London the same year. Gilbert and Sullivan found the clever repartee too good to resist and set it to music in the operetta "Cox and Box," so named because Mr. Cox appears on stage first.

CHAPTER 5

1.   When her son David was a boy, he asked his mother if she had ever loved anyone besides his father. She smiled and said she had once previously been engaged. When pressed for details as to who it was and what he was like and where he was now, she said she would tell him on her seventy-fifth birthday (she was then thirty-five) if he still wanted to know. She was living with that son and his family in Laramie on her seventy-fifth birthday, but he did not remind her of her promise. (J. D. Love, personal communication, 1989.)

2.   The *Shoshoni Pathfinder* was a kind of "Who's Who" of Fremont County, published in 1906 by Ed Wynn to commemorate the Chicago & Northwestern Railroad's extension to Lander, Wyoming, and the opening of parts of the Wind River Indian Reservation to white settlement. Its catch slogan was "Where rails end and trails begin." In addition to providing information about the railroad and the attributes of Fremont County, it contained photos of John G. Love, Superintendent of Schools Allie Davis, Eli Signor, Arthur H. Sanderson, and other notables of the region, biographical notes, and advertisements for local businesses. Prepublication publicity in the *Wind River Mountaineer* proclaimed: "The new publication will find its way to every corner of the globe and will be a complete directory and guide to the many thousands of settlers who anticipate invading Wyoming in the coming summer. The publication will absolutely eclipse anything of a similar character ever undertaken in the West." (December 29, 1905, p. 1.)

3.   To make the interpretation of John Love's financial gains and losses current, the gold standard in the years 1906–1910 was about eighteen dollars an ounce, whereas in the 1990s it is around four hundred dollars an ounce. (J. D. Love, personal communication, 1988.)

4.   Caroline Maude Holt was a 1903 Wellesley graduate and taught zoology there from 1903 to 1913. She received her M.A. from Columbia in 1908 and her Ph.D. in 1916 from the University of Pennsylvania, where she was the first woman medical student. She taught at Simmons College, in Boston, from 1914 until her retirement in 1953. She

then taught medical students at Vellore Christian Medical College for Women in South India for three years, accompanied by Florence Risley. (Wellesley Archives.)

5.   Winifred Hawkridge later traveled and wrote for the *Boston Herald,* where she could proudly say she "was at all times a total abstainer from the Woman's Page." She subsequently raised shetland ponies, wrote plays, married, had two children, and wrote a book about her travels in the "Golden West were people get things done" called *Westward Hobos.* (Wellesley Archives.)

6.   Lockwood was a beloved Wellesley English teacher for thirty-one years, poet and advisor to the Scribblers. Patricia Palmieri, in "A Social Portrait of Academic Women at Wellesley College 1900–1910," in *Adamless Eden, A Social Portrait of the Academic Community at Wellesley 1875–1920,* (Harvard, 1981, p. 365), says "Lockwood was a Milton scholar for whom 'teaching was her life.' She had an infallible memory and loved to challenge her students to walk up the highest hills in South Natick reciting *Paradise Lost* from memory. She never forgot a line."

7.   The *Rocky Mountain News* announced that Frank Waxham had filed for divorce from Ethel's stepmother, Alice, on February 14, 1907. Her financial speculations were draining the Waxham finances and those of his colleagues.

8.   The process used was sun printing. Film was put in a wooden frame under glass with light-sensitive paper behind the negative and exposed briefly to the sun. The prints were blue and white rather than black and white. In households without electricity, this was the common method used for printing photos. (J. D. Love, personal communication, 1989.)

9.   Ethel Waxham received her master's degree from the University of Colorado in literature. Her thesis, written in French and English, discussed "The Dramatic Theory and Practice of Maurice Mæterlinck."

10.   Florence Risley received her M.A. from Wellesley in 1911 and later did graduate work at Yale. For twenty-five years she served on the National Board of the YWCA and spent the years during and after the wars in France and Belgium. For her work there she received the *Médaille reconnaissance française.* She later taught in India with Caroline Holt, retired to live in Belgium and finally settled in Boston from 1965 until 1980. Her letters to Ethel Waxham, her children and grandchildren span seventy-five years. (Wellesley Archives and editors' personal experience.)

11.   The Wellesley friend, also known as "Muzzer Bear," who had been so ill with typhoid, Adrienne Muzzy, received her B.A. from Wellesley in 1905. She taught at Bristol High School in Bristol, Connecticut, from 1905 to 1906. From 1906 to 1907 she was in New Mexico and Colorado "recovering my amiability" and was returning East when she wrote this letter. In 1907 she "discovered library work" and in 1910 earned a B.S. from Simmons College in Boston. She worked as a librarian in the New York Public Library from 1908 to 1946, spending her vacations traveling with "The Parent" (her mother) or alone. (Wellesley Archives.)

12.   The Lander paper, *The Wind River Mountaineer,* found little that was too insignificant to print, i.e. local comings, goings, and announcements, such as lost dogs and sick children, forthcoming dances, and advertisements.

CHAPTER 6

1.   Laura Hibbard received her M.A. from Wellesley in 1908, studied at Oxford, and earned her doctorate at the University of Chicago in 1916. She managed to combine a successful scholarly career in medieval literature with marriage (but no children). She taught at Mount Holyoke from 1908 to 1916 and was a member of the Wellesley faculty from 1916 until her retirement. A friend later wrote, "She carried her learning and her labors so gayly that she seemed always to be engaged in joyous adventure rather than in grueling work." (Wellesley Archives.)

2.   Louise Dudley became and remained a good friend for life. (See Note 6 in Chapter 7.)

3.   John Love rode Brownie, another prized horse, thirty miles to find no letter at the post office in Moneta. When Western Union could not guarantee the delivery of messages sent, he saddled Punch and rode to Haily, at least sixty more miles, for a total of ninety miles that day. (J. D. Love, personal communication, 1988.)

4.   J. D. Love, "Dreams, Dams, and Disasters, 1908–1913." (unpublished paper, 1988) pp. 1, 4.

5.   University of Colorado Bulletin, vol. xiv, no. 4, 1914 (General Series no. 69, Library Series no. 2) contains a description and dates of chair positions Frank Waxham held, and two pages of references to articles he published about his work.

6.   Nora and her sister were known for their creative abilities. The Hyde Park High School paper lauded Nora's talents as a young writer. Her sister, whose name is not mentioned, made the theatre her career.

7.   Marcia's fiancé was Russell D. George. He later became State Geologist of Colorado.

CHAPTER 7

1.   Helen Watson was a friend and classmate from Wellesley, who graduated from Johns Hopkins University with an M.D. in 1910. According to the *Wellesley College Record,* after a three-year career as resident physician in the Women's Public and Private Medical Wards at Johns Hopkins, Helen exchanged her medical career for that of a wife and became mother to five children.

2.   Ethel Waxham and Donald McLean taught Sunday School together probably in Denver, and were friends at least since 1901. Although Ethel's address book shows at least seven of his changes of address, only two of his letters from 1908 to 1910 were preserved.

3.   Maud Thompson was a Wellesley classmate, who had worked with Ethel in a settlement house during one summer vacation. The *Wellesley College Record* shows that Maud received her B.A. in 1901, her M.A. also from Wellesley, in 1902, and her Ph.D. in classics from Yale in 1906. She is listed as a teacher, a socialist lecturer, and Education Emancipator. Maud's letters were all typewritten.

4.   The eye problems appear to have been a temporary case of eye strain, possibly due to fatigue, and Ethel wore glasses for several years. In later life, however, she only wore reading glasses.

5.   Faith Waxham did not find the groom to go with the bouquet and never married.

6.   Louise Dudley taught with Ethel at Kemper Hall. She had received her B.A. from Georgetown College in 1905 with a major in English literature and interrupted her graduate work at Bryn Mawr to teach at Kemper Hall. She was about to leave for a year of graduate study in Paris and England to research the topic, "The Egyptian Elements in the Legend of the Body and Soul." She returned to Bryn Mawr in early 1910, dissertation in hand, and was awarded her Ph.D. that June. She taught English literature at Mount Holyoke College from 1910 to 1911, and at Stephens College in Columbia, Missouri, from 1913 to

1914, before moving to Lawrence College in Appleton, Wisconsin. In 1918, she returned to France as a member of the International Red Cross, where she planned recreational activities for women working in munitions factories. In 1919 she returned to Stephens College where she remained, a revered faculty member, until her retirement in 1964. An innovator, she was a pioneer in the use of television for instruction and became well-known for relating interdisciplinary programs in the arts and humanities. She wrote *The Study of Literature* in the 1920s and a textbook entitled *The Humanities* in 1940. The liberal arts wing at the Stephens College Learning Center is named Louise Dudley Hall in her honor.

7.   Published in *Writing at Wyoming,* p. 12.

8.   Both Gertrude and Winifred had been classmates of Ethel's at Wellesley. Gertrude was in France to begin research for what was later to become her book *Tristan and Isolde, A Study of the Sources of the Romance,* published in 1913. Winifred Hawkridge wrote to the Wellesley class of 1906 *Record:*

> 1. Sailed for Europe, Oct. 1908 with the intention of studying drama at the Sorbonne. 2. Attended lectures at the Sorbonne, . . . my earnest pursuit of the drama was in vain, as Wellesley refused to accept this contribution toward the first lap on an M.A. 3. a frantic effort to see Life, beginning in a Paris Y.W.C.A. and ending in an English hydropathic resort. The highlights which flashed in between I will omit. They look shocking in print. . . . (Wellesley Archives.)

CHAPTER 8

1.   John Love's letter describing the "desperate circumstances" and the terms by which Ethel might benefit from his misfortune is missing.

2.   The ice was cut from the frozen water in the creek. Alkaline in nature, it was not fit for human consumption. The ice was packed in sawdust and stored in an ice house—a log cabin set deep into the hillside behind the main house—and used to preserve meat, eggs, and vegetables. (J. D. Love, personal communication, 1991.)

3.   J. D. Love, "A Part of Your Heritage," p. 8.

CHAPTER 9

1. She lived to be seventy-six years old.
2. John Love probably found "Rollicky Dick" Felton, his mother and sister, through an advertisement in a Western newspaper or magazine. Felton, having secured employment at the Love Ranch, proceeded to advertise for a wife. He sent the following message to a lonely heart's club publication: "Dashing young cowboy of twenty-three. My friends call me handsome. No flirts need apply. I mean business!" The Wolton post office was inundated with replies, but "Rollicky Dick's" luck with prospective wife candidates is a story in itself. He did not marry while at the Love Ranch. (J. D. Love, personal communication, 1991.)
3. A flowering tobacco appreciated for its evening fragrance. (Phoebe Love Holzinger, personal communication, 1990.)
4. A ranch situated along a stage or freight route, with facilities to serve meals and/or provide lodging for travelers. (J. D. Love, personal communication, 1991.)
5. These deaths were possibly due to selenium poisoning but more likely to some sort of virus. (J. D. Love, personal communication, 1989.)
6. John G. Love filed for a "Permit to Divert and Appropriate the Water of the State of Wyoming" on Love Ditch no. 2, which was to be 2.5 miles long and 4 miles wide. It was to be completed in two years. (J. D. Love, "Dreams, Dams, and Disasters, 1908–1913," 1989) p. 4.

CHAPTER 11

1. The herder was Thomas Mahoney. Other accounts of his ordeals and those of other herders lost in storms are recorded in A. J. Mockler, *History of Natrona County, Wyoming, 1923,* (privately published), p. 381, and in J. D. Love, *A Tough Breed of Men,* "Winter on the Open Range, Wyoming, 1909–1910," (unpublished account, 1983), pp. 4–7.
2. This particular fireless cooker was a long rectangular box divided into three separate compartments inside, with a securely fastening cover. Discs of soapstone were heated in a fire or conventional oven, and placed one apiece in each compartment. Food in containers was placed in the compartments, covered, and allowed to cook slowly, unattended, for hours. (J. D. Love, personal communication, 1989.)

3.   The brass imp was in the form of a door knocker, which was affixed to the guest room door at the Love Ranch, where it remained until the Loves moved away. (J. D. Love, personal communication, 1990.)

4.   The identity of the Harvard man remains a mystery. None of their correspondence has been found.

5.   It is not known who or what provoked this outburst—but several weeks later John Love sent Ethel a photograph of his ranch buildings taken by a Mrs. Williams who had recently visited the ranch. Unfortunately his reply was not saved.

6.   J. D. Love, "A Part of Your Heritage," p. 7.

BIBLIOGRAPHY

UNPUBLISHED SOURCES

Love, Ethel Waxham. "Rome Was Not Built in a Day." Undated, unpublished manuscript.

Love, J. D. "A Part of Your Heritage." Unpublished paper, 1968.

Love, J. D. "Winter on the Open Range, Wyoming, 1909–1910." In *A Tough Breed of Men.* Unpublished paper, 1983.

Love, J. D. "Dreams, Dams, and Disasters, 1908–1913." Unpublished paper, 1988.

PUBLISHED BOOKS AND ARTICLES

Bell, Tom. " 'Doc' Welty Left a Legacy." *Wind River Mountaineer,* vol. IV, no. 3 (July–September, 1988).

Guenther, Todd. "Gold, the Cariso, & South Pass City." *Wind River Mountaineer,* vol. VII, no. 2 (April–June, 1991).

Hyde, William DeWitt. *Apollo or Idas: The Choice of the College Woman, Address Delivered at the Twenty-seventh Annual Commencement of Wellesley College.* Cambridge: Riverside Press, 1905.

Love, Ethel Waxham. "At the Twin Creek School." In *Let Your Light Shine, Pioneer Women Educators of Wyoming.* Edited by Alpha Xi State Delta Kappa Gamma. Sheridan, Wyoming: Wyoming Print Shop, 1965.

Mockler, A. J. *History of Natrona County, Wyoming.* Published privately, 1923.

"Mystery in Divorce Case of Waxhams," *The Rocky Mountain News,* February 24, 1907.

Palmieri, Patricia. "A Social Portrait of Academic Women at Wellesley

College 1900–1910," in *Adamless Eden, A Social Portrait of the Academic Community at Wellesley 1875–1920,* Harvard, 1981.

Phillips, Stephen. In "Flowers of Parnassus—III." *Marpessa,* London and New York: John Lane, Publisher, 1902.

Rocky Mountain News. February 24, 1907, and June 9, 1910.

Shoshoni Pathfinder, Ed. Wynn and F. S. Smith, publishers, 1906. (No publishing company or place of publication given.)

Sprague, Marshall. *Massacre: The Tragedy at White River.* Boston: Little, Brown & Co., 1957.

"Teachers' Institute," *Wind River Mountaineer,* December 29, 1905.

Wellesley College Record, 1875–1912. A General Catalogue of Officers and Students, vol. I, (1906–1911), vol. II (1910–1915), vol. III (1916–1921), vol. IV (1920–1925), vol. V (1926–1931).

Woolf, Virginia, *The Letters of Virginia Woolf, Vol. IV 1929–1931,* Nigel Nicholson and Joanne Trautmann, Eds. Harcourt Brace Jovanovich: New York, 1979.

Wright, Anne. In *Let Your Light Shine, Pioneer Women Educators of Wyoming.* Edited by Alpha Xi State Delta Kappa Gamma. Sheridan, Wyoming: Wyoming Print Shop, 1965.

Writing at Wyoming, Laramie, Wyoming: Department of English, University of Wyoming, 1958. No editor named.

INTERVIEWS AND PERSONAL COMMUNICATIONS

Corbett, Jack, great-grandson of Gardiner and Mary Mills. Personal communication, 1989.

Holzinger, Phoebe Love, daughter of John and Ethel Waxham Love. Personal communication, 1990.

Love, J. D., son of John and Ethel Waxham Love. Personal communications, 1988–92.

Robinson, Kathy. Interview with Sandy Mills. Lander, Wyoming, October 2, 1967.

INDEX

Numbers followed by *a* refer to information in captions identifying photographs. Numbers followed by *n* refer to information in page footnotes. Numbers followed by (n.x) refer to information given in Notes section at book's end.

Abra, Ted (Hailey area), 42, 85
accommodations for travelers: hotels, 13, 68; meals, 12, 14, 17, 21; stage stations and road ranches: 11*a*, 17, 18, 19, 20, 21, 22, 24, 60
age, signs of, 196, 258, 274, 277, 292
Albuquerque, New Mexico, 1
alcohol: absence of, 80; abuse, 125, 164, 186; allusion to, 17, 83, 150; evils of, 37, 50, 55; medicinal uses, 145; recreation, 189, 241, 305; whiskey, 38, 45
Alger, Mr. (Hailey), 53, 54
Altar-bread woman, Mrs. Harris, 176, 181, 189
alternative professions, 64, 235, 310, 345, 346, 347, 373(n.5), 375(n.1). *See also* employment
alum, 62, 63
American Medical Association, 220, 224; convention activities, 221, 223, 224
Amoretti, Mrs. (Lander), 74
amusements: card games, 59, 68, 260, 266; for single women (Chicago), 167; horseback riding, 12*a*, 87, 117, 125, 129, 132, 135, 141, 144, 157, 163, 167, 215, 217, 235, 266; opera, 167, 206, 210; Red Bluff Ranch, 61, 66, 86, 92, 97, 124, 136, 144, 156, 260, 261, 266; roller skates, 218; symphony, 265; tennis, 235; Texas picnics and dances, 165; theatre, 118, 167; Twin Creek School recess, 41, 42; walking, 92, 139, 183, 191, 227, 257, 269
antelope, pet, 51, 63
Arapaho Indians, 74*n*

"Aspen Leaves" (poem by Ethel Waxham), 245, 376(n.7)
Assistant Chief of the Pugwash (Hailey area), 43, 100. *See also* Deane
Atkins, "Sunny" Jim (Lander), 59, 64
Atlantic City, Wyoming, 22, 35, 53, 58, 206, 207, 370(n.4). *See also* mining towns

bachelor life: bachelor quarters, 339; miseries of, 90
Bain, Tom (Hailey), 260, 266, 272
Baldwin girls (Lander), 58
Baldwin, Harry (Hailey area), 261
Bancroft, Elizabeth, 124, 125, 129, 131, 132, 136, 137, 140, 144, 151, 153, 154, 155, 156, 158, 161
Banis's (Hailey), 54
Barnes, Mr. and Mrs. Dick (Hailey area): Mrs. (heart seizure), 145; Mr., 101
Barrett, Mr. (Pueblo), 313, 314, 316, 327, 329, 333, 346, 347
Bates, Katherine Lee (Wellesley), 264, 264*n*
baths, 61; hazards of, 61, 92
Bayley, Dr. (minister, Denver), 351, 352
beauty: concepts of, 243, 248, 253; hunger for, 244; sacrifices to, 180
Beaver, Wyoming, 37
bedbugs, 60, 100
Bell Springs, Wyoming, 17. *See also* stage stations
Bent, Mr. (Hailey area), 81, 202
Bentra (Waxhams' cook, Denver), 250. *See also* domestic help
Berry, Marian (Wellesley), 112, 132, 133

Hailey, 10, 11*a*, 22, 23*a*, 25*a*, 43; Lost Soldier, 18, 19, 20, 21; meals, 17, 18, 21, 24; Myersville, 22; Reeds, 60
Stambough, Officer, 35
stenographer, 178
stereoscope ["first looks"], 207
Stevenson, Robert Lewis, "The rain is raining all around," 153
Stickney, Mrs. (Pueblo), 321
St. George, Miss (Kemper Hall), 175
St. Joseph Hospital (Denver), 1, 125, 152, 152*n*, 307
Stone and Timber Act, 212
stores: Altmans (New York), 16; Burnett's Store (Wind River Reservation), 154; Dresher Bros. (Omaha), 359; Scholar and Funks (Kenosha), 189; Spaulding Bros. (Chicago), 181; Sterns (New York), 16; Weltys' (Dubois), 16
strike, 148, 164, 327
Stringer, Arthur (poet), 230, 235
Strohm, Pearl (Wellesley), 225
suffrage, 229, 240, 247
Suffering Jim (Hailey area), 56
Sugar City, Colorado, 263
sulphate of copper, 297. *See also* medicine
sulphate of mercury, 297. *See also* medicine
sundial, 39, 85, 95
superintendents of schools, women, 9, 59, 60*a*, 69, 115, 286
Swedish royalty, King Gustaf V and Queen Victoria, 254
Sweetwater River, Wyoming, 3, 23
Sypes, Mr. and Mrs. (Atlantic City), 207

Taft, William Howard, 229, 234, 242
tailors, 211, 359
Tanhart, Margaret (Boulder), 268
teacher placement agencies: Albert Teachers' Agency (Chicago), 133, 233; Fisk Teachers' Employment Agency (Denver), 6, 9, 11*a*
teachers: character, 72; contracts, 345, 347, 350; life certificates, 286; N.E.A. meetings: Denver, 291–92, 294, 300–301; Pueblo, 337
teaching: 195; allurements, 272, 314; alternatives to, 223, 235, 283, 287; conditions, 7, 9, 112, 175; drudgery, 164, 196, 215, 259; duties, 122, 133, 175, 180, 183, 208, 209, 293, 316, 317, 327, 339, 341, 343; extra duties, 175, 181, 184, 333, 346; frustrations, 196, 214, 228; salaries, 6, 9, 196, 215, 228, 232, 238, 263, 272, 316, 329, 331; schedules, 175, 183, 240; substitute,

263, 268, lack of, 346; term, 6, 9, 38–41, 102, 103, 314; tutoring, 183, 303, 311, 342; wages, 228, 232
Tear, Mr. (Lander Institute), 70, 71, 72, 73, 74
telegraph service, 105, 187, 220, 335, 347, 361; cost, 105
telephone, 6, 48, 151, 240, 244, 314, 332, 335; cost, 244. *See also* conveniences
telescope, 90
temperatures, weather, 20, 21, 22, 41, 67, 78, 90, 91, 93, 208, 315, 317, 320, 329
Thanksgiving 1905, 51, 55, 103; 1908, 255–56
theatre, 118, 206, 264, 271; Denver: Baker and Co., 215, Orpheum, 278, 279; New York: New Star Theatre, 72; static, 146
theft: cattle, 42, 43; personal possessions, 184
Thin, Margery (Kemper Hall), 178
Thompson, Maud, 112, 228, 229, 230, 232, 235, 239, 240, 375(n.3)
Thoreau, Henry David, 129
Thornburgh, Major Thomas T., 36, 370(n.5)
Three Fingered Bill (Hailey area), 56
threshers, 63, 64, 65, 66, 74, 76, 77, 195, 307, 371(n.13); conventions regarding, 195, 371(n.13)
Thum(b), Susan (Kemper Hall), 173, 174, 178, 179, 180, 194, 207–8, 209
Tia Juana, Mexico, 113
tobacco, 42, 57, 275; chewing, 92
Tooley, Mr. (Pueblo), 332
toys: paper dolls, 194, 205; Christmas, 263, 268
tracheotomies, 1. *See also* medicine
transcendentalism, 259
transport, means of: freight wagon, 10, 16, 18, 143, 210, 298, 315, 323, 324, 335, 340, stage coach, 13
travel means: autobus, 289; automobile/machine, 54, 109, 152, 231, 289, 307, 342, 361; buggy/carriage, 2, 21, 47, 51, 53, 67, 75, 78, 79, 82, 90, 94, 102, 103, 105, 142, 146, 188, 196, 204, 206, 289, 359; cab, 172; hack, 188; horseback, 39, 42, 44, 51, 64, 78, 101, 105, 154, 184, 185, 186, 200; oceanliner, 242, 331–32; sleigh/sled, 18, 49, 55, 56, 67, 75, 77, 78, 88, 89, 91, 94, 207; spring buckboard, 24, 34; stage coach, 6, 10, 11*n*, 13, 17, 18, 19, 20, 22, 23, 24, 48, 70, 79, 91; streetcars, 52; train, 12, 13, 142, 148, 149, 150, 152, 154, 156, 164, 167, 183, 184, 185, 315, 324, 325, 326, 328, 337, 338, 342, 350,